TH

Surfing

WALLY FROISETH

DEDICATION

To my family and friends. Without their help, this project would not have been possible.

Second Edition
10 09 08 07 06   5 4 3 2 1

Published by
Gibbs Smith, Publisher
P.O. Box 667
Layton, Utah 84041

Orders: 1.800.748.5439
www.gibbs-smith.com

Design and principal photographic
editing by John Witzig

Printed and bound in China

First published in 1983 by Palm Beach Press.

Library of Congress Control Number: 2006927059

ISBN 0-9591816-4-4 first edition
ISBN 1-4236-0121-1 second edition (first Gibbs Smith edition)

THE HISTORY OF
Surfing

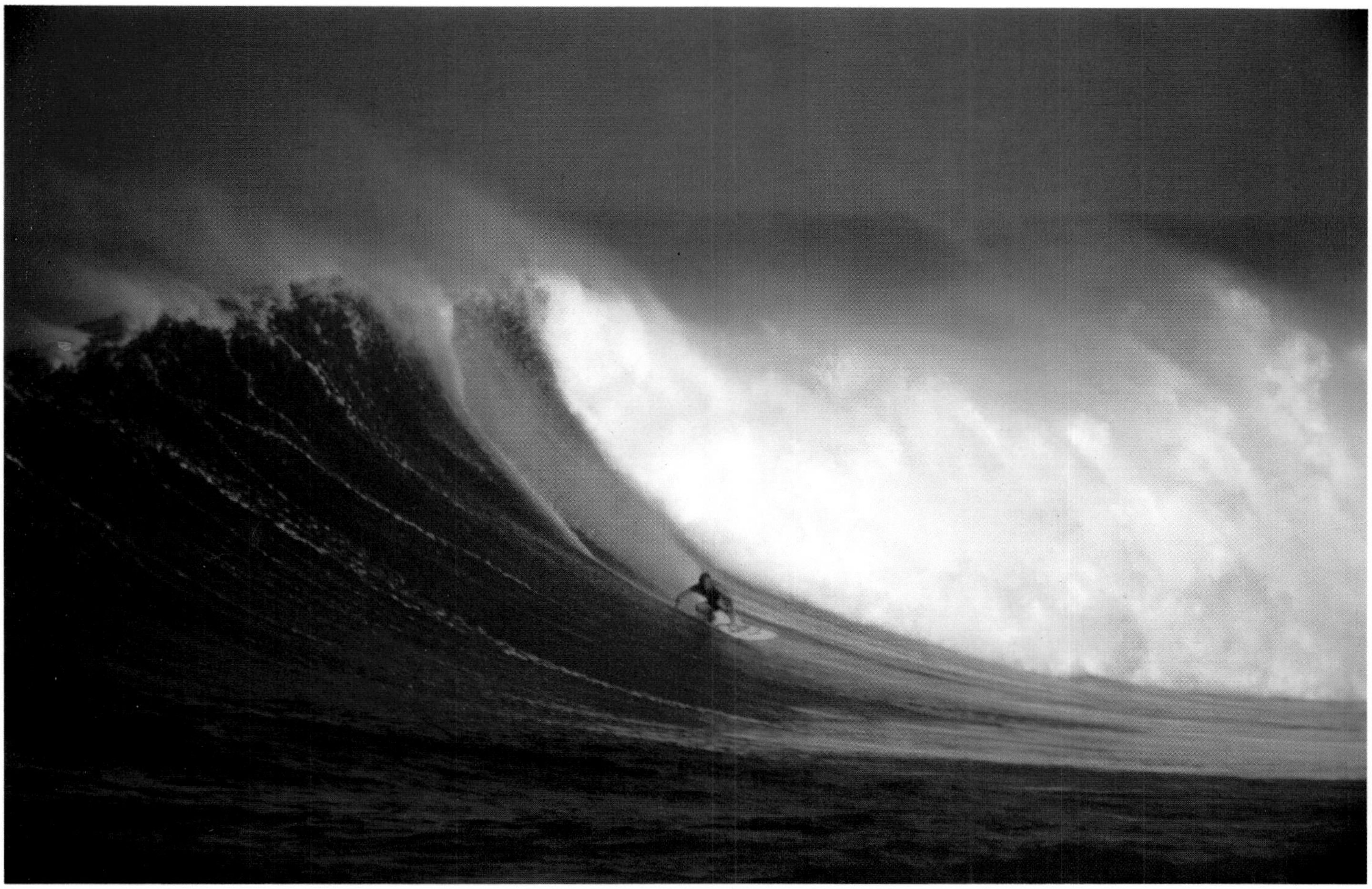

Nat Young — Sunset Beach, Hawaii, Nov. 1969.

NAT YOUNG
WITH CRAIG MCGREGOR
& ROD HOLMES

Gibbs Smith, Publisher
Salt Lake City

CONTENTS

PETER CRAWFORD

MIKE CORDESIUS

13

1

2

3

4

6

5

7

1. *Early engraving showing Wahine with surfboard.*

2. *The great Duke Kahanamoku with his surfing brothers.*

3. *Australian Open Surfing Championship at Bondi 1963.*

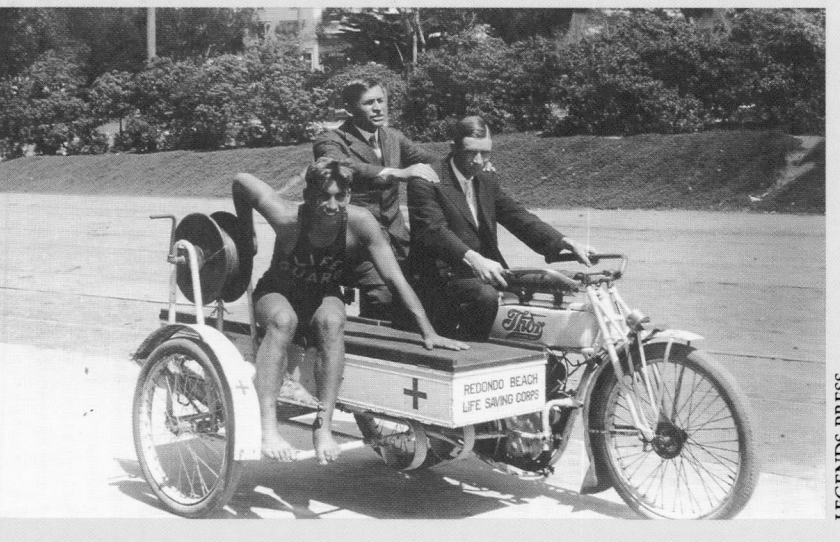

8

SURFER

Surfing has been around for a long time. Almost as long as humankind, to my way of thinking; or at least as long as there have been people and waves in the same place. That probably means Polynesia, and especially Hawaii, where we know surfboard riding has been carried on for centuries . . . since 400 AD at least.

The first surfers were probably 'unconscious' surfers: island fishermen who used waves as the fastest means of getting their canoes over the coral reefs and back to the beach with their catch. At Waikiki you can still see Hawaiians catching waves in their traditional outrigger canoes, laden with tourists instead of fish. At some still undefined stage in history, however, catching waves developed from being part of the everyday working skill of the fisherman to being a sport. Instead of *work* it became *play*. And this change revolutionised surfing; it turned into something which, in our own century, has spread from Hawaii across the face of the planet.

In Hawaii surfboard riding flourished to the point where it became an intricate part of the local Kapu religious/class system. Some beaches and types of surfboards were reserved for the ruling class; the commoners surfed different beaches, and on shorter boards. (As has happened before in history, it turned out the commoners had it right!). With the arrival of Western missionaries in Hawaii, however, the sport went into a decline. The missionaries imposed their own Christian values on the islanders and substituted Church and school for the supposedly pagan practices of surfing and games. The old Koa or Wili Wili surfboards became beached abandoned, and faded out of the culture. For all we know the sport

of surfriding could have disappeared altogether.

It didn't. At the start of the 20th century Hawaiians living close to Waikiki began surfing for the pure fun of it. It was no longer work, or religious ritual, but sheer pleasure. George Freeth, the son of a Hawaiian woman and an Irish sailor, introduced surfboard riding to the United States mainland; in 1907 he rode a shorter, chopped down version of the boards which had been used by the ancient Hawaiians, and which can be seen in the Bishop Museum in Honolulu. A superb Hawaiian swimmer and surfer, Duke Kahanamoku, used the same sort of board to introduce surfing to Australia in 1915. The sport was beginning to spread. It reached South Africa, Japan, New Zealand, South America, Britain, France, in fact everywhere waves break. In the space of little over half a century it exploded to become, after swimming, the most popular water sport in the world.

Today surfing is an incredibly complex sport: maybe, as some claim, it is even an art. It's developed all sorts of forms: kneeboards, wave skis, paddleboards, mats, boogie boards, and, latest of all, windsurfing. All are in this book, as part of the history of how we have learnt to ride waves.

For me, board riding is at the very centre of surfing. And as the sport evolved, so has the surfboard; in fact you can just about trace the history of surfing by looking at the design evolution of the surfboard. The early Hawaiian boards were solid redwood planks, and that dictated the way they were ridden; straight into the beach, or at best across the line of the wave. Then came Tom Blake's hollow paddleboards, which became the

standard board on the Californian and Australian coasts. On the beautiful point breaks of Malibu, Rincon and Makaha, surfers like Wally Froiseth and Pete Peterson rode narrow, solid 'hot curl' boards and experimented with ways of beating the curl and turning on the wave face. Then came the lighter, shorter balsa board, followed by the first fibreglass-and-resin boards and designers like Bob Simmons and Joe Quigg. A new generation of surfers . . . Phil Edwards, Mickey Dora, Dewey Weber, to name just a few . . . ushered in the hot dog style of surfing in the mid 50s.

About this time surfing became not just a sport but a cult; it was the time of *Gidget, The Endless Summer* and The Beach Boys. The Californians introduced their Malibu boards to Australia and a few years later, in 1962, an Australian, Midget Farrelly, turned the tables on them and won the first unofficial world championship. It was the beginning of a long but friendly rivalry between Australia, the United States and Hawaii for dominance in world surfing.

Meanwhile the surfboard evolved still further. Bob McTavish, George Greenough and I chopped a couple of feet off the length of our Malibus, introduced V-bottoms, and when I won the world championship in San Diego the 'new era' began. Boards got still shorter and lighter; the rails became more refined; surfers experimented over the years with swallowtails, channels, stingers, flutes, twin fins and three fins. Surfing styles evolved too. From the early static, stand-up approach surfing evolved through turning and classic styles to the nose-riding of the Californians. Then came the Australian 'power' method of surfing, which was much more ag-

4. *1926 Australian Surfboard Champ. C.J. 'Snowy' McAlister.*

5. *The first Surf Safari to the coast of California by the Hawaiians Ross Takaki (left) Wally Froiseth (centre).*

6. *The colourful character Tubesteak of Malibu.*

7. *Corky Carroll, U.S. Men's Open Champion '66, '67 and '69.*

8. *This is how they covered Redondo Beach in 1920. The reel was used for paying out a torpedo rescue can to the bather in distress.*

9. *The Aussi surfboat, a real crowd pleaser at surf carnivals, especially in big seas.*

BUD BROWNE

9

DR. JACK BALL

Top: *Surfbathers at Manly, 1906.*

Above: *Members of the Palos Verdes Surfing Club in action. Formed in 1936, the Club was California's first.*

Right: *Windansea in San Diego where in 1953 Bob Simmons lost his life while surfing*

JEFF DIVINE

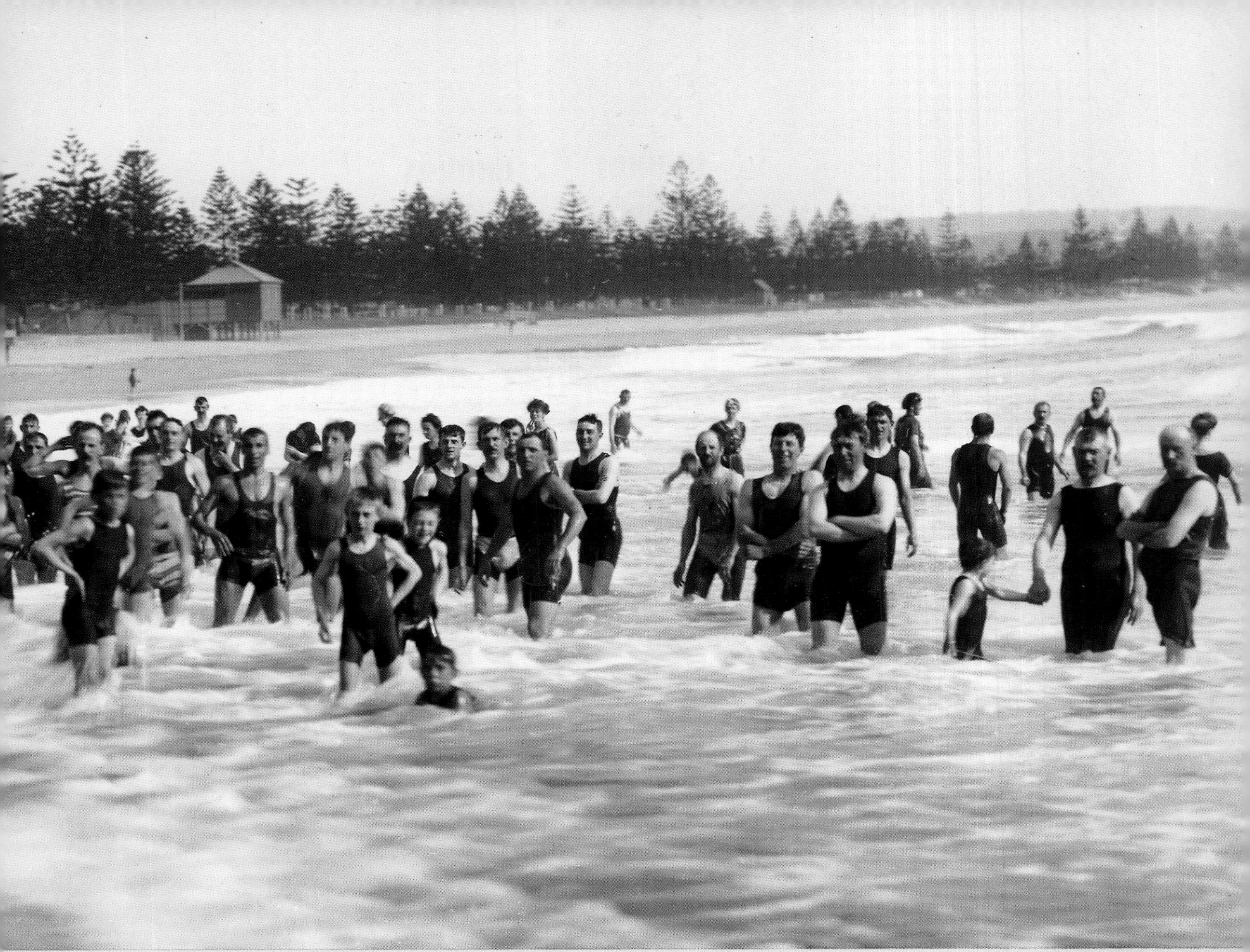

N.S.W. GOVERNMENT PRINTER

GEORGE SAMANA

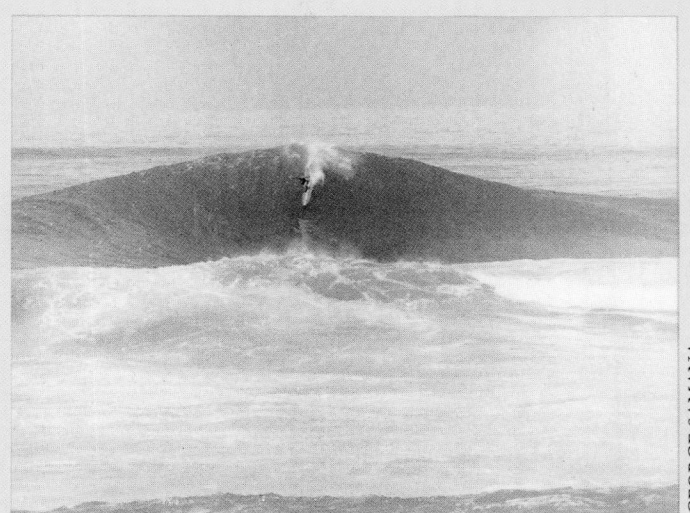

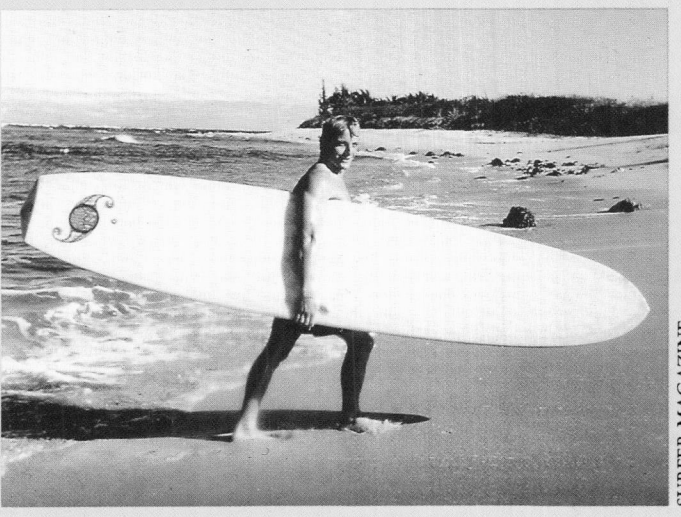

The West Peak — Sunset Beach, Hawaii.

SURFER MAGAZINE

Bob McTavish with a vee-bottom Fantastic Plastic machine: Sunset Beach, the winter of '67/68.

Wally Froiseth at 'First Break' Waikiki as few have ever ridden it; especially on a solid wood 'Hot Curl' board without a fin (inserts).

JOE QUIGG

ART BREWER

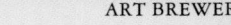

JOHN WITZIG

RON STONER

1. *An institution in American surfing — the '60's Surf Woody.*

2. *Two legends in Hawaiian surfing Dick Brewer (left) and Buzzy Trent.*

3. *Pat Curren in the early days of riding mountains.*

4. *Exponent of the classic style, Bill Hamilton in sweeping cutback.*

5. *Bopping Bob McTavish. The Guru of the new era in the mid 60's.*

6. *The delicate art of nose riding as demonstrated by one of the best — Steve Bigler of California — Claude Codgen looks on in appreciation.*

gressive and radical than the old approach. Surfers like Hawaiians Jock Sutherland and Gerry Lopez and later South African Shaun Tomson switched the emphasis to tube riding. Surfers began carving tracks out of the big Hawaiian waves instead of just getting the hell out of there on big guns. It was then all refined and developed by surfers like Jeff Hakman, Reno Abellira, Terry Fitzgerald, Michael Peterson, Ian Cairns, Peter Drouyn and Peter Townend. Out of this came the rip-tear-and-lacerate manoeuvres of today and surfers like four times world champion Mark Richards, Tommy Carroll, Mark Price, Richard Cram, Hans Hedemann and Tom Curren. Looking at what the hotties are doing to the wave face right now, you think: what next?

Artificial waves? Windsurfing? A breakthrough in technology which radically changes the surfboard, and therefore what you can do on it?

Whatever happens, one thing will remain: the waves. I've surfed all over the world now, and I'm still amazed at the variety and richness of surf which different breaks have to offer. I suppose my favourite breaks are the ones I'm most familiar with, because I live with them, constantly checking the bank, wind and swell: the Wedge, at Whale Beach, on Sydney's north side, especially during the cyclone season; and Narrabeen, because there are so many good surfers out there that it raises your own surfing. Further along the New South Wales coast I like Angourie. I was one of the first to surf there: it's a very predictable wave, breaking right over a reef, and you can surf it (as I have) even during the night. In Hawaii you can't go past Sunset. It will always be a very challenging wave, very complex, never doing the same thing twice; when you first arrive there you are terrified. No country will ever replace Hawaii as the site of the ideal surf breaks. In California my favourite break is Malibu, but it's rare to get it without crowds. That's why I love the beautiful waves at Blacks, below the university in La Jolla; you have to walk down the cliff face to

State of the Art 1981. Professional Surfing: M.R. at Burleigh.

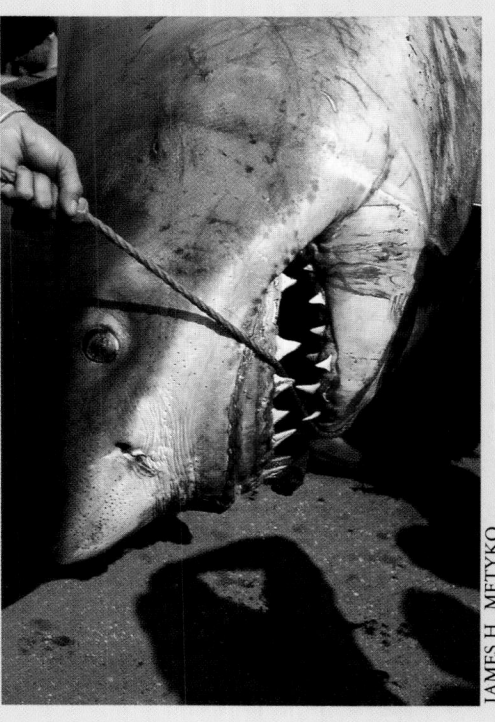

A 14 ft Great White: 2500 lbs.

STEVE WILKINGS

ISLAND STYLE

Top: *Reno Abellira at Sunset Beach, Oahu, Hawaii.*

Above: *North Shore line-up.*

Top right: *Wayne 'Rabbit' Bartholomew at Burleigh Heads, Queensland, Australia.*

Right: *Burleigh line-up.*

SATO

JEFF DIVINE

JEFF DIVINE

1. *The Master Swordsman — Gerry Lopez, carving at the Pipeline.*

2. *David Nuuhiwa is synonymous with nose riding but he is particularly skilled in the tube.*

3. *Patron Saints of surfing.*

4. *Tommy Carroll "The Little Aussie Battler" continuing the tradition of power surfing.*

5. *Tom Curran — 1982 World Amateur Champion — the hottest Californian to emerge since Rolf Aurness.*

6. *Margo Oberg in the curl. Girls have always surfed but not as well as men.*

7. *Windsurfing — the wave of the future?*

PETER SIMONS

JEFF DIVINE

DARRELL JONES

PETER CRAWFORD

DAN MERKEL

More surfers — the same number of waves.

get there, it's unpopulated — you have to put out some energy to get some rewards, and I like that.

Then there are the surfers themselves. I'm going to make a movie about the history of surfing, and one of the reasons is my admiration for the older surfers who have created the surfing tradition we've all inherited. I think of people like the great Tom Blake, who first put a fin on a surfboard, and his theory that nature is God. I've come around to that way of thinking more and more; if you do something like surfing at a sufficiently committed level then that's your religion; you can feel the energy and ride on it. And when I was a kid I was trying like hell to be a direct copy of Phil Edwards. I still think kids have the right to mimic their heroes, because that's the way they learn; and when the kid eventually gets better than his hero, there shouldn't be any animosity. Phil was a tall guy, like me, and his smooth, functional style suited me exactly; but I was putting a lot more power into my surfing, and there came a time when I realised I was doing two turns on the wave to his one. That process is inevitable: just as Wayne Lynch, Michael Peterson and, I guess, Mark Richards took over some

of the things I was doing and pushed them further. That's how surfing develops.

I feel very open, very unpossessive about it all. Even proud. I mean, surfing crosses countries, colour, religion, everything — I think that's fantastic. That's what the rest of the world should be like. Surfing still gives me a charge whether it's me doing it or someone else. I love how electric Tommy Carroll is: how he can make his board accelerate to three times its speed in the distance of a couple of boards. All over the world other surfers are doing other things; surfing is now practised wherever waves break on the planet's surface. Each country is playing its part in the development of the sport. However, we must never lose sight of the essence of surfing. The reason our forefathers went surfing is the same reason we go surfing today . . . good fun.

As the rest of this book shows . . .

●

29

C.J. HEDEMANN

Above: *By the end of the 19th century few Hawaiians were surfing. The sport was kept alive, however, at Waikiki by surfers such as this.*

Right: *Hawaiian legends and chants tell of incredible surfing feats by men and women. This early engraving showing Wahines in action was titled: "Surf Swimming by Sandwich Islands."*

BISHOP MUSEUM

SURFING ROOTS

Nobody is quite sure when the Polynesians began to surf, but Hawaiian chants which date back to the 15th century AD tell stories of surfing exploits which seem to show that surfing was a major part of Hawaiian life long before that. For as long, perhaps, as the Hawaiians had existed as an independent race. And though we know that the Tahitians, for instance, had long practised surfing it was Hawaii which was the source of the sport's great expansion.

The first Western man to see surfing in action was Captain Cook, the great British navigator who came across Hawaii in the late 1770s on one of the voyages of exploration which also led to the European discovery and settlement of Australia. When he sailed into Kealakekua Bay, in Hawaii, he was astounded to see the Islanders catching waves on boards and wrote a lovely description of it:

"The surf, which breaks on the coast around the bay, extends to the distance of about 150 yards from the shore, within which space the surges of the sea, accumulating from the shallowness of the water, are dashed against the beach with prodigious violence. Whenever, from stormy weather or any extraordinary swell at sea, the impetuosity of the surf is increased to its utmost height, they choose this time for this amusement . . .

"Twenty or thirty of the natives, taking each a long narrow board, rounded at the ends, set out together from the shore. The first wave they meet they plunge under, and suffering it to roll over them, rise again beyond it, and make the best of their way by swimming out into sea. The second wave is encountered in the same manner as the first; the great difficulty consisting in seizing the proper moment of diving underneath it, which, if missed, the person is caught by the surf and driven back again with great violence, and all his dexterity is then required to prevent himself being dashed against the rocks.

"As soon as they have gained, by these repeated efforts, the smooth water beyond the surf they lay themselves at length on their boards and prepare for their return. As the surf consists of a number of waves, of which every third is remarked to be always much larger than the others and to flow higher on the shore . . . their first object is to place themselves on the summit of the largest surge, by which they are driven along with amazing rapidity toward the shore . . ."

Captain Cook also saw Islanders surfing in canoes at Tahiti; here is a description he wrote in December, 1777:

"On walking one day about Matavi Point, where our tents were erected, I saw a man paddling in a small canoe so quickly and looking about him with such eagerness of each side, as to command all my attention. At first I imagined that he had stolen something from one of the ships and was pursued, but on waiting patiently, saw him repeat his amusement. He went out from the shore till he was near the place where the swell begins to take its rise and, watching its first motion very attentively, paddled before it with great quickness, till he found that it overlooked him, and had acquired sufficient force to carry his canoe before it without passing underneath.

"He then sat motionless and was carried along at the same swift rate as the wave, till it landed him upon the beach. Then he started out, emptied his canoe, and went in search of another swell.

"I could not help concluding that this man felt the most supreme pleasure while he was driven on so fast and so smoothly by the sea . . ."

The Hawaiians have always been great water-people and seafarers, and people have been arguing about how they arrived on the Islands for centuries. The Mormon Church believes that some early Mormon ancestors left the west coast of Central or South America and found their way into the Pacific, where they became part of the Polynesian nation. Many anthropologists, however, think the immigration of the Polynesian people into the Pacific was from the west, from Asia, rather than from the east. Thor Heyerdahl's epic raft voyage popularised the possibility of Polynesians emigrating from South America, but nearly all the scientific evidence points the other way. Whatever the truth, we know that the Hawaiians developed a subtle system of laws, known as Kapu, which is a variation of the Tahitian word Tapu (or taboo). A hereditary caste of nobelmen, or alii, dominated the commoners, and surfing became a part of this system: certain beaches and types of boards were reserved for the alii. The Hawaiian word for surfing was *he'enalu,* which is a word rich in meanings; the first half, for instance, can mean 'to change from a solid to a liquid substance' or 'run as a liquid'; *nalu,* the second part, can refer to the surging motion of a wave, the foaming of a wave, or the slimy liquid on the face of a newborn child. The ocean had the status of a god (Kanaloa). And when a surfboard was made there was an appropriate ritual to accompany its creation.

Only three types of tree were used to make the ancient surfboards: the wili wili, the ula (or breadfruit), and the koa. Once a tree had been selected a red fish called Kumu was placed at the foot of its trunk. The tree was cut down, and the fish placed with a prayer in a hole dug at the root. After this ceremony the surfer chipped away at the tree with a stone adze until it was reduced to the size of the board he wanted: 14 to 16 feet long for the alii, 10 to 12 feet long for the commoners. After it was completed the board was pulled down to the beach and placed in a canoe house (halau). Granulated coral, called pohaku puna, and a rough kind of stone called oahi were used for smoothing the rough surfaces on the board and getting rid of the adze marks. Finally the root of the Ti plant or a pounded bark called hili was used to give the board a glossy black finish.

Before the surfboard was used in the sea, however, there were other ceremonies to be performed. It had to be dedicated, and the traditional rituals were religiously observed by those responsible for creating the board. In this way the making of a surfboard became a creative act which joined man and the sea.

A great deal of what we know about early Hawaiian surfing is due to chants which were handed down from generation to generation and were not written down until the early 19th century. Then Hawaiian scholars such as Samuel Kamakau began to record the chants which they remembered from their childhood; Kamakau, for instance, recorded an incident which occurred in the life of Umi, a famous chief who ruled over the entire Big Island and Maui during the late 15th and early 16th century. Kamakau writes that Umi, as a young man, was a fine surfrider and one day 'a certain chief of Laupahoehoe noticed Umi's skill'. Says Kamakau:

"His name was Paiea, and he knew all the surfs and the best one to ride. It was the one directly in front of Laupahoehoe, facing Hilo. It was a huge one which none dared to ride except Paiea, who was noted for his skill. Gambling on surfing was practised in that locality. All of the inhabitants from Waipunalei to Kaula placed their wager on Umi, and those of Laupahoehoe on Paiea.

The two rode the surf, and while surfing Paiea noticed that Umi was winning. As they drew near a rock, Paiea crowded him against it, skinning his side. Umi was strong and pressed his foot against Paiea's chest and then landed ashore. Umi won against Paiea, and because Paiea crowded Umi against the rock with the intention of killing him Paiea was roasted in an imu (oven) in later years when Umi became the supreme king of the Big Island."

With the coming of missionaries into Hawaii in the early 19th century the sport of surfing went into a decline. The evangelists and Protestant missionaries who swept across the Pacific were determined to convert the Islanders to Christianity, and in large part they succeeded. The missionaries considered surfing a hedonistic pursuit and a distraction from the Christian religion; no doubt they were aware, too, of the religious and cultural significance of surfing in the Hawaiian community, and realised that it could be a focus of cultural resistance to Western customs. If we are to go by contemporary artists' impressions and Europeans didn't understand the technique and art of surfing; their drawings portray naked natives sitting on bits of wood on top of waves, and don't display any real perception of what was going on.

The repression of surfing in the Islands coincided with a general suspicion throughout Europe of bathing in the sea. For surfing to be accepted by Western culture it had to overcome a lot of prejudices . . . which, eventually, it did.
●

Top right: *1779 at Kealakekua Bay, engraving by John Webber, official artist who accompanied Captain James Cook on his 'discovery' of the Hawaiian Islands.*

Below: *Waikiki in 1865 with morning glory vines planted by the Royal Family covering the beach.*

BISHOP MUSEUM

Right: *European artists had difficulty in really understanding what the Hawaiians were doing in the surf.*

Far right: *The Bishop Museum in Honolulu houses the world's finest collection of ancient Hawaiian surfboards.*

Below: *Drawing by 'Pellion' artist on ship 'Uranye' French expedition 1919 showing house of Prime Minister.*

BAKER/VAN DYKE

SURFING MAGAZINE

RAY JEROME BAKER/ROBERT E. VAN DYKE

BATHING AND BODYSURFING

In Europe during the 18th century bathing in the ocean in any form was hardly considered civilised behaviour. There was a general belief that outdoor bathing helped spread the epidemics that swept England and the Continent during the Middle Ages. During the second half of the 19th century, however, the old prejudices against bathing began to disappear. . . In order to bridge the gap between the Victorian moral code (Queen Victoria was on the throne in England) and the desire to bathe in the sea the bathing machine was invented. The English machine, designed to promote modesty and decency, was basically a wooden box on

1906: The western world took to the ocean en-mass — in the correct attire of course.

wheels. These so-called machines were drawn by a horse into the sea where its occupants, once they had changed into bathing costumes, would emerge well-hidden by the machine to take the plunge. Slowly the public began to develop better methods of swimming and in 1896 swimming races were included in the Olympic Games.

In the late 19th century the Australian public had only just begun to venture into the water. The colonies had their own particular type of bathing machine which had a net around the perimeter to protect the swimmers against shark attack. Most people were content to promenade on the piers and the men who pioneered open-sea bathing had to do so before the hour of dawn, as it was illegal to bathe in a public place between 7 am and 6 pm. Bathing often took the form of piling your clothes on the sand and running naked into the surf, where you kept your feet very firmly on the bottom. Not long after the men had begun bathing women took to the sea as well and in 1899 the ladies at Manly, Sydney's main north-of-the-harbour beach, made a request for dressing sheds; these didn't materialise for quite a few years because community attitudes had not changed enough to formally condone women bathing. More than one local Manly newspaper was concerned that, if any of the increasing number of bathers drowned, the council would be held responsible. This led to the police patrolling the beach every morning and trying to make sure nobody stayed in the water after 7 am.

Needless to say, Australians began to ignore the law and started surf bathing during the day between 7 am and 6 pm. One particularly regular offender was a boy called Fred Williams, who was a fine swimmer and who became a public figure when, at Manly, he made the first publicised

N.S.W. GOVERNMENT PRINTER

rescue of another swimmer who had got into difficulties in the surf. One summer's morning, when he was swimming in the corner at Manly, he saw something which really excited him: coming towards him out of the foam was a dark-skinned, woolly-headed boy who was smiling and yelling with delight as the wave carried him to the shore. It was, as far as we know, the first time bodysurfing had occurred in Australia, and the boy was a Polynesian Islander called Tommy Tanna. It seems he had been brought to Australia to work as a garden boy for one of Manly's wealthy families. Tommy was no teacher, but he was only too willing to show Fred how to body surf. Williams became so good at it that he began to pass the skill on to other swimmers and body surfing began to spread up and down the coast.

The irony here is that those Manly families which brought such pressure to bear on the authorities to enforce the daylight bathing law were the employers of Tommy Tanna, and without their bringing an Islander to work in the garden it might have been years before Australians learnt to body surf.

Finally Manly Council extended the hours for bathing until 8 am. Notice boards went up with information as

The Australian and South African Bathing Machine: Colonial designers added a shark-proof cage to the European invention.

Below: *Fred Williams was shown how to body-surf by Tommy Tanna, a South Sea Islander.*

to the penalities: a fine of up to two pounds for bathing during the prohibited hours, and ten pounds for wearing a costume which did not cover the swimmer from neck to knee. Sea bathing increased all along the populated coast from Coogee in the south to Manly in the north. Attempts to police the time limit were difficult because it was easy to recognise the local constabulary, and when plainclothes police were brought across the harbour from the city of Sydney they sometimes caught the wrong men. In those days it was usual for the crews of the 18-footer racing yachts to sail across the harbour to spend a noisy Saturday afternoon along the Corso and on the ocean beach, and on one occasion it was some of these men that the visiting police arrested. The magistrate practically laughed the case out of court.

Then along came Gocher. Full name, William Henry Gocher, editor and owner of a local newspaper called the Manly and North Sydney News. On Sunday, on the opening day of the surf season of 1902-3 (it was the first day of September in those years) Gocher walked along Manly beach, climbed the hill at the northern end and descended the other side to where many surfers went . . . a beach called Freshwater. He told the surfers he intended to force the issue of restricted bathing hours; he would use his newspaper to inform everyone of his intention to bathe at midday the following Sunday. If the police arrested him the matter would serve as a test case and all would know where they stood. Gocher's guess was that the bathers would be on the right side of the fence. After all, the beaches were the property of the *public,* not merely a few jaundiced ratepayers who wanted the bathing laws enforced.

Gocher advertised what he was going to do, went swimming — and no-one took any notice. The noonday sun blazed down on his balding middle-aged head, and no-one cared, least of all the police. Next week he appeared again, but the affair of the sailing club men had dampened the enthusiasm of the police to arrest any-one. On his third attempt, which he publicised much more widely, Gocher succeeded in drawing quite a crowd — so much so that a few of his friends who had meant to share the bathing exhibition with him got cold feet when they saw the crowd and stayed on the beach.

This time the police acted. Gocher was escorted from the water and questioned, but the police brought no charges against him. And so Gocher won for Australians the right to bathe in the sea whenever they wanted to. Yet Gocher himself was English. He was born in Suffolk in 1856 and emigrated with his two brothers to Australia about 1872. In 1884 he worked in Sydney as an artist painting portraits, and in 1901 stood for the Senate, coming 49th out of 50 candidates. He failed again when he stood for the State parliament in

1901 and 1904. By this time he had moved to Manly and had started his newspaper, and no doubt was looking for causes to champion. He was probably something of an opportunist and, like all newspapermen, was searching for a good story when he decided to defy the restrictions upon public bathing. But at least his stunt worked.

In November 1903 Manly Council reluctantly decided to allow all-day bathing. Similar moves were taking place at other beaches. At Bondi, Frank McEllone and the rector of St Mary's church at Waverley had their names taken by police for bathing during the day, but the pressure for surf bathing was irresistible. Manly was really the centre of the new push. The population had doubled within a few years, and so had house rents. The surge in popularity of surfing led to drownings, still the number of surfers doubled, trebled and quadrupled. In 1902 seventeen people drowned at Manly beach. It was obviously something would have to be done.

1. *The Sly brothers — Australia's first lifeguards.*

2. *Lyster Ormsby (right), inventor of the surf-reel with members of the Bondi Surf Club, 1908.*

3. *Surf carnival at Newcastle Beach, 1908.*

4. *Members of the Manly Surf Club, 1908.*

1

2

BONDI SURF BATHERS LIFE SAVING CLUB

MANLY WARRINGAH & PITTWATER HIST. SOC.

3

4

BONDI SURF BATHERS LIFE SAVING CLUB

MANLY WARRINGAH & PITTWATER HIST. SOC.

RAY JEROME BAKER/ROBERT E. VAN DYKE

RAY JEROME BAKER/ROBERT E. VAN DYKE

Above: *Waikiki in the 1920's. But it could have been any of His Majesty's colonies when conditions were right.*

Left: *The surfoplane was the device most older Aussie surfers first used to ride waves*

Below: *Ocean piers were a great source of amusement around the turn of the 20th century.*

N.S.W. GOVERNMENT PRINTER

N.S.W. GOVERNMENT PRINTER

Below: *Coogee, NSW in 1908. New found freedom for some, but not everyone's cup of tea.*   Bottom: *Newport in 1915: now a densely populated suburb on Sydney's northern beaches.*

N.S.W. GOVERNMENT PRINTER

RAY JEROME BAKER/ROBERT E. VAN DYKE

All over the world, the beach was very much the place to be in the late 20's.

One of the first attempts at setting up a rescue organisation was by the Sly Brothers, of Fairy Bower, who started tackling the surf in an old ship's lifeboat they had converted into a fishing boat. Manly Council insisted they wear a uniform, which the brothers looked upon as a bit of a joke; also they felt the rescue work interfered with their fishing. But from their lifeboat developed the Australian surfboat, with its four oarsmen and big sweep oar at the back, which over the years became standard equipment with local surf clubs.

These surf lifesaving clubs were to develop into a unique Australian institution, but their beginnings were unpromising enough. A Life Saving Society had been formed in 1894 and had set up rescue equipment at the most popular Sydney beaches: Manly, Bondi, Coogee and Bronte. This consisted of a pole in the centre of the beach with a coil of rope and a circular lifebuoy attached, but the heavy surf made this gear almost useless. In 1906 the Bondi Surf Bathers' Life Saving Club was formed by local surfers, including Lyster Ormsby, Percy Flynol and Sid Fullwood. The same summer Manly Council appointed a paid lifeguard, but for some reason the idea didn't catch on and it was the surf lifesaving clubs which took over the rescue work. A club was formed at Bronte in 1907, and another at Manly in 1908; the movement began to spread to other beaches, and eventually the Surf Life Saving Association of Australia was formed. The lifesavers developed their own methods of rescuing people from the surf, including the reel-and-belt method which has since been taken up all over the world . . . basically, a beltman towing a line makes the rescue and is then hauled back to the beach by other lifesavers manning the reel.

There is some controversy over who designed the first surf reel. Most say Lyster Ormsby, and this seems a reasonable assumption. The actual building of the first reel was done by a coachbuilder, Mr Olding, who said that in 1903 a committee of four from the Bondi club, including Ormsby, visited him. Mr Olding says that the reel was never mentioned and no plan, design or measurement was submitted to him, but leaves open the question of what exactly the committee *did* discuss with him. The important thing is the reel was made, and it worked. It was put on public

display at Bondi in 1906 and two days later the first rescue using the reel took place. The swimmer who was dragged out of the surf was someone who was to go on to become a legend in Australian aviation, Charles Kingsford Smith. However, the sea was still to claim his life when some 30 years later he was lost during a historic flight over the Indian Ocean. Certainly the reel has since helped save the lives of thousands of surfers. And, from those tentative beginnings, the surf lifesaving movement grew to become a highly skilled and experienced organisation with its own carnivals, rituals and sporting culture.

Today, surfboard riders may save as many people who get into trouble in the water as lifesavers do. Personally, I'd save at least one person a month.

N.S.W. GOVERNMENT PRINTER

That's understandable, because surfboard riders are often out there on the edge of the rip coming out from the shore; if a swimmer gets caught in the rip we can haul him onto a board and get him back to the beach. Of course, we're not trained to handle swimmers who've become unconscious, and we're not really on the lookout for them; we're looking for waves. There is an element of glamour attached to being a club lifesaver, but there's no doubt the movement fills a genuine need.

Australia's fascination with the ocean continued to grow through the early part of this century. The only setback occurred in 1907 when the mayors of Waverley, Randwick and Manly, in whose municipalities the most popular surfing beaches were located, issued a directive that all bathers, irrespective of sex, had to wear skirts! This was provoked by the fact that men were lying on the beach wearing V trunks and women were wearing light, gauzy material which when wet clung to their bodies too closely to be 'decent!' The councils decreed that surfers should wear a costume which consisted of 'a guernsey with trouser legs, reaching from the elbow to the bend of the knee, together with a skirt, not unsightly, attached to the garment, covering the figure from hips to knees'. The same pattern would serve women as well as men; both sexes had to be covered apron-fashion.

Needless to say, the bathing public would have none of this. In order to mock the regulations the bathers organised a march from Bondi to the city, with a dead seagull on a stick as a banner. Many men wore petticoats, some with yards of lace and embroidery trailing in the dust behind. Some wore red flannels; others decorated themselves with ballet frills around their bulging bellies. A few wore chaff bags with the ends lopped off or kitchen curtains. It was a hilarious occasion, with the law flaunted once again; after that the Australian authorities fell in with what was being worn in Europe and America, and local surfers wore woollen neck-to-knee costumes . . . without skirts.

As the years went on, surf bathing and body surfing grew in popularity and became a national sport throughout Australia. The lifesaving movement grew with it. The next major step forward had to await the arrival of the surfboard. ●

EONI   EHUKAI   KNUTE   FRED   HILO   DAVID   DUKE

Dude Miller.   H. Nainoa.   K. Cottrell.   F. Wilhelm.   Hilo Boyd.   H. Coelle.   D. Kahanamoku.   Steamboat.   H. Anahu.

Dowd.   Kim Hai.   L. Kaupiko.   T. Hjorth.   Joe Bishaw.   W. Kahanamoku.   Genoves.   Holstien.   Lewis.   S. Kahanamoku.   Landa.

Pua Kealoha.   Lady Langer.   E. Hiebtrey.   Stubby Kruger.   Duke P. Kahanamoku.   H. Prieste.   A. Beckley.   H. Awana.

Top: *The famous Beach Boys of Waikiki who were responsible for the renewed interest in surfing.*

Above: *The Beach Boys performed crazy stunts such as riding their boards with dogs, chairs, ukuleles and adoring lady tourists.*

HAWAIIAN REVIVAL

In Hawaii, in the early 20th century, the Islanders began to reawaken to the gift of the waves. As the influence of the missionaries began to decline surfboard riding was taken up again, but the only place where this was done regularly was on the gentle sloping waves of Waikiki, on the island of Oahu. Not only native Hawaiians were surfing, but the sons and daughters of Europeans and Americans who had made their homes in Hawaii took up the sport as well.

One of these was George Freeth, who was born in 1883 of Irish and Hawaiian parentage. In 1900, at the age of 16, he taught himself to ride standing up on the board instead of lying down. The board on which he accomplished this was a solid, heavy, 16-foot *Alia* design. The story is that it had been given to him by his uncle, a Hawaiian prince, and the board is now a treasured item in the Bishop Museum in Honolulu.

Freeth was an innovator and experimented with shorter boards by cutting the old 16-foot boards in half. These short boards were a great success, and in the spring of 1907 he was brought to Redondo beach, in California, to demonstrate surfboard riding as a publicity stunt to promote the opening of the Redondo-Los Angeles railroad owned by Henry Huntington — who gave his name to Huntington Beach. Freeth stayed on in California to become the first lifeguard, and in this way brought the art of surfboard riding to the United States. He became a national hero and earned both the Carnegie Medal for bravery and the Congressional Medal of Honour when in a particularly violent storm in December, 1908 he made three trips through mountainous surf to rescue seven Japanese fishermen. At least 78 people owed their lives to his work as a lifeguard. He was a great swimmer as well as surfer, and in 1912 he would almost certainly have been selected to represent the United States at the Olympic Games had it not been ruled that he was a 'professional' because he was a paid lifeguard. At the age of 35 he died in San Diego during a national influenza epidemic; locals said that

Freeth exhausted himself rescuing several swimmers at Oceanside and became an easy victim of the virus.

Freeth was a great man; he had the build of a surfer and by "standing on the water" at Redondo he began the move of surfboard riding out of Hawaii through the rest of the world.

Surfing rapidly began to catch on in the United States. When conditions were warm and sunny the beach became the new place to be. Californians ventured in automobiles to Corona Del Mar to watch the surfing and enjoy the beach. People on the mainland of the United States discovered Hawaii as a holiday resort, and the Islands became America's vacation funland. In order to accommodate this phenomenon Waikiki was developed, and hotels sprang up on the beachfront amid the palms and next to the gentle surf. For American tourists arriving there for the first time it was an exotic experience; the luxury ocean liners would come in to berth at Aloha Tower, to be greeted by Hawaiian guitars, ukuleles, singers and hula dancers. The tourists would be showered with leis and quickly transported to one of the two modern hotels, the Moana in Waikiki or, on the other side of the island, which they reached by railway, the Haleiwa Hotel; there they would be free to wander over the palatial lawns which ran right down to the beach. In Hawaii they had two unfamiliar alternatives to swimming: the outrigger canoe and the surfboard. Nowhere else in the world is quite like Waikiki for the first experience of surfing. The water is a constant 76 degrees F., so it is never too cold to surf. Fanned by trade winds, the waves are long in forming, slow to break, and then run for a great distance over a level coral bottom.

Naturally a team of lifeguards was needed to protect the tourists and keep them safe from drowning, and this was recruited from Hawaiians who lived in the area. One family that lived close by was the Paoa-Kahanamokus. They had one daughter and five sons, David, Sargent, Louis, Sam and Duke. Duke was the

eldest, and his name came not from Hawaiian royalty but from his father, who was called Duke in July 1869 when the Duke of Edinburgh made an official visit to Hawaii and some families named their sons after him. Duke, as the eldest son, inherited his father's name. He was born in 1890 and he and his brothers all grew up surfing and swimming around Waikiki, but Duke was extraordinarily gifted, and he went on to become one of the great surfers in history.

As the tourist industry grew Duke and his brothers came to be employed on the beach as 'beachboys'. The amount of time they spent in the water was amazing: up to eight hours a day. As a result they became extremely skilful surfers and began developing new manoeuvres . . . standing on the board backwards, head stands, stepping from board to board, sliding both left and right with the breaking wave, and the ever-popular tandem with both a dog and a lady tourist clinging on for dear life.

It was inevitable that Duke, like George Freeth before him, should end up in the United States. Indeed in 1912 he was chosen to represent America at the Olympic Games in Stockholm, Freeth having been disqualified. Duke took an easy first in the 100-metre freestyle to become the world's fastest sprint swimmer, a position he held until 1929 when a lanky kid from Chicago called Johnny Weismuller beat him. Duke introduced surfboard riding to the U.S. east coast and on the way to the Olympic Games enjoyed a surf in California as well.

It was Duke who brought surfboard riding to Australia. In 1912 C.D. Paterson, of Manly, had returned from Hawaii with a solid, heavy redwood board which a few local bodysurfers had tried to ride, but couldn't. Then three years later the New South Wales Swimming Association invited Duke Kahanamoku to swim at the Domain Baths in Sydney, where he broke his own world record for the 100 yards with a time of 53.8 seconds. While he was in Australia he

1

RAY JEROME BAKER/ROBERT E. VAN DYKE

3

BISHOP MUSEUM

2

LEGENDS PRESS

44

4

1. *Duke Kahanamoku (right) in 1920 with Norman Ross, former World and Olympic long distance swimmer.*

2. *George Freeth, the man who took surfing from Hawaii to the United States mainland. Californian land developer, Henry E. Huntington brought Freeth to California in 1907 to promote the opening of his Redondo — Los Angeles Railroad.*

3. *1928, Tom Blake significantly contributed to surfboard design. Inspired by ancient Hawaiian boards he developed the hollow board and is credited with being the first to add a fin to a board.*

4. *1924 Redondo Beach Fashion Show and Bathing Beauty Parade.*

5. *Maxie Mitchell at Waikiki.*

6. *Pacific Systems Homes, Swastika Model first company to commercially produce boards. Swastika deleted in 1939. Sold new for under $40, constructed of laminated Redwood and Balsa, covered with varnish, rails are full with square upper edge and rounder lower edge — length 10' wide-point 23", nose 21", tail 22", tail block 22".*

7. *Checkerboard Cosmetics are not new as shown by this 1930's beach boy.*

5

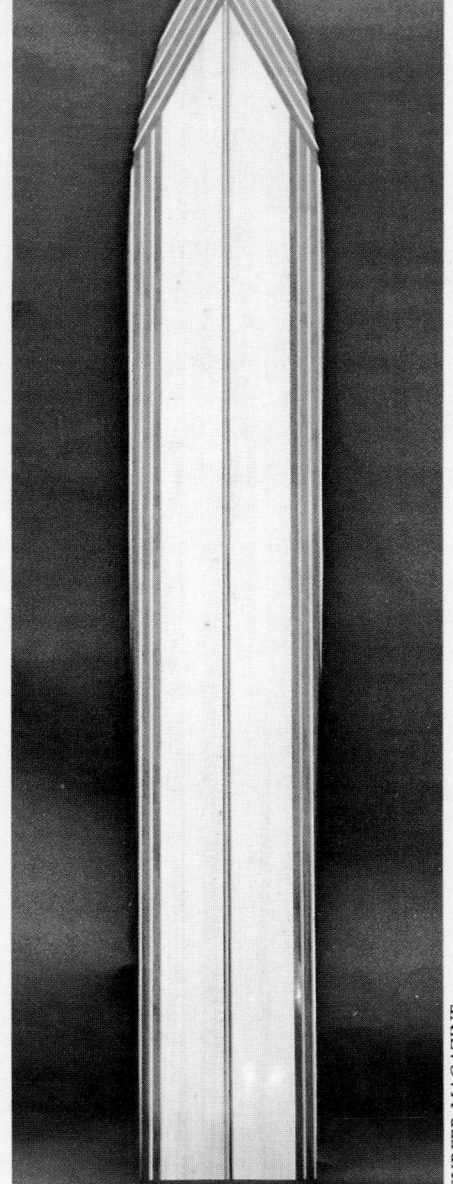

BISHOP MUSEUM

6

SURFER MAGAZINE

7

JOE QUIGG

Top: *1920's. The grand old ladies of Waikiki. The Moana and Royal Hawaiian Hotels.*

Left: *Waikiki 1918. The tourist industry was flourishing, hotels dotted the beachfront. Note the biplane over Diamond Head.*

Jack London, the famous writer (left) and his wife next to him on the beach at Waikiki with Alexander Hume Ford, founder of the Outrigger Canoe Club.

SNOW McALISTER

15th Jan. 1915 Duke Kahanamoku introduces surfboard riding to Australia. This historic photo shows the Duke emerging from the surf at Freshwater after giving a display of surfing on a board he made in Australia from sugar pine.

made a tour of the beaches and chose Freshwater to give an exhibition of the art of surfboard riding. He didn't know about the old redwood board in the district so he set to work to build his own out of a piece of sugar pine supplied by a surf club member whose family was in the timber business.

Sunday morning. A clear, brilliant day. Spectators were milling around to watch. Manly Surf Boat was on hand to give Duke assistance to drag his board through the break — an offer he laughed at good naturedly. Picking up his board he ran to the water's edge, slid on and paddled out through the breakers. He made better time on the way out than the local swimmers who escorted him. Once out beyond the break it wasn't long before he picked up a wave in the northern corner, stood up and ran the

board diagonally across the bay, continually beating the break. Duke showed the crowd everything in the book, from head stands to a finale of tandem surfing with a local girl, Isobel Latham — who at the time of writing is still alive and told me the story of that memorable day.

Among those watching was a 10-year-old Manly boy called Claude West. He was so impressed by what Duke did that he managed to get the Hawaiian to coach him in the art of board riding, and when Duke left Australia he passed the board he had made on to the youngster. Claude soon became a proficient board rider, and other surfers began to imitate him. Claude proved himself a great surfer: he won the Australian surfing championships from 1919 to 1924 and was responsible for demonstrating the benefits of the surfboard in

rescue work; on one occasion he rescued the then Governor-General of Australia, Sir Ronald Munro Ferguson. West went on to build many surfboards fashioned like the one he had inherited from Duke; he was a good craftsman, having learnt to fine-plane making coffins for an undertaker. In 1918 he tried to make a lighter surfboard by chipping out the centre of a solid board and covering it with a lighter wood but the experiment proved unsatisfactory. Plywood had not been invented at this stage, and waterproof glue was unheard of. All timber was sun-dried instead of kiln-dried and the sun quickly cracked the thin outside veneer, letting the water in.

But the hollow board, the next major step in surfboard design, was on the way.

●

Duke (centre left) and his Californian friends clowning it up at Carona Del Mar about 1925. These pics are taken off 16mm film found in Los Angeles county dump and given to Leroy Grannis. The other surfers are unfortunately unidentified.

HEYDAY OF THE HOLLOW BOARD

After World War I the surfboard changed. Boards became longer, lighter, narrower, and hollow. The man responsible for this was Tom Blake, who around 1920 moved from his home in Wisconsin to California. In 1924, aged 22, he sailed for Hawaii and became hooked on surfing; later the same year he was back working as a lifeguard in Santa Monica and it was here he built the first hollow board. The design was influenced by the ancient boards he had seen at the Bishop Museum in Honolulu. He purchased a solid slab of redwood 16' long, 2' wide and 4" thick. It weighed around 150 lbs — too heavy to be of service as a surfboard, even when shaped. So to lighten it he drilled hundreds of holes in it from top to bottom, each hole removing a cylinder of wood four inches long. Then he left the holey board season for a month. After the wood had fully dried he covered the top and bottom surfaces with a thin layer of wood, sealing the holes. He then shaped the board in a design adapted from the ancient Hawaiians. It finished up 15' long, 19" wide and 4" thick, looking like a cigar. Its weight was only 100 lbs, because it was partly hollow.

With this board Blake won every paddle board race he entered for several years. He was a strict vegetarian and a marvellous athlete, swimming just seconds behind Duke Kahanamoku and Johnny Weismuller, in fact even beating the Duke once. Duke and Blake were great friends and rivals and spent much time together, surfing, attempting world records, and acting in the early days of Hollywood. Weismuller is remembered for his role as Tarzan, the Duke as 'Old Ironsides' and 'The Medicine Man' and numerous parts as a Hawaiian chief, and Blake as a stuntman for Clark Gable and others. In the late 'twenties, while the Duke and Weismuller were working in Hollywood, Blake was working in Santa Monica, building lighter and lighter paddleboards, finally getting the weight down to 60 lb through the aid of a wood frame covered with a thin layer of redwood. He was a

tireless inventor; as well as being concerned with being the fastest paddler, he modified his board shapes for riding waves.

Surfing was becoming more popular and in 1928 Tom won the first Pacific Coast Surfing Championships, held at Corona Del Mar. He used two boards that particular day, one for paddling and one for riding waves. Some old-timers say it was the first time they ever saw a board turned but others, like Hoppy Swartz, are reputed to have already done this. The

turning manoeuvre was executed by dragging either the left or the right leg in the water.

Tom's adopted home in Santa Monica was in the same area as Malibu and in the summer of 1926 Tom and his friend Sam Reid pulled their 10' x 18" wide-tailed wave-riding boards from the back seat of an Essex and proceeded to walk a couple of miles from the end of the coast road to a desolate, crescent-shaped beach well within the Ringe Ranch, Malibu. The waves were not big that day, but it was the first time Malibu had ever been surfed. Tom Blake actually rode the first wave there.

The story of Malibu is very interesting. Rancho Malibu had been handed down to Rhoda May Ringe in 1905 when her husband Frederick died. She built her own railroad from the pier in Malibu to the northern end of her ranch at the Ventura County line. In 1926 Rhoda May Ringe was forced to give up a long-standing fight she had waged against the 'intrusion' of government authorities; the Roosevelt

Highway, or U.S. 101 as it is now known, was going through her 26 miles of coastline, like it or not. She had fought a battle with the authorities for 17 years, had been ridiculed by the press for standing in the way of progress, and had gone four times to the Californian Supreme Court and twice to the U.S. Supreme Court. She completely exhausted her considerable fortune and died in Santa Monica in February 1941. The Ringe family, however, lives on with Rhoda May Ringe's grandson, Ron, still living in the Malibu area and being active in the Malibu Historical Society. It's interesting to consider that had his grandmother gone along with government access to her land she would probably have been able to keep her ranch and thus all the coastal land from Topanga to the Ventura County line.

In 1930 Tom Blake and the Duke moved from California back to Hawaii. Surfing was slowly catching on along the mainland but the Depression, the lure of friends and relations to surf with and a more relaxed lifestyle attracted them both. The tourist industry still survived in the islands, providing 'beach boy' jobs. Surfing was accepted as a fact of life and was growing in popularity through fierce club competition. This had intensified since the inception of the Outrigger Canoe Club in Waikiki in 1908 by Alexander Hume Ford and others who were aggravated by the way hotels were covering all the access to the beach. The trustees of the late Queen Emma's estate turned over a very valuable piece of property to the Outrigger on condition that it would perpetuate the traditional water sports which the Queen had been so fond of. Within a few months there were over a hundred members. Around the same period the Hui Nalu Club was formed by John D. Kaupiko and friends in order to give the Outrigger some competition in canoes, swimming and paddle boards. Duke and his brothers were early members, winning many victories for the club in Kamehameha Day celebrations and numerous other contests. Blake continued winning competitions. He patented his method of construction of the hollow paddleboards and it was officially adopted by the United States lifeguards as the best method of saving lives in the surf. Blake also developed the first keel or fin, which greatly increased the stability and manoeuvrability of his boards. In 1983 age 80, after years of living, study and learning, he still has the same belief that he carved in stone somewhere in Wisconsin in 1964: *NATURE = GOD, THOMAS E. BLAKE.*

The man responsible for Blake's hollow style of construction being introduced to Australia was Frank Adler, a Maroubra surfer who got the idea from an American magazine which showed Blake's board. Adler first used his hollow board in surf club competition in 1934 and easily outpaddled other surfers who were using solid boards. It didn't take long for the new hollow style of boardbuilding to catch on, and hollow boards began to dominate the Australian east coast surfing scene.

In those days surfboard competitions were 'either a race or display depending on conditions that day.' Generally speaking the surfboard was frowned upon by officials of the surf life saving movement, because they believed it was undermining the established reel-and-belt method of rescue. Exactly why they felt this threat has never been clear, because the value of the board had been proven by Claude West in the 1920s. Perhaps the first real dissension within the ranks was at the 1926 Australian championships in Newcastle. Halfway through one swimming event several sharks were sighted close to shore. Instead of suspending the contest the board riders were sent out, which left quite a nasty taste in many board riders' mouths. That brings to mind a more pleasant story of the surfer who won that particular race in Newcastle. 'Snowy' McAlister, a well-known surfer over the years, was leading by a slight margin when they rounded the buoy. He paddled onto a big green swell and after riding for some time standing up he decided to

Balsa Paddle Boards with lid.
Showing construction of Hollow Board.

Hollow surf ski and boards became standard equipment for Aussie Clubbies. Bondi Beach Australia 1945.

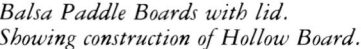

Below: *Preston 'Pete' Peterson. Pacific Coast Surfing Champ 1932, 36, 38, 41.*

WALLY FROISETH

SUN HERALD

JOE QUIGG

do a head stand. This manoeuvre took so much concentration and strain that Snowy rode the wave in this fashion clean up onto the beach. Snowy's trance-like state was interrupted by an official tapping him on the calf and telling him he had won! Upon feeling the sand with his fingers over the gunwales of the board Snowy relaxed his head stand to collect his three guineas for first place.

One particular development that can be attributed to Australia around this period is the invention of the surf ski by G. A. 'Saxon' Crackenthorp. It probably evolved out of the use of canoes in the surf at North Bondi. Because you paddled the ski with an oar, sitting down, it was easier to ride than a board. Originally the skis were 8' long and 28" wide and made of heavy cedar planking, but this gave way to plywood over a light timber frame. Surf club competition drew the skis out in length and eventually another man was used to gain more speed and make it more of a team sport; this led to the standard two-man double ski, a sort of tandem bike on water. In contrast to the surfboard, the surf ski was quickly adopted by the Surf Life Saving Association as official lifesaving equipment. Surfboards, however, were tolerated by officials because so many loyal club members used them, displaying their club badges painted on the decks together with the club's colours running in pin stripes around the rails. The surf club was a tremendously prestigious institution during this period. Australian girls liked the idea of going out with one of those 'bronzed gods' and the surf club ranks swelled to reach 8454 members in 1935.

In a way it was all a foretaste of the rivalry between lifesavers and surfboard riders which broke out after World War II. But for the time being the board riders were still part of the club movement and all regarded themselves as, first and foremost, 'surfers.'

SNOW McALISTER

Above: *Hot young surfer C.J. 'Snow' McAlister. 1917.*

Right: *Snow's winning wave. Newcastle 11th Feb. 1928.*

SNOW McALISTER

DR DON JAMES

PHOTOS DR. JACK BALL

BETWEEN THE WARS

Between World War I and World War II surfing boomed in California. Compared to the rest of the United States mainland the west coast provided ideal beaches and surf breaks. As the popularity of the automobile increased surfers could go further and further afield in search of waves; they spent weekends at San Onofre, Long Beach, or Palos Verdes. Surfers were a radical, colourful group within California's expanding population. They were an incredibly healthy lot, spending long days down at the beach, engaging in friendly competition, encouraging their girls to surf, and partying long into the night. They successfully combined normal working-class lives with the excitement of being the first group of surfers.

In Hawaii a new generation of surfers was growing up which was to contribute to surfboard design and the art of riding big waves. When Duke Kahanamoku was spreading the surf-

1939 San Onofre. (L to R) Tooley Clark, Jim Bixier, Don Oakey, ?, Dorian Paskowitz, Lloyd Baker, Pete Peterson, Guard Chapin, Vincent Lihnberg, Lorrin Harrison.

ing gospel overseas these surfers were still kids; they hung about Waikiki Beach and rented boards from the Waikiki Tavern Bath House for 25 cents a day. There were still only a couple of hundred surfers in the area, and they restricted themselves to the beaches from Diamond Head down to Honolulu harbour. The typical board of that time, in the late 1920s, was still a solid redwood from six to nine feet long, flat-bottomed, with the edges just barely turned up on the bottom side. Surfers would buy a redwood plank at the local lumber yard, take it home, chop it into rough shape with an axe, and then whittle it down with a plane and knife. The finished board was invariably flat, heavy, and about 3½ inches thick.

LORRIN HARRISON

Going surfin' — *San Onofre in 1939. A
Californian surfing ritual. The white auto is
an Auburn Speedster.*

One of the new generation was Wally Froiseth, a great surfer who went on to help invent the narrow-tail 'hot curl' surfboard and was among the first to ride big waves on Hawaii's north shore. Later on he organised the annual Makaha surf contest, which became one of the most successful contests in the world. By this time the Outrigger Canoe Club and the Hui Nalu Canoe Club had been formed at Waikiki: The Outrigger was a rather posh country-club-style outfit, and Froiseth and his friends weren't members. "We were what was known as the 'Tavern Boys' or the 'Empty Lot Boys' really," says Wally, who still lives in Honolulu. "We started right next to Prince Kuhio's beach home on Waikiki; they had a big empty lot with this big Banyon tree there, which is still there now, and we used to keep our boards stored inside the tree roots when we went home. Next day we'd come down, go surfing all day, and put our boards back there. We were kind of on the lower end of the beach, so to speak. At that time we knew about every board on the island and everybody that surfed. There were just the beach boys, a few others."

There wasn't much competition — "people would just surf," says Froiseth. "Fellows like Hawkshaw and the Big Rock and Duke would do crazy stunts, you know, sit on a board with a chair and play ukulele, standing on their heads, that kind of old-time thing. When I was a kid these beach boys would take us out to surf tandem when the waves got big, those of us who were not afraid. So of course I got kind of enthused about big surf, larger and larger waves for more of a challenge, because in those days you just caught the wave and slid a little angle, you couldn't do what you can with a modern board.

"We had a lot of problems with the boards. We would call them sliding tails, which means the back of the board would slide around in front and dump you off. The tails were about 12 to 14 inches wide, just flat, wide boards. We got pretty disgusted with it; we were trying to get across and make the wave and not get caught by the white water, sometimes we wanted to make longer and bigger waves, and these small flat boards were just not getting across. The waves at Diamond Head are pretty steep, pretty hollow, something like Sunset, so we came home and decided to work on it. I don't know whose idea it was, John Kelly or Fran Heath

55

or myself, probably mostly Kelly, we took a hatchet and just chopped off the back sides of each board and went out in the surf and tried again, brought them back in and chopped a little bit more . . . until, that way, we got a tail that was small enough to allow the stern to sink in a little. You could get a little control and speed and not have the tail slide around in front and dump you; it let us get across on a fast and steep-breaking wave. No fin. Solid red-wood. John Kelly made the first all-new board with the narrow tail, and mine was the second, and we got it to work pretty good. It was a pintail, about 4 inches wide; I have mine that I made downstairs.

"Then we started to vee them a little bit, put a V on the bottom; we'd shave a bit more off, you know, keep going in and out until we had it down to a point where that V would hold and give a good angle on the wave so we could get across. And then we really started to make the waves. We were making waves that nobody else could possibly make. It was kind of a big thing and a lot of people started copying. That phase of surfing was, I guess, our contribution, we improved it somewhat from the old early boards.

"It was very critical, the exact shape of the V. It was only about the last quarter of the board. So that when you're on a slide, on the slope of the wave, you've got an angle so that the tail of your board won't slip down. It made it more directional; you could steer, but you had to make a long curve, not like the later era. A lot of guys made V bottoms but they made the top of the V too sharp and it still didn't do them any good. It would just slip right out. What we used to say at the time, it had to have a calculated drag.

"We could change direction by lean-ing back. We weren't dragging our feet too much anymore. We used to have to turn it by dragging our feet in the water, but now you could turn it by tipping it . . . you had to get your weight back and then lift up the bow, and slowly turn around in the other direction, then step forward into trim. You had to get way back on the board with all your weight be-cause those redwood boards were all heavy, like 90 pounds."

Froiseth remembers that the surfers at the Outrigger Club weren't too pleased with what the new generation

56

was doing. "They were all mad at us because we were making waves. We were passing them. And we were kind of like, well, the mob-across-the-track kind of guys." Other sur-fers, however, began cutting down the tails of their surfboards. Among them were some of the first Califor-nian surfers to make the trek from the mainland to Hawaii, such as Lorrin 'Whitey' Harrison and Preston 'Pete' Peterson.

Peterson was the best mainland surfer of the time; in 1932, 1936, 1938 and 1941 he won the Pacific Coast Surf-ing Championship. Pete grew up in the entrance to Santa Monica Canyon where his parents had the bath house on the beach. He remembers well the surfing exhibitions by the Duke. In 1920, at the age of seven, he acquired his first board. It was 12' long with an 11" wide tail, 18" at its widest point, and made of solid redwood which for some obscure reason had to be shipped from Oregon via Hawaii. It had no rocker, egg-shaped rails, and the redwood planks were held to-gether with lag bolts running inwards from the rails.

In 1932, at the height of the depres-sion, Lorrin 'Whitey' Harrison tried to stow away on a ship to Hawaii but got caught and was transported back to San Francisco. He spent that night in the slammer — and stowed away again the next morning! After two-and-a-half days hidden in a lifeboat he gave himself up, but at least this time he made it to Hawaii. Mean-while Pete had paid his way across, but he eventually ran out of money and ended up moving into the same house in Waikiki as 'Whitey' and they became close friends. Later Whitey and Pete stowed away back to the U.S. mainland on the U.S.S. *Re-public* masquerading as members of a contingent of 1,000 soldiers being shipped back to California. Stowing away became a surfing tradition that continued right into the 'sixties. Whitey made four or five successful trips in this manner, but he was forced to abandon it when the laws against stowaways were tightened up.

Whitey and Pete were two of Califor-nia's early lifeguards. Pete Peterson had a big, strong physique and later got into movies as a stuntman; for in-stance, he worked on *Jaws* and *Jaws II* as stunt co-ordinator. He was also a diver and became involved in deepwa-ter salvage. In 1967 he came to Aust-ralia and gave some great displays in tandem events. He died in Santa

WALLY FROISETH

JEFF DIVINE

WALLY FROISETH

Above: *San Onofre summer of 1946. Dave Rochlen with surf and paddle boards in background.*

Right: *The Cove, Palos Verdes.*

Below: *San Onofre Club contest.*

Left top: *Wally Froiseth was a great innovator. Here he is with the template drawn on the board he cut down to stop the tail spinning out in Hawaii's powerful waves.*

Left centre: *Mickey Munoz with Balsa/Redwood hot curl and San Onofre style boards.*

Left bottom: *Two of Wally's Balsa Redwood combinations.*

Monica in early 1983, not long after I had talked to him about the early days of surfing for this book.

Back in the winter of 1932, Pete and Whitey surfed all over the south shore of Oahu, on every coral reef from Diamond Head to the entrance to Honolulu harbour. They rode waves all day long on both boards and outrigger canoes, enjoying the unfamiliarly warm Hawaiian water. While surfing at Waikiki one morning, Pete spied an interesting looking board under another surfer. The statistics were about the same as his: 10' long by 2' wide, with a wide, square tail, but the timber was completely different. It was balsa. Back on the beach, Pete picked up one of these new blondcoloured boards and discovered they were half the weight of his redwood one. Apparently they had been made in Florida, and the balsa came from South America. They had been given several coats of varnish to keep the water out, but this tended to crack under pressure, especially where they were knelt upon. The weight was the quality that made these boards fantastic: only 30 to 40 pounds. Who made them is a mystery, as are the surfers who rode them. But they represented such an advance on the old, heavy redwood boards that surfers began shaping their boards from the new timber, which soon began to be in great demand and hard to get.

Pacific Ready Cut Homes, in California, was the first company to produce commercial surfboards. The company was owned by Meyers Butte, operating out of Vernon in Los Angeles, and in 1937 it employed Whitey Harrison to shape boards for it. Four boards a day for $100 a month. They were constructed of laminated redwood and balsa which could be milled and joined with the recently available waterproof glue, basically using the lightness of balsa down the middle and the strength of the redwood around the rails. Varnish protected the outside; the rail shape was full with a square upper edge and rounded lower edge. The typical board was 10' long, 23" wide, and 22" across the tail block, and was known as the Swastika Model because of the distinctive logo the company used. It wasn't until years later 'Whitey' found out that the person responsible for the Swastika, a guy named 'Dutch', was a Nazi! After 1939, when war broke out in Europe, the swastika insignia was no longer used. With all that timber and labour

57

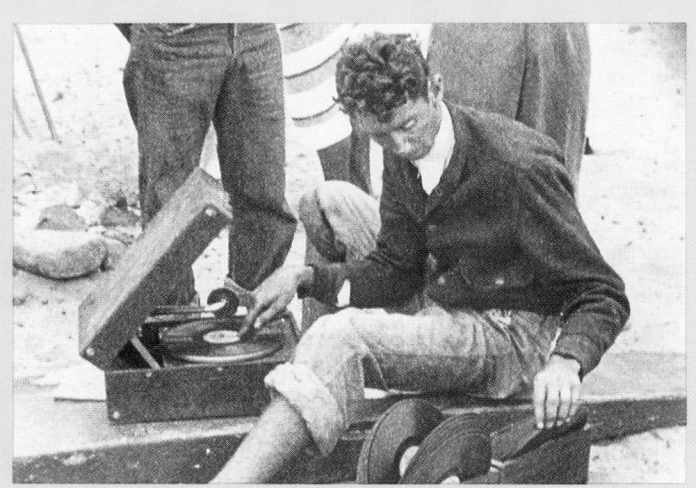

they still sold for under $40 each.

Wally Froiseth took up the balsa/redwood boards, too . . . but only for tandem riding, which he liked. For his own surfing he preferred the new pintail redwood board he had helped develop. Froiseth tried cutting down on the tail of balsa boards and shaping a V into the rear section, but "it just didn't work that good. Because it was too buoyant. Even though the tail was narrow, it was thick and wouldn't sink in. It floated too high," he explains. "I owned about the sixth or seventh balsa board in here; I got it for tandems. We'd walk up the beach, ask some girl: 'Hey how about going surfing tandem?' In those days everybody would go out . . . we never asked for any favours . . . we just wanted people to enjoy the sport. So I had my solid redwood and I had this balsa for tandem, you know."

Froiseth and his friends were the first surfers to ride the big waves at Makaha and Sunset beaches — well, the first since ancient Hawaiian times. A friend of theirs was given the job as a look-out on a radio tower construction site in the area and used to ring up if the surf was big. "We found this place at Makaha, no just past Makaha actually, as we went out on a vacation from high school camping and spearfishing and when we came back we saw Makaha beach breaking beautifully so we stopped and bodysurfed," says Froiseth. "Then we talked it over and said, next weekend let's bring our boards over. Which we did. We had a terrific surf and were really stoked. Then we spread the word around; we used to take guys out and we'd lose them, one way or another. The waves would be too big and they'd be scared of them, they weren't used to that size of wave — or it'd be flat! The Duke started coming out there in '39, because he heard that the surf was big and he liked big waves."

"And then a couple of times we didn't see good waves over there and went up to Sunset, and were the first ones to actually surf Sunset. It was '39; another guy and myself. And of course with the kind of boards we had, you know, as steep as Sunset is, almost every wave, we used to talk about making one wave out of ten. How big was it that first day? They were way overhead, probably 20 foot. In fact we almost had a disaster. There was me and my brother and another guy who used to go out with us all the time. This guy lost his board and got caught in the current, my brother went out to rescue him but they couldn't get in, you know, tandem, against the current, with a solid wood board. I had to go out and tow another board out, so each of us had boards."

"A lot of times we'd take out guys but they wouldn't go surfing. They'd be too afraid. At that time very few did surf big surf."

America's involvement in World War II had quite an effect on surfing. Surfers went away to war in all the services, but mostly into the navy. John Kelly was one of these. In order to get some surfing excitement during the long breaks at sea he took to dragging a rope behind the back of his destroyer and bodysurfing behind the ship. One day however, the rope

RAY JEROME BAKER/ROBERT E. VAN DYKE

Above: *1942 — barbed wire on Waikiki. Only military personnel were allowed on the beach.*

Right: *1949 Waikiki tavern. Meeting place of 'Empty Lot Boys' in the '30s. The words 'Hale Auau' mean 'bath house'.*

Left: *These shots from Dr Jack Ball's 16mm film 'Californian Surfrider' show the very beginnings of the West Coast surfing lifestyle. Good old San Onofre is an institution to this day.*

RAY JEROME BAKER/ROBERT E. VAN DYKE

broke and John watched his ship sail over the horizon! In good surfing style he kept his cool and eventually the Navy came back to his rescue.

Woody Brown was another great surfer from this era. He did not fight in the war because of his strong pacifist beliefs; Woody had been raised an atheist, and he was somewhat an introverted youth who liked to escape the trappings of civilisation by flying. "I needed to get away from the Earth," he wrote later in life. "There is no crime or hatred when you fly, the truth is central to me."

He had an extraordinary career. In 1938, he built a glider from a kit and set the world distance record with a 263-mile flight. When he landed in Texas he was given a hero's welcome, inundated with telegrams, and paraded throught the streets of Wichita Falls with a police escort and a brass band. However, this jubilation was short lived, because his wife died during childbirth just a few days later. Woody was devastated. He left the United States determined to lose himself in the obscurity of travelling the world, and arrived in Hawaii on the first leg of this journey in 1941 just as war broke out. Naturally all travel was halted so Woody was stuck in Hawaii. He rode around Oahu on a bicycle, absolutely alone, but the Hawaiian people picked him up and showed him how to surf and fish. Eventually he married a Hawaiian woman.

As Woody's surfing ability increased, his adventurous spirit sent him to the north shore to hunt for a bigger challenge. At this stage big waves had been surfed by only a few, including Wally Froiseth and Dickie Cross. Woody and Dickie were great surfing mates and used to tackle Sunset together, but one day they overreached themselves. Wally Froiseth tells the story:

"They went out at Sunset and it got bigger and bigger and they couldn't get in. Then it got just like all the way across where there's no break in the surf, just continuous. One of those huge days. So they paddled down the coast and they paddled all the way to Waimea Bay. Well, they were sitting there when this huge set came. Dickie started to paddle for it, to take off on it. And Woody told him "no, no, don't take it, it's all the way across the bay. There's no chance of you going any place." But the last thing he saw was Dickie dropping into it; we never saw him again. The wave outside of Woody was bigger yet. He had no chance to get out of it. It must have been a huge wave because, you know, they were both good surfers and they could read the swells . . ."

Dickie Cross drowned; Woody Brown was found unconscious on the beach. He recovered, but he didn't do much surfing after that. He took a job as a surveyor on Christmas Island just after the war and, while there,

saw his first double-outrigger canoe. This inspired him to design and build a twin-hulled boat that could surf Waikiki's breakers . . . and the original catamaran was born. In order to prove the design he sailed to California in one. Then he returned to Hawaii and could be found sailing his cat for tourists at Waikiki right up till 1983.

Like so many surfers, he turned to the Bible in later life and found understanding in his personal translations of the holy book. He wrote these findings down in a book called *The Gospel of Love* published in 1981. Perhaps the best insight into Woody Brown is provided by this quote from his book: "I have always had a talent for taking a complicated subject and making it simple."

Maybe the last word should be Wally Froiseth's. On his second trip to Australia the Duke brought back a surf ski, which had never been seen in the Islands before. Nobody expected to be impressed but Froiseth, with his typically open mind, was. "Yeah, it impressed us," he says, years later. "It was something new, something we'd never seen. It was great. You know, my thinking is . . . every area has contributed something. I don't care where they are, these guys have contributed. Nobody can say that they did the whole thing. There's just no way. Nobody's got all the brains. Nobody can think of all aces. It's good."

•

Wally Froiseth (left) and a proud Dicky Cross just before his tragic death at Waimea Bay.

WALLY FROISETH

EVOLUTION OF THE MODERN BOARD

The modern surfboard is generally associated with one man, Bob Simmons, but this is not correct. Bud Morrisey, Guard Chapin, Matt Kivlin and Joe Quigg were just as influential as Simmons and individually all of these surfers helped to develop the modern surfboard. The period right before, during and after World War II in a lot of ways was similar to 'the magnificent men in their flying machines' era. All five of these surfers were tireless inventors, constantly experimenting, trying every idea they could dream up, shaping it and surfing it as quickly as possible. Ideas overlapped during this period; every conceivable design concept was tried, including multi-fins, hollow boards, short boards, concaves, low rails, almost everything you could possibly think of. Bud Morrisey was the oldest and therefore the first of his push. He was a loner who surfed around Redondo up to Topanga and is one of the first surfers Joe Quigg saw ever walk the board instead of the strike a pose Jack Dempsey-style of surfing instigated by Blake and Peterson. He made boards for friends in the Redondo area, including 'Adie' Bear and Tooley Clark, two of the Palace Verdes Surf Club's hottest surfers. He married one of the original girl surfers, Mary Ann Hawkins, and raised a family in Venice only a few miles from where he had grown up and surfed.

Guard Chapin was a member of the prestigious Palace Verdes Surf Club. He was the step-father of the legendary Mickey Dora and one of the better surfers in that particular club. He significantly changed the accepted San Onofre style of rail. The plan shapes were similar to the old San Onofre outlines. Guard even turned the rail down in the back and used nose blocks to give lift in the nose — all prior to World War II.

How Bob Simmons came into surfing is an interesting story. He was a gifted academic, a graduate of the Californian Institute of Technology, and was considered to have a brilliant career in engineering ahead of him when he had an accident on his

Rennie Yater's collection of historic boards.

FIBERGLASS MATERIALS

DON BALCH

motorcycle. His right arm was so badly mangled the doctors told him he would have to exercise it constantly or they would have to amputate it. Sitting in a hospital bed wondering what to do Bob became friendly with another patient who suggested he try surfing; the paddling would exercise his arm and riding a surfboard would give something of the same feeling as riding a motorcycle.

Simmons was discharged from hospital in 1935 and took up surfing, buying one of Guard Chapin's old solid redwood surfboards. His arm was always to be withered and lacked strength, but slowly he began to build up some muscle tone in it. He was very conscious of his health; he was considered by his early surfing friends to be an eccentric because he took to a pure vegetarian diet, living in his old Ford, and wandering up and down the coast in search of waves. In a way he was the first 'hip-

pie' surfer, the forerunner of an entire generation. Around 1945 he went to work for Guard Chapin building garage doors and started to build his own surfboards as well. Naturally his first boards were copies of Guard's but within a year he had developed those ideas and improved on them. The most significant contribution he made was the scarfed nose lift that stopped the boards from pearling. As you can see by the photographs of that era, many surfers were reluctant to give up their old San Onofre-type boards and had Simmons scarf another piece on the nose and fair it in to create nose lift.

Simmons was the first modern board builder and a dedicated surfer, usually first out in the morning and last in at night. By constantly travelling the coast he received an abundance of orders. If you really wanted one of his boards you had to pay for it up front and sometimes you had to wait for a year to get a new Simmons 'spoon'. Simmons shaped every one of these personally and Joe Quigg and Matt Kivlin did all the glassing and finishing.

Wars have always sped up the pace of technology. The period leading up to World War I was one in which chemists searched for waterproof glues which would bond timber together; that led to surfers having a means of holding all the pieces of timber together instead of using bolts running from rail to rail. Plywood was a refinement of this bonding; it made the first fighting aircraft a reality and led to the box-frame plywood-covered surf/paddle boards that were so much a part of the Australian surf club scene. Fibreglass, resin and styrofoam came out of World War II. Preston "Pete" Peterson was actually the first person to build a fibreglass surfboard; he did this in June, 1946 with the help of Brant Goldsworthy, who had a plastics company in Los Angeles which supplied component parts for aircraft in World War II. The board was constructed of two hollow moulded halves joined together with a redwood central stringer and with the seam sealed with fibreglass tape.

GEORGE SAMAMA

Above: *Matt Kivlin — a big man (6'3")
with a smooth flowing style.*

Right: *Kivlin waxing-up his first Malibu
board at Tijuana Sloughs, 1950.*

Left top: *The great Bob Simmons at Malibu
on styrofoam sandwich board.*

Far left centre: *Twin skegg, spoon nose, slot
rails, clutch handles, triple glass, on
Simmons' high speed surfing vehicle.*

Left centre: *This timeless shot of Simmons
(left) and a bunch of locals could be anywhere
in the world when surfers get together.*

Left bottom: *Malibu summer of 1951.*

JOHN ELWELL

Brant Goldsworthy and his partner Ted Thal, were the first to sell fibreglass and resin to the private sector. The first resin manufacturer was the Bakelite Corporation. Those early resins were of the same viscosity as the resins used today but the catalyst was a paste-like vaseline that had to be thoroughly mixed with the resin. The drying time was totally dependent on the amount of sunshine and naturally one side dried while the rails were still tacky. Because it made the boards look ugly compared to the shiny varnish already available it took a little time to gain acceptance, but because resin was much more protective, change was inevitable. Experimenting with resin and glass was a frustrating experience. Because of his diligent enquiries to every chemical company in Los Angeles, Joe Quigg was suspected of being a German spy! Another time Quigg remembers walking into Ted Thal's one-room shop (now a huge corporation) and seeing little bottles of stuff that had

just arrived at the Thalco Chemical Company. Ted didn't know what it was, but the label read 'setting fluid — highly explosive' and that made him suspect it was the catalyst he needed. Joe pleaded with Thal to let him have some; Thal, however, declined. Frustrated, Joe remembered that one of his friends, Dave Sweet, had an uncle who was in the plastics department of Douglas Aircraft so Joe persuaded Dave to contact his uncle and get some setting fluid. When Joe came back to Dave's house a couple of days later he saw Dave in the backyard putting out a fire which had occurred from a particularly hot mix! Because it was proving so hard to get he drove back to Ted Thal's office, identified the suspicious stuff in the little bottles, and persuaded Thal to part with it and some other funny stuff called pigment or tint.

Joe and his friend, Matt Kivlin, left for the Islands in 1947. They were excited about the prospect of surfing

warm water and good waves, especially after Joe's long term in the navy during the war. Joe was in the Islands when Simmons wrote saying that he had built his first light board and it was in the twenty-five-pound range. He had never built anything like this before and that was late 1949. Simmons had had fibreglass and resins for three years but did not choose to use these materials for their lightness but only as protection around the nose of his redwood boards.

Simmons didn't go to war. Instead he worked at Douglas Aircraft and continued to build surfboards. Naturally he had the jump on everyone else; he was familiar with a light fibreglass cloth which gave him the possibility of making lighter boards, but he didn't use it until 1949. Ironically Simmons delayed using the cloth because he believed that heavier boards were faster and he fastidiously stuck to this idea. Even his 'sandwich'

JOE QUIGG

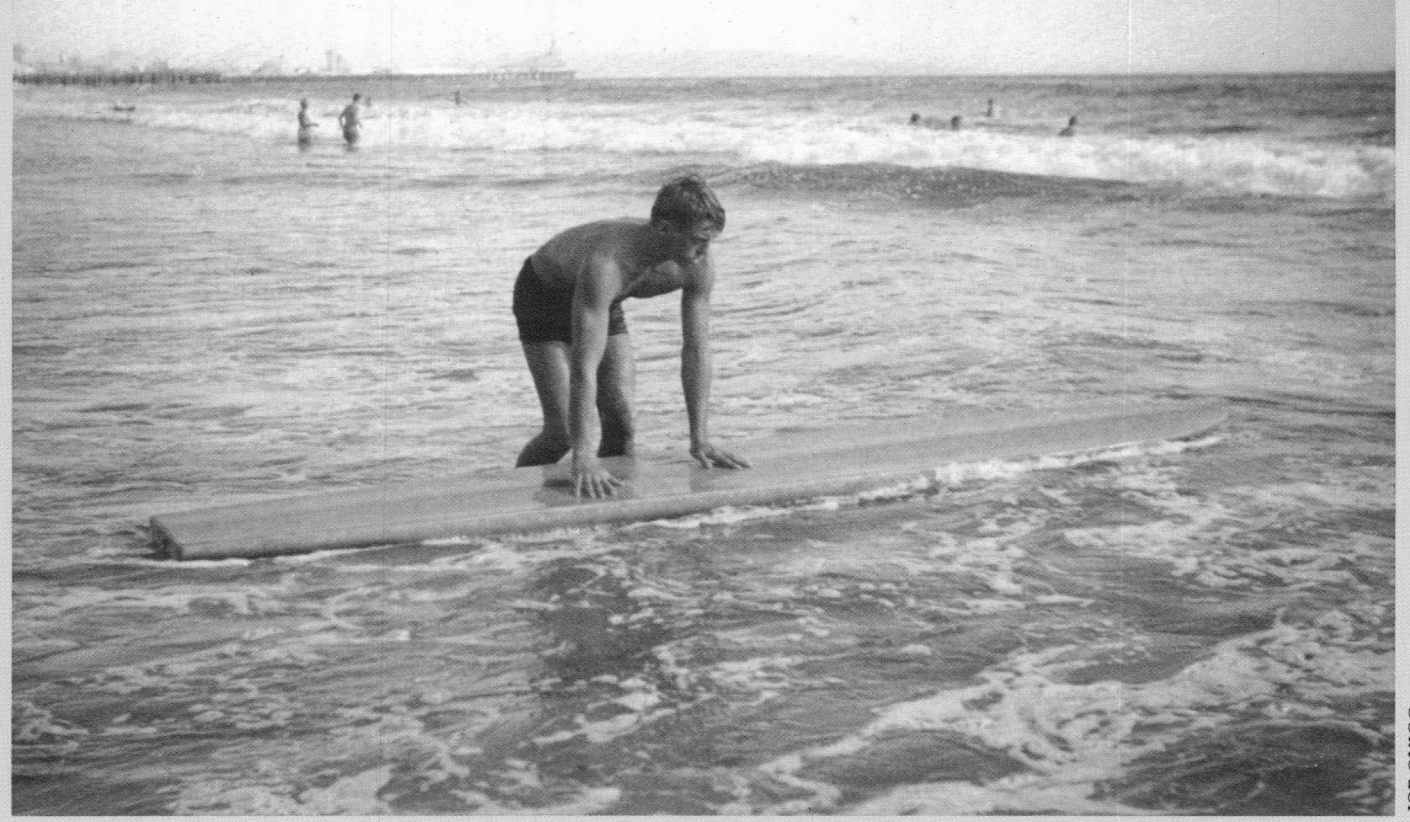

Top: *Joe Quigg testing the world's first fibreglass board made by Pete Peterson and Brant Goldsworthy, August 1946.*

Right: *Who said the Aussies invented the short board? (L to R) Joe and Jack Quigg, Moon. 1932.*

Below: *Rincon Queen of the Coast.*

JOE QUIGG

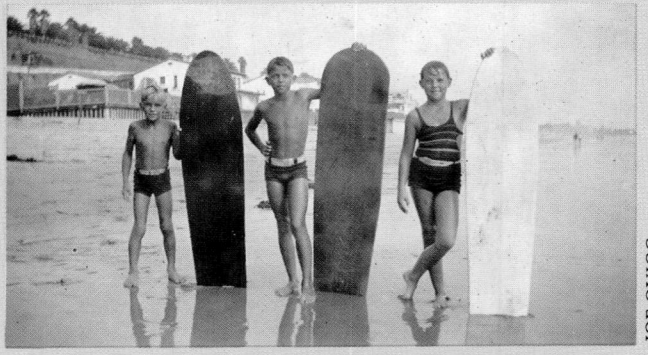

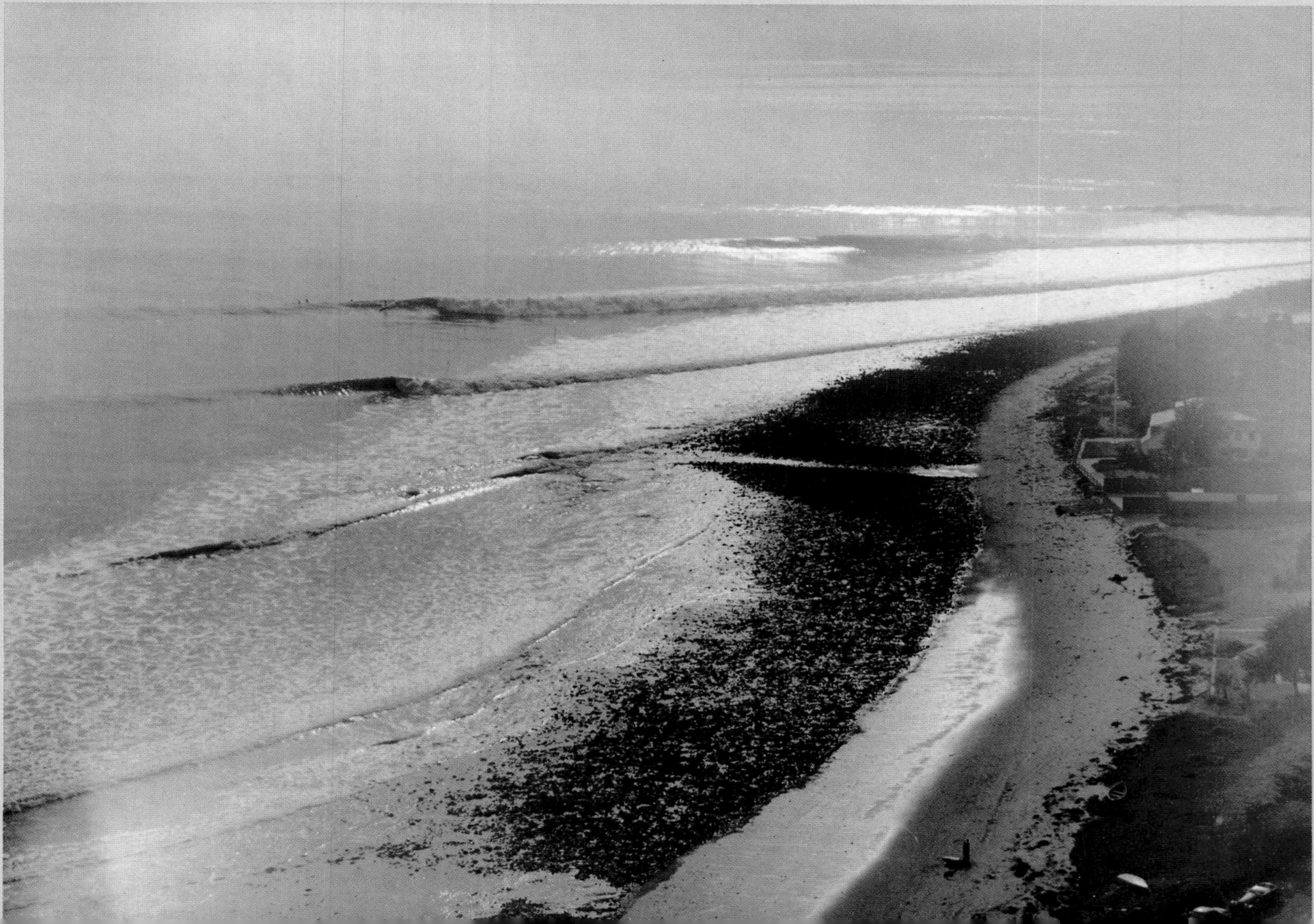

JOE QUIGG

JOE QUIGG

Left: *Dave Sykes 1942 — a loner who showed up when the surf was good.*

Below: *Joe Quigg at Malibu 1951. Perfect trim from point to pit.*

Above: *Dave Sykes at Malibu 1946. When the Malibu boards came in, many surfers wouldn't give up their old San Onofre style boards. They had Simmons' scarf and shape, balsa nose lift.*

JOE QUIGG

1

2

3

4

5

6

7

8

RENNIE YATER

1. *Tom Zahn at Rincon.*

2. *Tom Zahn and Joe Quigg with 1950s Quiver.*

3. *(L to R) Dave Rochlen, Preston Peterson, Tommy Volk.*

4. *Wally Froiseth gluing balsa and redwood planks before shaping.*

5-8 *The original surf safari. Wally Froiseth and Russ Takaki sailed from Honolulu to the Californian coast. Bought an A Model Ford, surfed from 'Frisco to San Diego and took the steamship home.*

Above: *Big south swell Malibu early 50s.*

Right: *A stoked Russ Takaki at Malibu.*

board, as it was called — it had a light styrofoam core with thin plywood on the deck and bottom, plus balsa rails, and was covered with glass — was heavier than the balsa boards that his glassers Matt Kivlin and Joe Quigg were making at the same time.

Both Kivlin and Quigg had started surfing before Simmons. Because they grew up in the Malibu area they were full-on surfers. They paddled around together and built boards with Simmons. The first Malibu boards were built by Joe for his girlfriend, Aggie, although she was not the person who ended up surfing it. It was a radical nine-foot-six-inch long board and eventually wound up in the hands of a local surfer named Leslie Williams. He ended up wailing on that board, becoming the hottest surfer in the area and turning faster than anyone else. Simmons got very upset about

this board and his partnership with the others broke up over it, especially when Matt Kivlin wanted to build a 'potato chip' for *his* girl. Matt was a big guy, about 6'3" tall, who organised all the parties for the Malibu Yacht Club (the first Surf Club in the area) and was by far the most consistent surfer at Malibu in the late 'forties and early 'fifties. When he started to ride his girl's nine-foot-four he reached the height of excellence.

Joe Quigg married his girlfriend Aggie and moved to the Islands permanently around this period. Matt Kivlin eventually quit surfing to further his studies in architecture. By this time everybody wanted a Malibu board, but who was going to build them? Simmons took a trip to the Islands in 1950 and wrote that he was disappointed with the performance of his boards on the Island waves. They were too wide in the tail and spun

out. He came home to surf his native California and one day in 1953, while surfing at Windansea in San Diego he disappeared. His body was found three days later by Mike Diffenderfer and several other La Jolla surfers.

67

THE AGE OF SURF CLUBS

In Australia the surfboard was entrenched in surf club activities right through to the 'sixties. The Surf Life Saving Association had gone from strength to strength and had almost 10,000 members by the season of 1939-40. Affiliate clubs had been firmly established in almost every coastal country town in New South Wales and in all the other States as well.

It was a tremendously prestigious thing to be a member of your local volunteer surf club. The new probationary member had to undergo a series of difficult tests in order to gain his bronze medallion, which meant that he had qualified in the world's most efficient method of rescue and resuscitation. Upon paying his club fees he was assigned to beach patrol duty on a roster system which required him to sit on the beach for hours every weekend, keeping watch on the swimmers, setting up flags to show where it was safe to bathe, and occasionally rescuing people who got into difficulties in the surf.

The surf was so new and exciting to the public in those days that the patrols were kept busy blowing their whistles at straying swimmers, dabbing iodine on crying kids' bluebottle stings, sounding the shark alarm, and rescuing the odd maiden in distress. As a reward for all this vigilance service the recruit gained access to 'the club'. By this stage almost every beach that had a surf club could also boast a club house, which was usually paid for by donations from grateful rescued victims or handouts from smart council officials who were willing to pay this small concession instead of having to employ lifeguards. Spending time inside or around the club house was the best thing about being a member. It was here that you learnt how to walk and talk like a lifesaver, and if you proved yourself in the social aspects of the club you might even be accepted into the boat crew.

The club always had a dance on Saturday night and often someone from the boat crew would organise a keg on Sunday afternoon. Surf club men were traditionally big drinkers, and it was usually during one of these sessions that the recruit was introduced to the more social aspects of being a member. Quite often the first thing that happened was the recruit was given a nickname. Everyone in the club had one, and the new name was usually a slingoff at some aspect of his physical appearance — protruding teeth, big feet, a big nose, the colour of his hair — but the important question was whether or not he could take the name and the 'baiting' that went with it. For instance, one of the things the probationary member had to take in his stride was having the hose periodically turned on him and his mates while they sat in the sun talking to the girls or watching the beach football!

When I was a kid I used to hang around the Collaroy Surf Club, but I was too young to do patrol duty. At the time they called me Nat (it should be Gnat) because I looked so small on my board, which was nicknamed the Queen Mary. It was a secondhand board made of redwood and balsa covered with fibreglass and

Bondi Surf Carnival 1927.

had been built by Bill Clymer, an early Brookvale boardbuilder who now builds surfboats out of space-age materials. The Queen Mary has long since disappeared, but my own nickname has stuck; even my close surfing mates forget my real name is Robert.

Sometimes when the boat crew had consumed a little too much alcohol on a Sunday afternoon and needed a little exercise they dug a big hole in the sand and tried to bury the new recruits alive. Then there were the stunts. 'Legs' Lane was always good for one, especially when he had had a few too many. Ambling over to a picnicking group of people who had arrived to enjoy their day at the seaside in buses, Legs would climb into the driver's seat, start the bus, and take off out of the parking area with the bus driver and passengers running up the street after him. That was a good stunt! Legs almost got to be boat captain from that.

Right from the start of the new member's involvement in the surf club he was involved in competition. In the beginning it was play, but as he got better at the games he realised that club rivalry was not just a game. The association encouraged this competitive involvement; they organised an extensive season of surf carnivals where all affiliate clubs would compete for the prestigious position of being Australian champion. When a carnival was not scheduled for a particular weekend, club members would train relentlessly and compete against themselves. They would compete in every aspect of surf club ritual, from the regimented Rescue and Resuscitation drill with its belts and reels to beach events such as the relay race and the greasy pole event, where two men would sit on a pole with a sandbag each and try to slog the other man off the pole. The surf club was an entire way of life.

In the 1930s and later, surf boat races were the big spectator event . . . especially in big seas. For years these boats didn't change in basic design from the first one owned and operated

Presented to the S.L.S.A. of A.
by the Publishers of
'PARADE' MAGAZINE
1956

as a fishing boat by the Sly brothers at Manly. That was a regular ship's double-ended lifeboat, built before the turn of the century; it served its purpose well by being able to be carried to the water by the brothers, and being stable enough for them to move around in while pulling in fish. With the advent of bathing the boat was used to haul in bodies as well as fish, and the brothers found themselves spending as much time saving people as fishing. After a few years the Sly brothers gradually lost interest in lifesaving. The council had supplied the fisherman-patrol with high necked blue-and-white jerseys to be worn with black bowler hats, but these became fishy and got lost and eventually Manly Surf Club decided the arrangement wasn't working. They had a special rescue boat built for themselves based on the design of the Slys' lifeboat, but they added watertight bulkheads and sawed off the stern. The surfboat was born.

The greatest boatman of this era was Harold 'Rastus' Evans. He captained his men with a passion few had seen before, training three nights a week and spending all weekend with his crew, who rowed miles in secrecy so that other boat crews would not see their style. In order to win a race they would do almost anything. Some of the worst acts of bad sportsmanship were committed as the boats rounded the buoy before heading for the beach; often Rastus's sweep oar would be thrust under the paddles of an oncoming rival, preventing the men on one side from rowing at all. Sometimes the crews would carry scars and bruises that added up to nothing less than assault and battery. Often crews came back to the beach in a furious temper; in one particular incident two crewmen jumped out and began fighting on the beach until officials intervened.

The officials then changed the rules, and each boat had their own buoy to round. This stopped a lot of the hand-to-hand combat, but after rounding the buoys the crews faced the real battle of how to get back to the beach without being swamped. Bending like slaves under the orders of the sweep, the oarsmen would find themselves looking back at a mountain of water which they were about to attempt to ride. Although the boats' design had been modified to ride waves, they were not suited to holding a given course under anything but perfect conditions. On a

big green wave the displacement hull would sit firmly in the water and the sweep could steer well enough, but when one of these 18'-27' long, 8'-9' wide crafts came plummeting down the face of a huge dumper, the result was often disastrous. More often than not the force of the white water hitting the back of the boat would force it to slew off course. No matter how much strength the sweep had in his arms and body, the sweep oar could only take a certain amount of pressure before wood was cracking, splinters were washing up onto the beach, and the men were swimming for the shore.

Certainly the surf boats did cost clubs quite a bit in equipment but they fostered a good team spirit. They were primarily used for racing, being virtually useless for lifesaving; they were too slow to get moving in an

emergency and it was much more luck than good management that got them beyond the break in any kind of heavy surf. As crowd-pullers at the surf carnivals, however, they were great. Everyone loves seeing a good wipeout!

The surf lifesaving clubs had an incredible record of "no lives lost while patrol on duty" until a fateful day in February 1938, which has gone down in the history books as Black Sunday. On that day the extreme mid-summer temperatures, which Sydney gets sometimes, had sent tens of thousands of bathers onto the met-

ropolitan beaches. Down at Bondi the beach and the shore break were crowded with people enjoying a vigorous surf. "Earlier in the day the high tide and rough sea kept most people from showing themselves too game and they didn't give us much trouble," said Tom Meagher, Bondi senior beach inspector at the time. "But in the afternoon as the water shallowed with the fall of the tide, some got a bit cockier and there was a gradual edging out toward the end of the sandbank." Immediately inshore and to one side of the sandbank was a deepish channel cut by the waves receding to open ocean. The club captain, Carl Jeppesen, had recognized this as a potential trouble spot and had the patrol on duty bring down extra reels, which were set up immediately opposite the channel.

Shortly after 3 o'clock in the afternoon the waves went flat for a short period and then, a series of five or six bigger waves came crashing in. These waves swept over the heads of the bathers on the bank, knocking many off their feet. As one wave surged up the beach, the next followed close behind it. No interval between the waves permitted the water to recede through the normal channel and it banked up to the high tide line. As the last waves of the set came rolling in a massive volume of water surged towards the channel, sweeping the sandbank clear of everyone on it. Some two hundred bathers were in serious trouble; mothers were crying for their children, people were shouting for help. Several beltmen raced into the sea, taking advantage of the extra lines, but their efforts to bring assistance to the ones furthest out were hampered by the panic-stricken swimmers who were fighting for their lives just beyond the edge of the bank. Dozens gripped the line. When the linesmen saw what was happening, with the beltmen submerged by the weight of so many people dragging on the line, the 'haul in' order was given. Every line came in with ten or twenty people clinging to it. Luckily many Bondi clubmen were on hand that afternoon, due to the regular Sunday competition, and they helped handle the emergency. They snatched up anything which would help support people in trouble and swam out with these floats into the surf.

The clubmen began bringing in drowning victims, one by one. In a short space of time the beach resembled a battleground, with bodies everywhere being given the resuscitation that would give life back to most. "There were at least 40 to 50 people that didn't look as if they'd be any good," Tom Meagher said. "They had to be treated on the beach, but as breathing was restored in each case we sent the worst cases to the clubhouse where the casualty room overflowed in a couple of minutes. Then we sent them to the wrestling mats on the clubhouse floor and when there was no more room there, we sent them up onto the flat roof. It was literally a matter of putting them wherever we could find a few feet of space." There were doctors among the bathers on the beach and within minutes they and police and ambulance officers arrived to give assistance. Dead and living were all brought ashore. The ones that could not recover by themselves had to be worked

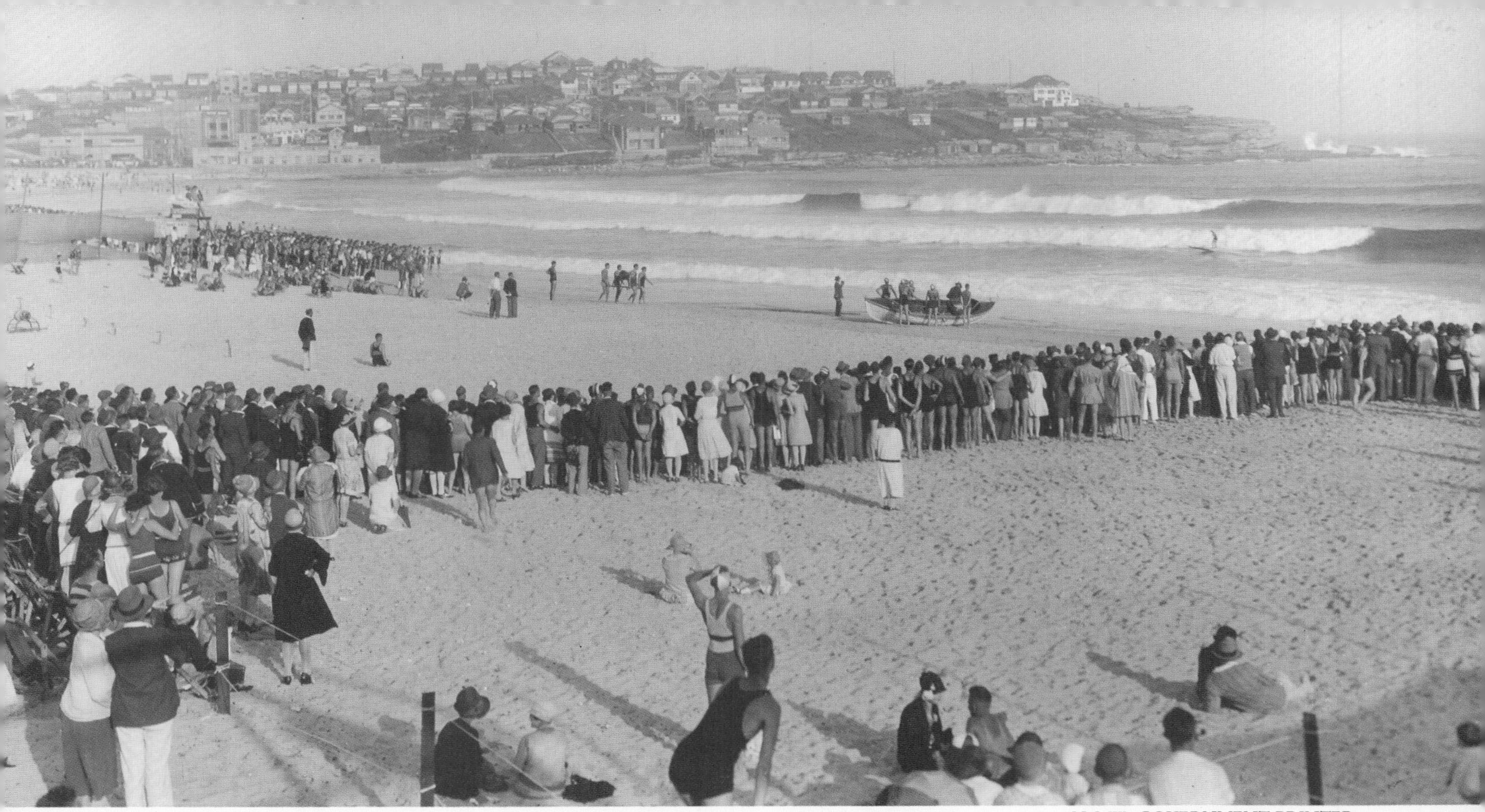

upon; the resuscitators formed into relays, relieving each other as the strain became too much. One youth, black in the face and given up for dead, was restored to life after 90 minutes of work, and two more apparently hopeless cases were brought back to life. In at least two other cases breathing was partially restored before the victims died.

The final tally of dead was five — all men. For the most part they were young, and all from different walks of life. The saddest sight was a German cook who came ashore with his wrist twisted in the lifeline. He had looped the line about his wrist himself and had used his other hand to hold up a drowning girl by the hair, keeping her clear of the water . . . but had himself drowned while doing it. The girl was in a bad way when eventually brought ashore, but she recovered.

Her rescuer was beyond all aid.

No awards of merit were ever made to individuals in connection with the rescues on Black Sunday. Individuals could not be singled out. The clubmen had functioned as a single lifesaving unit; the authorities considered that the fact so many lives had been saved was enough reward.

"The lifesavers merely did their duty," club captain Jeppersen told the coroner at the inquest. It was left to an American doctor then visiting Australia, who had witnessed what had happened on Black Sunday and had helped with the work of resuscitation, to say the last word: "This rescue business is a labour of love," he told the coroner and the court, "the like of which the world cannot show anywhere else."

Above: *Surf Carnival 1927.*

Left: *The sweep or steersman could not see the situation they were in. He gauged it by the amount of terror on the oarsman's faces.*

Right: *Tropical gentleman. Newcastle Feb. 6th 1932. Standing: M. Reece, L. McJachrow, R. Harris, 'Snow' McAlister, A Rose. Sitting: J. Drinkwater, F. Bennett, L. Crumb.*

MALIBU

PHOTOS DR DON JAMES

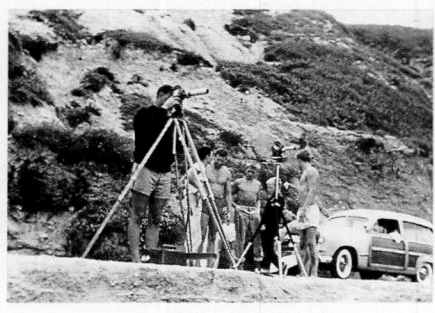

DALE VELZY

Top: *A surf stoked Buzzy Trent exploding into the 50s.*

Above left: *The Birth of Surf Movies.*

Above right: *Third from left, Hobie Alter.*

Right: *'The Little Man on Wheels' — Dewey Weber.*

Below: *Fading forehand turn by Dewey Weber at Malibu.*

LEROY GRANNIS

After the war California was well and truly off and riding waves. Well, some of it. The surfing population grew to 5,000, with little colonies of dedicated surfers springing up at Windansea, Oceanside, Laguna, Huntington Beach, the South Bay, Malibu, Santa Cruz and good old San Onofre. They were all aware of each other's existence through the movement of lifeguards up and down the coast. These lifeguards formed a strong, prestigious movement which had begun with Freeth at Redondo and spread to other places; they were responsible for patrolling the surfing beaches of California from towers erected every mile or so along each beach. In the early years they were State-controlled; later the county took over their administration. Because the job paid well, and it put them right where they wanted to be, most of California's finest surfers were lifeguards at some stage of their careers.

Most surfers, however, stayed in their own area surfing with friends under conditions that were uncomplicated and loads of fun. When the surf was up, they went surfing. When the surf was down, they hung around the beach listening to surf stories. It was on these occasions that they got to hear what was going on in the other surf spots. A few older surfers travelled everywhere telling tales whenever they stopped. Simmons had been one of these traveling prophets until his death in 1953; others were 'Opai' (Tom Wert), Jim Fisher, Lorrin 'Whitey' Harrison, Barney Wilkes, and all the old San Onofre regulars. Doc Ball was another of these; he published a book in 1946 called *Californian Surfriders* and made a 16mm movie which was shown to friends and lent to surfing clubs. The stories of this group of surfers often included tales of Malibu and how good the waves were up there, and how it seemed that the centre of California surfing had moved from San Onofre up to Malibu and was part of the search by surfers for a more challenging wave on which the new style boards could be ridden.

A colourful Manhattan Beach local named Dale Velzy had moved to Malibu around 1948; he wanted to ride better quality waves than his native South Bay could offer, and he wanted to refine his surfboard designs. However, Malibu was still quite isolated and he found there was only a limited market for his labours of love. So Velzy moved back to

South Bay, opening a shop in Venice. He was well liked, having been the unofficial shaper of the Hermosa Surf Club; he was forced to move his shaping trestles from there to under the pier when the other members complained about the amount of balsa shavings strewn all over the club room! He was in the merchant marines during the war and while in Guam scrounged up some ply off his ship and proceeded to build a hollow paddle/surfboard to give him some exercise. He rode it or paddled it in Guam and Malaya and even took it to Australia, where he ended up giving it away on one particularly memorable night of darts, beer and Aussie sheilas.

Velzy was a colourful character, and his shop in Venice proved to be a great success. With all the knowledge he had gained from the experiments of Kivlin, Quigg and Simmons on rail shapes, tail shapes, bottom shapes and outlines, he was inundated with orders to the point where he couldn't keep up with them and still ride waves. So he offered a keen local surfer named Hap Jacobs the chance to learn to shape and become a partner in his thriving business. Velzy's new 'pig board' really caught on. Every hot young surfer on the coast was soon riding one . . . Mickey Dora, Dewey Weber and Phil Edwards, to name but a few. These Velzy/Jacobs sticks were synonymous with the new 'hot dog' era. Turning by bending and pushing was now a breeze, walking the nose something every good surfer could do, and even the head dip and quasimodo were coming into vogue.

When Velzy brought out his 'sausage board' he had almost more money than he knew what to do with. He went out and bought the most prestigious car he could think of, a gull-winged Mercedes, adorned himself with gold, and gave all the better surfers their boards for free. He decided that surf movies would be big one day and took a keen young surfing shutter-bug named Bruce Brown into a local camera store, peeled off a few thousand dollars, and bought Bruce all the equipment to shoot his first movie, *Slippery When Wet*. He even bought all the hot surfers tickets to go to the Islands to star in Bruce's movie and was responsible for sending Mike Bright to the surfing championships associated with the Olympics in Australia in 1956, which was when the first Malibu boards came to Australia.

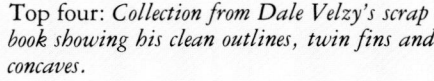

Top four: *Collection from Dale Velzy's scrap book showing his clean outlines, twin fins and concaves.*

Above: *50s Velzy/Jacobs Malibu Board.*

Above right: *Stylish cutback by Dale Velzy at Manhattan Beach.*

Right: *Hap Jacobs with a good example of the Velzy/Jacobs partnership.*

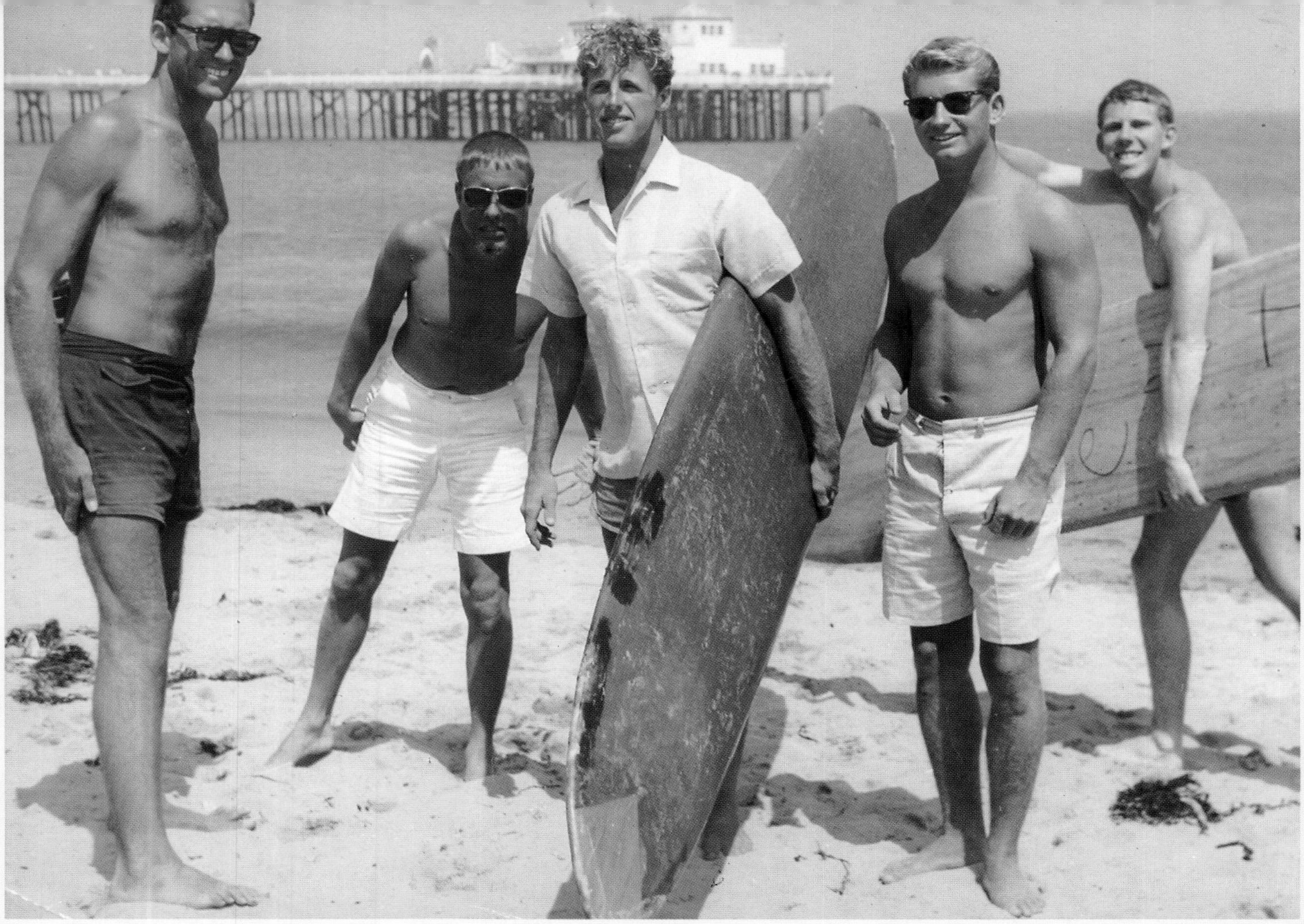

EVANS FAMILY

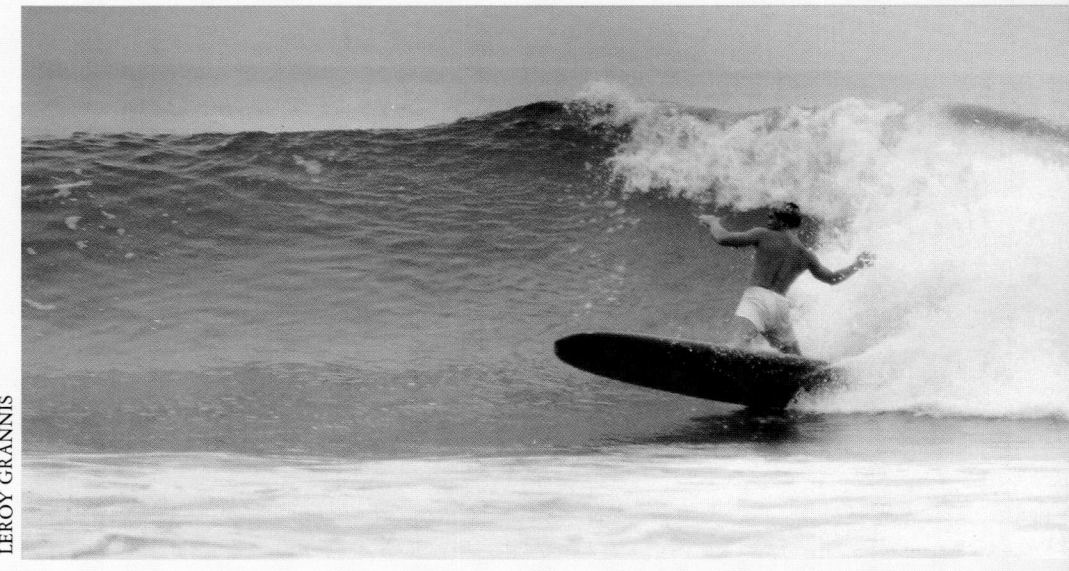

Above: *(L to R) Peter Cole, Tom Howard, Kemp Aaberg, John Sprout and Bubblehead.*

Right: *'The Malibu Lizard', Johnny Fain.*

Below Mickey Dora — casual grace in full trim.

LEROY GRANNIS

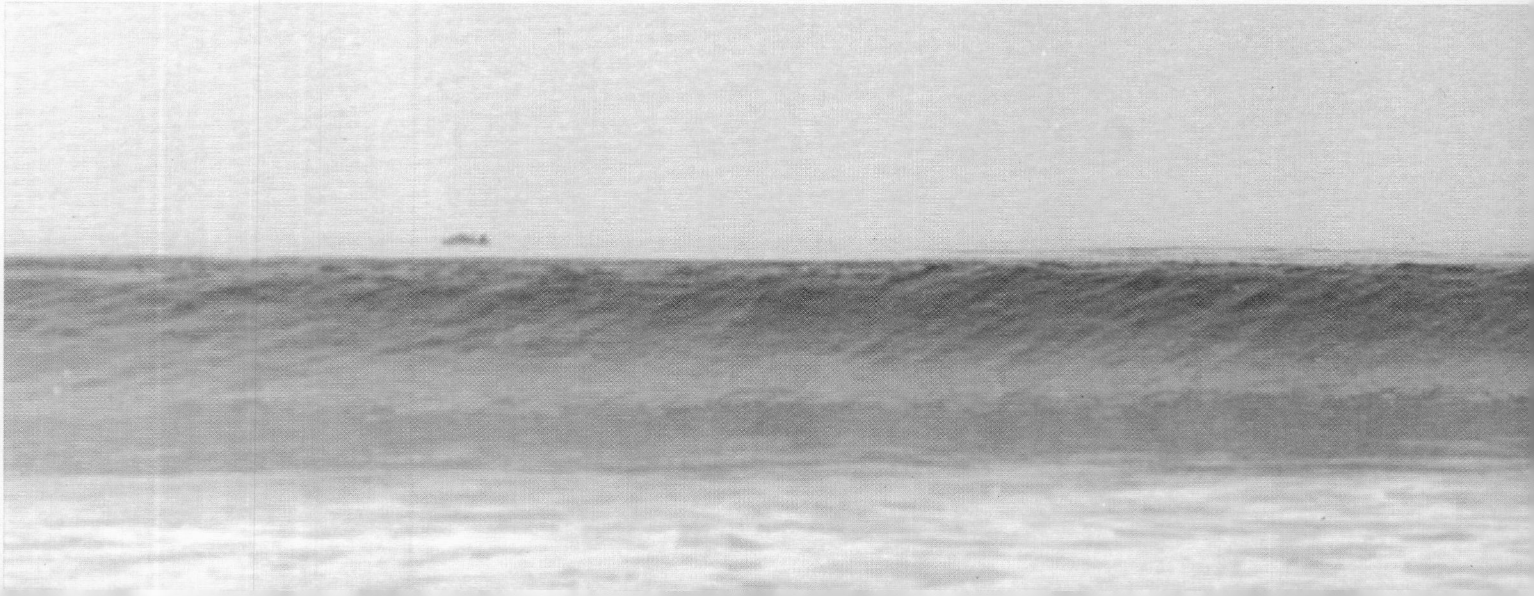

GEORGE SAMAMA

Left: *Bob Cooper in repose.*

Below: *The great Lance Carson in full flight.*

Bottom: *Dora's car — A 1932 Roller purchased for $300 from Hollywood film baron, Saul Wetzel's widow.*

RENNIE YATER

GEORGE SAMAMA

Balsa boards were not rapidly replaced by foam; foam came on slowly after years of experiments, so at this time there were still lots of balsa boards around. Pacific Systems Homes, who had built those first redwood and balsa swastika boards before the war, changed their name to General Veneer; as well as supplying the veneer they imported all the South American balsa. Competition was so fierce between the rival surfboard manufacturers every time a new shipment arrived, it became obvious some substitute had to be found.

The very first board manufacturer to experiment with polyurethane foam was David Sweet in Santa Monica, probably through his uncle at Douglas Aircraft. Hobie Alter in Dana Point was certainly the first manufacturer to seriously develop the potential of foam with the technical assistance of fellow surfer and good friend, Gordon 'Grubby' Clark, who was a chemistry graduate. Clark refined the balance of chemicals to be poured into the mould and now, 20 years later, is the world's largest supplier of foam blanks, including windsurfer blanks. Originally they weren't as concerned with reducing the weight of the boards as with finding a replacement for balsa, which was becoming difficult to get hold of. Dale Velzy had expanded again, incorporating a factory in San Clemente in his business, close to Dana Point. One day he caught sight of Hobie on his way to the San Juan county dump with a truck-load of blanks. He followed and watched Hobie breaking up the blanks. Some had deep holes, others were distorted with unexplained shrinkage; but gradually the bugs were worked out until Hobie was able to produce the first polyurethane foam surfboards. They were all pastel opaques at first in order to cover the defects.

By this time the Malibu 'sausage' board had become the standard board. Matt Kivlin had quit surfing because it was becoming too crowded. Joe Quigg moved to the Islands, building boards in his garage and later opening a shop on Ward Avenue. And a young lifeguard named Greg Noll, with a strong physique and an aggressive nature, was in constant demand for his surfboard building ability. He was a fine athlete, competing in Australia in the 1956 Olympic Surf Carnival. He finally opened a shop in his home town of Manhattan Beach. In the early 'fif-

Above: *Phil Edwards (left) and Hobie Alter discuss bottom shapes over one of Gordon 'Grubby' Clark's blanks.*

Above right: *The definitive drop knee turn, by two of the greatest. Mike Diffenderfer (inside) and Phil Edwards.*

Right: *Phil Edwards, father of the classic or functional style of riding.*

Far right: *Clean forehand turn by Edwards.*

Rennie Yater made Rincon his home break in the late 50s.

ties accepted good Californian board design was between nine and eleven feet long and around twenty-two inches wide, with either a square or a round tail. The boards weighed around twenty pounds and lightness was a sought-after quality. The early foamies were covered with a double layer of ten-ounce cloth saturated with as little resin as possible. The cost was between $75-$80 and California's new surfers couldn't get enough of them. Just before the Jacobs/Velzy partnership broke up they were making 160 a week, all custom orders. Mickey Munoz, the Patterson brothers, George Rice, Bob Cooper, Mickey Dora, Dewey Weber and the great Phil Edwards, all of these surfers helped usher in the 'hot dog' style of surfing.

Riding on the long lines of Malibu gave so much time that walking the board and trimming in the front third of the board became *the* new manoeuvre; so did stalling the board so the curl could catch up. One surfer who was exceptionally good at this style was Bob Cooper. Joe Quigg had made him an 11'6'' long, 20½'' wide, 6½'' narrow-tail model out of foam. It was based on the 'hot curl' boards of the 1940s that Woody Brown and Wally Froiseth had used in Hawaii. It required no fin, having instead a deep, curved displacement hull that nestled the board in the water. It was a perfect solution to the problem of how to outrun the curl as the wave accelerated around Malibu's perfectly shaped point. Critical turning was not possible without spinning out, so smooth, flowing manoeuvres and fast footwork were necessary.

Phil Edwards, one of my idols, ushered in the more functional style of surfboard riding with smoother, more graceful movements. He was another advocate of the 'hot curl' board, riding a balsa one constantly for almost two years. Phil had started surfing in Oceanside in 1947. Luckily his mother supported his surfing habit and by the summer of '51 he was chasing surf all over the Californian coast, from Rincon in the north, where he had to wear a woollen neck-to-knee to keep out the cold during winter, to Malibu and his home breaks of Oceanside and San Onofre during summer. In the summer of '52 Phil was staying in Doheny State Park, surfing Onofre and the surrounding areas, and

SURFER MAGAZINE

Bud Browne, at 65, vegetarian, born July 12, 1912. Body surfer — whose talent with a camera entertained the surfing world from the 50s into the 80s.

amazing everyone with his casual footwork. Phil rode with a style that allowed him to strike a pose beyond the necessities of balance, and turned surfing into an art form.

When he was only 13 years old Phil had already established a name for himself. During a big swell in the summer of 1953, when everyone in the area was out at Salt Creek, a local surfer called 'Key Hole' was wowing the crowd with ride after ride all the way to the beach. Phil paddled out to join him and obviously there was a lot of pressure on the young kid, but he came through with some good rides in his own inimitable style. As the swell grew in size a few of the crew, including Phil, went down to check out Dana Point. This day Phil decided to tackle Dana. 'Burrhead' Driever, another local surfer, who was looking after Phil in his first big surf experience, went out with him. The story goes that Phil and Burrhead took off on a wave together. Burrhead was yelling "Head for the green!" when Phil cut back towards the curl. He just cut back, flipped another turn, ran to the nose, and caught up with the astonished Burrhead. The word soon spread and Phil Edwards was the new standard to judge by.

Mickey Chapin/Dora was the hottest surfer in California during this period, and Edwards' guiding light. Dora travelled the coast continuously and it was inevitable that Edwards should run into Dora and the two of them would cruise around together putting on displays of fancy turning and fast footwork. Then, in the winter of 1955, they both decided to look for bigger waves. That meant only one place: Hawaii. ●

JOHN SEVERSON

Greg Noll 'The Bull' in distinctive striped trunks at Waimea Bay.

BIG WAVES BIG GUNS

Hawaii is the home of big waves. Yet it wasn't until the mid-'fifties that surfers regularly began to tackle the big swells that build up along the north shore, and most of the early big-wave riders were in fact Californians who had come to Hawaii to do just that.

About the winter of 1955 a San Francisco paper published a front page photograph of three surfers screaming across a giant Makaha Point wave; they were George Downing, Wally Froiseth and Woody Brown. That shot blew everyone away, all up and down the coast. Keen surfers had already seen Bud Browne's early surfing movies of big-wave riding in Hawaii, but seeing that shot in a mass-circulation paper made everyone realise what Hawaii could hold in store for them. After that every winter, about November, a crew of Californian surfers made the pilgrimage to Hawaii with the intention of riding waves at Sunset Beach and Makaha.

Phil Edwards and Mickey Dora both made the journey in 1955. Phil remembers taking his favourite 'cat board' with him: 7'10" long, 24" wide, with a 17" tail. In the winter of 1957 the Californian surfers in Hawaii included Greg Noll, Mike Stang, Mickey Munoz and Del Cannon. Some Californians had already made the move permanently: Ray Beatty, Bob Sheppard, Jose Angel, Fred Van Dyke, Pat Curren, Peter Cole, John Severson, Bruce Brown, Jim Fisher, Buzzy Trent and a few others. Both John Severson and Fred Van Dyke had come to the Islands through their enlistment in national service. 'Silvertongue' Severson had been clever enough to persuade the army to let him start a surf team of which he and Van Dyke were the first enlistments. On strict orders to go out and surf for their country, they proceeded to ride waves all over Oahu.

Severson remembers his first brush with big waves only too well. He paddled out at Makaha on perhaps the first big swell of the year. Perfect ten to twelve feet, glassy bowl surf with no-one out. After pushing back all the adrenalin induced by steady doses of Fred Van Dyke's scrapbook and Fred's stories of Waimea Bay closing out, being sucked into a lava tube, and being dragged out to sea by rip tides, John finally found the line-up. A big blue glassy peak showed about half a mile out and he paddled around to a take-off position, trying to keep his appointment with his first big-wave experience. Without knowing about the infamous Makaha bowl, John stood up just as the wave was leaping up to form the bowl. The board and John parted company, John falling through space until he hit the wave again and was pitched over the falls. Eventually he came up very alone and a long way from shore. Most surfers can identify with this first Hawaiian experience.

Still more Californian surfers began leaving the mainland, with a dream of riding giant island waves: Kemp Aaberg, Mike Diffenderfer, Al Nelson, Little John Richards . . . the list goes on and on. In a reverse movement many Hawaiian surfers came over to work on the mainland. Kimo Hollinger started to pour foam for Velzy/Jacobs, the Californian board builders. Two hot young Hawaiian gremmies named Donald Takayama and Harold Iggy came over to learn to shape from Greg Noll and Velzy/Jacobs. Some of Hawaii's finest surfers . . . Chubby Mitchell, Joey Cabell, 'Buddy Boy' Achoy, Lord 'Tally Ho' Blears . . . stayed for varying amounts of time before returning to the Islands.

Pat Curren was a classic character as well as an amazing surfer (he is the father of Tom Curren, one of the hottest young competitors in the 1983 pro season). He camped on a vacant lot near Pipeline so he could go surfing whenever he wanted to . . . and it was Pat who was responsible for naming the big-wave boards 'elephant guns'. He decided that if an elephant gun was needed to hunt elephants, then it would also be needed to hunt big waves. Later the name was shortened to 'guns'. Big, strong and designed for speed, they became the standard equipment of the big-wave hunters of Hawaii.

●

SURFER MAGAZINE

The ultimate challenge.

BRUCE BROWN

UNKNOWN

GEORGE SAMANA

PHOTOGRAPHY UNLIMITED

4. *Mike Doyle (on the outside) at Makaha Point.*

5. *"Land-sakes, wait 'till I tell Maud back in Shady Gulch!"*

GEORGE SAMANA

1. *Greg Noll — after putting on a little bulk, the lean hungry hottie from Manhattan Beach, Calif., took to the bay like there was no tomorrow.*

2. *Caught inside at Waimea. Cowabunga!!*

3. *Waimea is no place to learn to surf.*

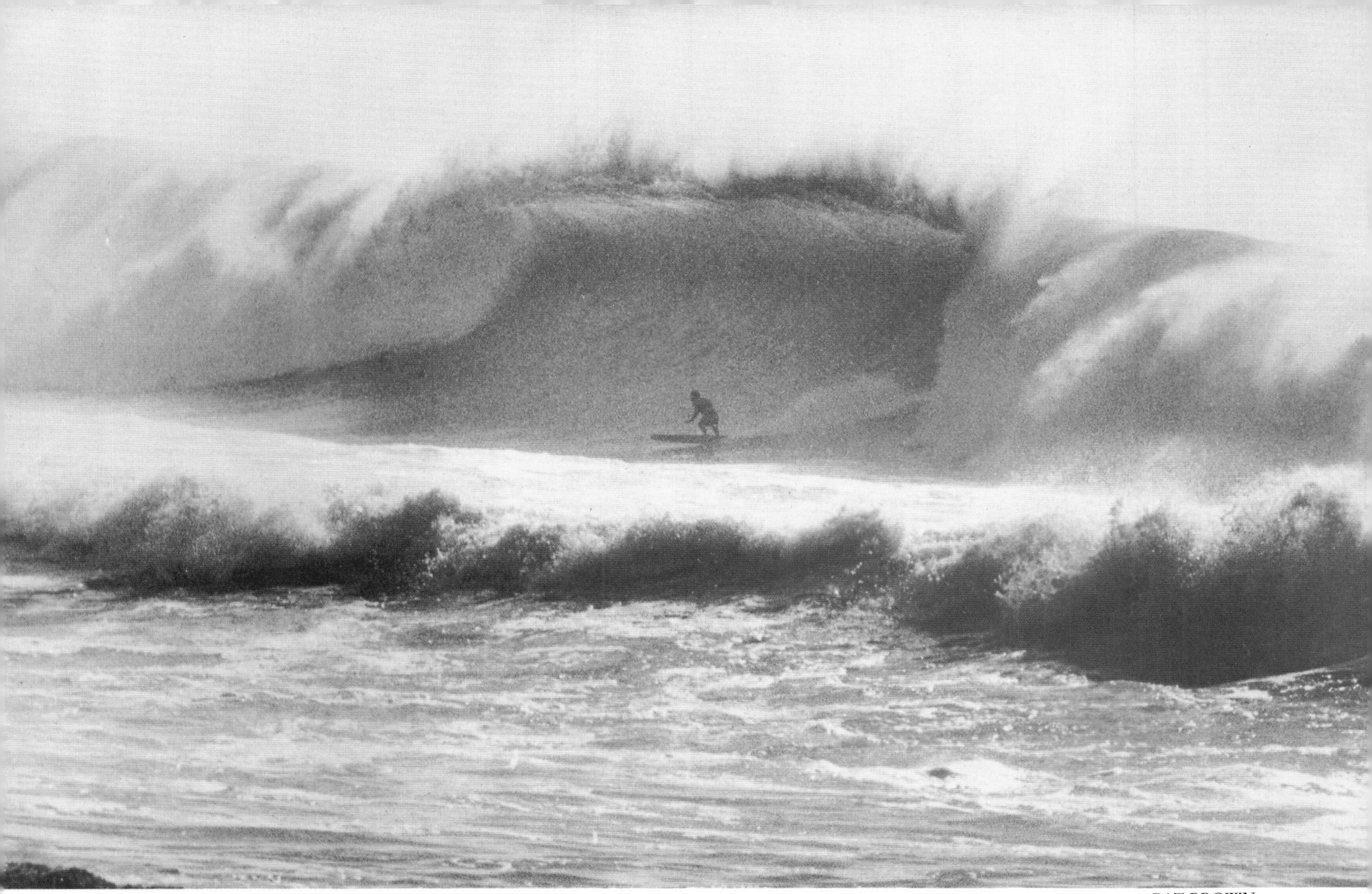

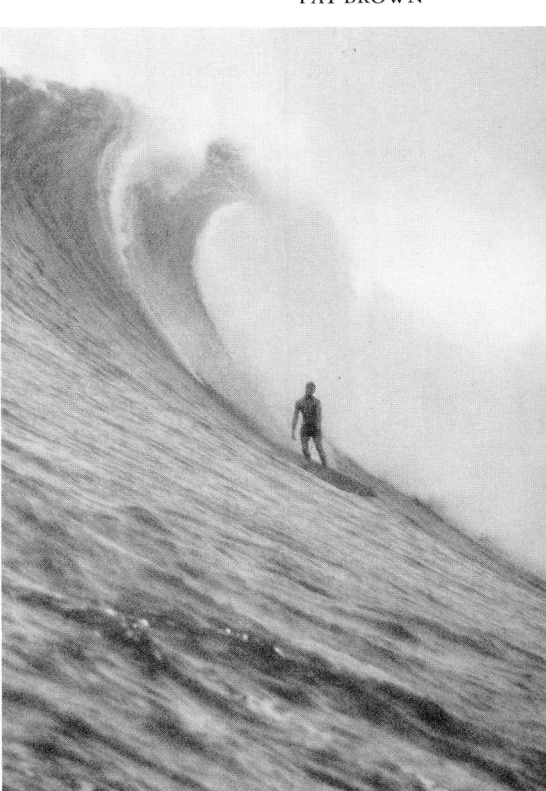

PAT BROWN

Above: *Pat Brown (Bruce's wife) shot this at Makaha in the early 60s. Despite many attempts nobody has ever been able to identify the surfer — Did he live?*

Right: *Another casualty from the Bay — It still happens.*

Far right: *Paul Gebauer, an extremely talented surfer; at Sunset.*

Below: *Makaha 1965. Land developer Chinn Ho chats with Fred Van Dyke and the Duke.*

Below right: *Buzzy Trent with an early elephant gun.*

SURFER MAGAZINE

JOE QUIGG

SURFER MAGAZINE

SURFER MAGAZINE

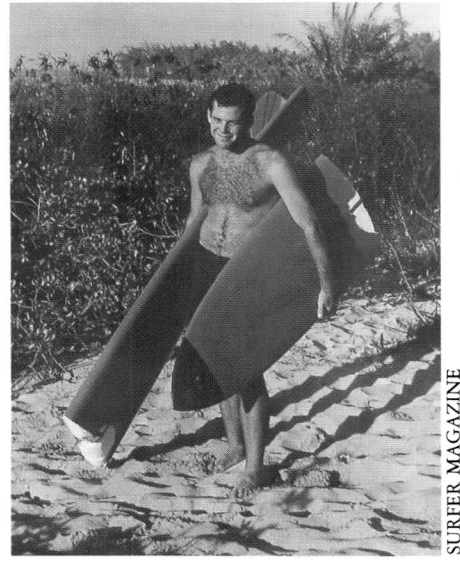

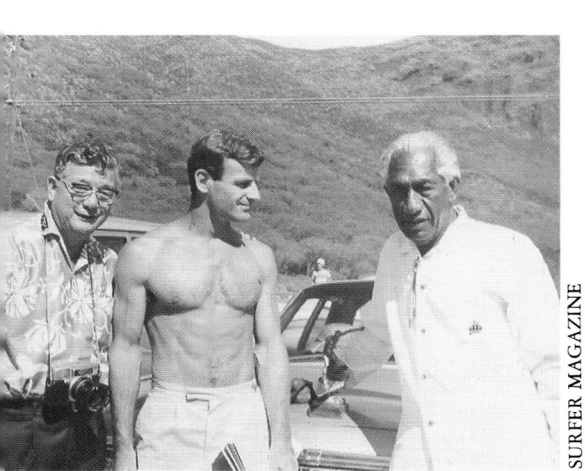

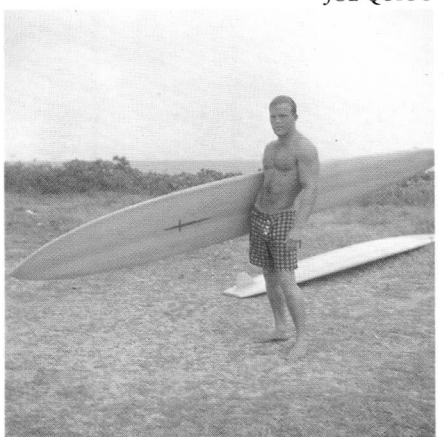

B ack in California, the surfing scene exploded. This was the time when surfing became not just a sport but an entire culture, with hundreds of thousands of young people modelling themselves on a surfing lifestyle. Surfing invaded music, fashion, films, slang, TV, magazines, the whole bit. A new breed of American beach boys developed, a sort of later equivalent of the Hawaiian beach boys who had become professional surfers in the years before World War II. The new breed spent their time lifeguarding, surfing and just having fun; music, parties, waves, boards, girlfriends. They began wearing brightly coloured baggie trunks and, in winter, wetsuits developed from Navy frogmen's outfits. There was little smog in those days, huge kelp beds just off the Californian coast kept the waves glassy much of the time, and surfers found they could surf all year round. It wasn't long before surfing had developed from sport to culture to — cult.

SURFIN' U.S.A.

Probably it was the Gidget movies, books and magazines that did as much as anything to bring surfing to the masses. Malibu had become a prestige area, and many sons and daughters of the wealthy people who lived along the coast became involved in surfing . . . and the 'surfers' who went with it. At the time these included Dewey Weber, Mickey Munoz, Kemp Aaberg, Bob Cooper, Mike Doyle, Jim Fisher, Mickey Dora, Johnny Fain, Tom Morey, Robert Patterson and 'Tubesteak', who was the man responsible for naming Gidget. According to Tubesteak himself, about the last week in June 1956 he, Mickey Munoz and Mickey Dora was standing on the incline above Malibu, checking out the waves, when a young surfer in a baby-blue ski parka pulled a new Velzy/Jacobs board from the rear of a Buick convertible and headed off down the path.

"Hey," shouted Dora, hassling the new arrival. "Go back to the valley, you kook!" shouted Munoz. The stranger got such a shock he stumbled and the board tumbled to the rocks below. Tubesteak told the others to shut up and went to help and discovered the new arrival was a girl. A very short girl!

"For Chrissake," mumbled Tubesteak, "it's a midget, a girl midget, a goddamn gidget!"

The girl was not amused. "I'm not a gidget," she yelled. "My name is Kathryn — and you can keep your filthy hands off me, you creep."

Tubesteak laughed. "Hey Gidget, see you around."

PHOTOS SURFER MAGAZINE

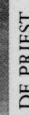

ED DE PRIEST

That was a statement which was to mean more than Tubesteak thought. Kathryn's father was a writer, and he wrote a book about his daughter's summer adventure which became a bestseller. Columbia made the first of its Gidget movies, glamourising the West Coast surfing life, and suddenly everyone seemed to be going surfing. It was the 'in' thing to do. By the summer of 1956 the surfing craze was in high gear. Surfers had built the two famous grass shacks at Malibu which appear in the Gidget films, one in the pit and another out on the point. The offshore santana winds blew regularly all that summer and there was a consistent glassy swell. It was a time when Dora could be seen flying across the face of a five-foot wall, executing a perfect 'el spontaneo' while the crowd on the beach went wild. Munoz might be next up with an immaculate Quasimodo, followed by Cooper with an 'el telephono' from point to the pit. And then came the first annual luau.

It was the end of summer, first Monday in September, and everyone who surfed in California seemed to have heard about the party. All the regulars came, plus Mike Diffenderfer, L.J. Richards, Ole, Jack Haley, Hap Jacobs, Allan Gomes, Chick Edmondson, Hobie, Hynson, Rusty Miller (later to settle down at Byron Bay on Australia's east coast), Tim Dorsey and Robert August. The air was filled with good vibes and loud music. A bonfire was lit, and out of one of the Malibu grass shacks came the legendary 'surfer girls': the gorgeous Linda Benson, luscious Juicy Lucy, ravishing Ramona from Pomona, and then Sally from the Valley, Marion the Librarian and fi-

Frames from the 60s: Everybody's gone surfin', surfin' U.S.A.

nally, to the most applause, Shirley from Temple City, Gidget and Mandos Mary. Tubesteak put a torch to the grass shacks. The first annual luau was drawing to a close and so was an era in American surfing.

Hot dogging was in. Nobody knows how the name arose, but everybody knew what it was; fast, radical manoeuvres (for the time), nose rides, hanging five, hanging ten, stalling, running to the nose, drop-knee cutbacks, head dip, wave scratch, and much else. One of the kings was Dewey Weber, who was into amazing arm gestures as well as having been a member of Groucho Marx's Yo Yo team and in his youth, a model for Buster Brown shoe commercials. Sometimes it was hard to tell the difference in the surf between Weber and Johnny Fain, the 'Malibu Lizard': they were both about 5'4" in height, with long blond hair and muscular physiques. Johnny was younger and more or less took over Weber's role as

BRUCE BROWN

LEROY GRANNIS

WALLY FROISETH

PHOTOS SURFER MAGAZINE

83

the older surfer got into raising a family and developing his surfboard business. And what a business! As time went on a new surfboard market opened on the east coast of the United States, and the Californian board builders began shipping large consignments across the country to East Coast surfers who were buying boards 'off the rack'. Both Hobie Alter and Dewey Weber increased production drastically and extended their plants to cope with the demand. Hobie went from making 20-30 boards a week to 100 a week. Weber was employing something like 10 glassers. When I worked for him in the late '60s as a design consultant the top production shapers and glassers were making $25,000 a year, more than twice a schoolteacher's average wage.

But this is getting ahead of the West Coast story a bit. California's unique point breaks would never change but they were getting more crowded, especially on weekends, and the more serious surfers had to travel further afield to find uncrowded quality waves. One surf spot they infiltrated was Camp Pendleton. It had two dominant points, named 'Uppers' and 'Lowers', which not only had good waves but provided surfers with a challenge by forcing them to run the gauntlet of marine guards. One classic story is about Jack Haley, who sneaked into Trestles wearing a Napoleonic officer's coat and sabre; the marines drove up with the intention of kicking him out, but Jack challenged them to a duel and they all left laughing. That was in the early days; the officers' patience wore thin as the number of surfers increased, and in the final years of the 1950s they would round up vanloads of surfers and escort them back to the camp gates, taking their names, confiscating their surfboards and sometimes even prosecuting them for trespassing.

Around the time when Mickey Dora was a surf star, and years after Mickey had been the first lifeguard in the area, he was apprehended for being on the base. Back in the sergeant's office he gave his name and watched while the sergeant turned from red to purple, his eyes popping. Reaching up, leaning over the table, grabbing 'The Cat's' shirt, he pulled him closer for direct eye contact and managed to shout at the height of his tantrum that he had had two other Mickey Doras that day, ten in the last week and over five hundred in the entire

84

summer. Every surfer who was picked up by the marines was giving his name as either Mickey Dora or Phil Edwards!

Right next door to Trestles is Cotton's Point, a tempting surf spot overlooked by the Cotton family's beautiful Spanish-style villa, which was to become the western White House in President Nixon's reign. In the early 1950s the local surfers had developed a method of sneaking into the area by nosing their cars up to the guard chain, pulling on the car emergency brake lightly, jumping out and holding the chain up while the car coasted under; it only remained to drive up the side entrance track and to stow the car in the bush for the 'sneak' to be complete. There was only one guard but he was a fanatic; Mr Carney, hater of surfers and dedicated to protecting the estate

with a shotgun. He fired at surfers many times but nobody, fortunately, was ever hit.

During this exploratory period of surfing in California surfers discovered many new beaches and point surfs, only to be kicked out by irate ranchers who insisted that the surfers scared their cattle, broke their fences down and caused chaos to normal farm life. The Holister ranch north of Santa Barbara was one such discovery; John Severson, who had turned his hand to movies as well as magazines, put together a 'surf safari' into this area in 1959. He and his friends were given the boot from Government Point, at the most northern end of the ranch, but they camped at the other end in Gaviota Park instead and next day set off to explore the coast to the north. From the top of one bluff all they could see was perfect point

1

2

after point stretching off into the distance, with off-shore winds holding up six to eight foot barrels. They had found paradise! Young Mike Doyle was the star of the day. A few other surfers made camping trips to this area in 1959, including James Aurness and his son Rolf. Everywhere you travelled there was a tremendous feeling of openness and adventure; it seemed that around every bend there was a new surfing spot to name and try out.

Mexico was the ultimate 'safari', and many Californian surfers burned down Highway 101 and over the border in their board-laden 'woodies'. The Blue Fox nightclub in Tijuana was a favourite surfer haunt; it had bizarre sexual floor shows and strong tequila. Back in Los Angeles, at the surf movies, the surfers would brag about what they had seen. These

movies had been made on a semi-professional basis for some years; in 1959 the first highly publicised screening was held at Santa Monica High School, where just about everyone who rode a board converged to see a collection of movies by Bud Browne, Don James and Walt Hoffman. Someone set off a firecracker, the lights went out and everyone sat mesmerised by sequences of waves at Sunset and surfers like Buzzy Trent and Jim Fisher coming down and proning out on huge Makaha waves. Screenings of surf movies soon got a reputation for being rowdy, undisciplined events; swastikas, iron crosses and other pieces of Nazi paraphernalia showed up on surfers; a thousand surfers would shout "sieg heil" in unison when the lights went out on a South Bay surf screening. Brown-eyes became commonplace at Malibu, where surfers flashed them at

freeway motorists; at Trestles surfers exhibited their bottoms to the passing San Diego train. Surfing was getting a bad name; something had to be done, and in August 1961, the United States Surfing Association was formed. It helped make surfing and surfers more acceptable.

This was also the era of surf music. Dick Dale was a typical Southern Californian surfer who used to take his guitar down to the beach and play music in between surfing his new 9'6" board. "There was a tremendous amount of power that I felt while surfing and that feeling of power was simply transferred from myself to my guitar when I was playing surf music," he explained. "I couldn't get that feeling by singing so the music took on an instrumental form." Dick became 'King of the Surf Guitar' and because of his popularity scores of garage bands sprang up which were dedicated to playing the new 'surfing music'. Santa Ana High School had a lot of students who were surfers and two of these got together in the late summer of 1961 to form the basis of a group called The Chantays. They were an immediate success at school dances. The following year, while they were looking around for something to call an instrumental melody they were working on, they happened to watch a Bruce Brown movie in the school auditorium and decided to call the tune *'Pipeline'*. The song took off, became No. 1 around the world, and surf music became the new cult sound.

By 1963 the Beach Boys had appeared. Surf music was no longer just an instrumental sound but had developed lyrics which celebrated the whole Californian experience, from

SURFER MAGAZINE

3

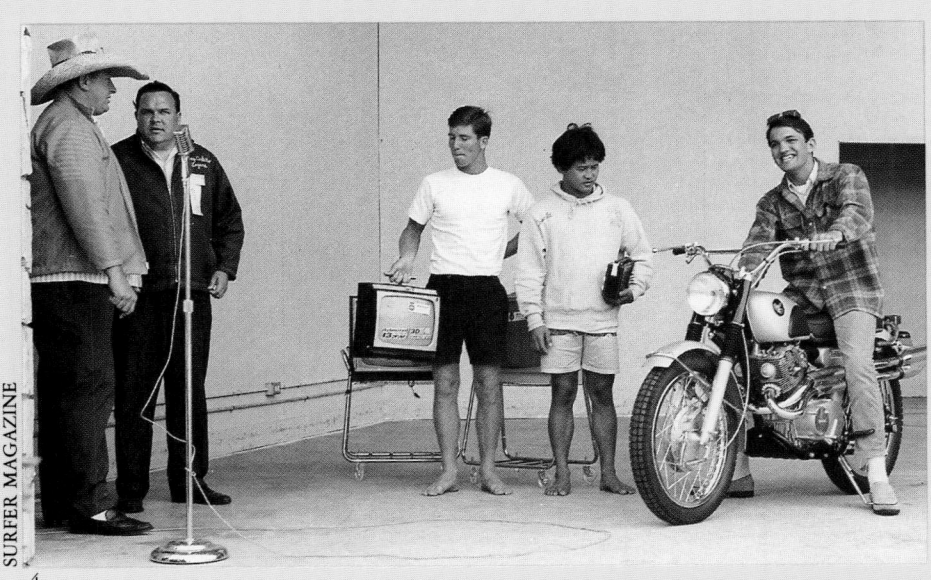

SURFER MAGAZINE

4

1. *Paisleys of the 60s.*
   Harold Iggy, Mike Tabling and Dewey Weber.

2. *Every picture tells a story. PR shot of Duke Corporation.*

3. *(L to R) Harold Iggy, Butch van Artsdalen, 60s girl, Joey Cabell, Mickey Munoz, Donald Takayama.*

4. *John Peck 1st, Steve Bigler 2nd, Donald Takayama 3rd.*

surfing to hot rods to high schools. 'Surfin' USA' was the Beach Boys' first hit, in April 1963; they became one of the world's major recording groups and Brian Wilson developed into one of the finest songwriters of the 'sixties. He wrote songs for Jan & Dean as well as the Beach Boys and for other surfbands such as the Safaris, the Hondels and the Legendary Masked Surfers. In order to keep up with the surf sound rhythm surfers began dancing a stylized, easy dance, it wasn't very beautiful to watch, consisting of two stomps on one foot, then two on the other, but it felt good. Oh yeah, and it was new. Everything was new. Surfing, surf music, the stomp . . . it was a good time to be young, Californian, and a surfer. ●

RON STONER

1. *Surf Sound.*

2. *A young Mike Doyle.*

3. *John Peck at Laguna.*

4. *Surf movies: 1961.*

5. *Peter van Dyke with charred board after a bush fire swept Trestles.*

6. *John Peck 1964.*

Above: *Mike Hynson at Cojo Point, Holister Ranch, mid-60s. "From the top of one bluff, all we could see was perfect point after point stretching off into the distance. We had found paradise . . ."* John Severson, on first surfing the Ranch, 1959.

SURFING MAGAZINE

1

SURFING MAGAZINE

2

LEROY GRANNIS

3

BRUCE BROWN

4

RICH SIFON

5

SURFING MAGAZINE

6

HUGHES

1. *Bruce Brown (left) and Mike Doyle.*

2. *Board bumps: legacy of the 60s.*

3. *The drysuit: forerunner of wetsuits.*

4. *Ten in a camper: 'The Endless Bummer'.*

5. *The Mickey Mumble.*

6. *Mike Hynson at Haleiwa, Hawaii.*

Above: *Mexico was the ultimate safari for Californian surfers in the 60s. They burned down Highway 101 and over the border in their board laden Kombis.*

7. *Bill Fury at Huntington Beach, Calif.*

1

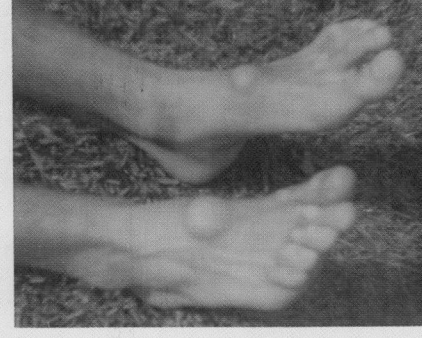

NORM SNOW

2

DR DON JAMES

3

PHOTOS BRUCE BROWN

4

SURFER MAGAZINE

5

DARRIN

6

RON STONER

7

"*Getting ready to bury this junk with the rest of the trashy rot that keeps bugging me! Scrap metal tokenism as a grubby little payoff to keep me in line and my mouth shut. Such outside pressures will never succeed in making me a lap dog for the entrenched controlling interests who have turned our once great individualistic sport into a mushy, soggy cartoon.*"

— Mickey Dora

THE OZ CONNECTION

Modern surfing was late arriving in Australia, and when it did it came not via Hawaii but from California. In 1956 a group of lifeguards came to Australia on a tour which coincided with the Olympic Games being held in Melbourne. The group was led by Tom Zahn and included Mike Bright, Bob Burnside and Greg Noll. They brought with them, for the first time, the new Malibu boards, three of which were made by Joe Quigg. Actually Hollywood film star Peter Lawford had brought a Malibu board with him to Sydney before that, when he was on location in Australia shooting the film *Kangaroo*, but nobody ever saw him surf it. The Californians, however, surfed their new boards all up and down the east coast from Avalon to Torquay and in doing so utterly changed the nature of surfing in Australia. Officially the local surfboard team thrashed them in the paddle races, but what startled the local surfers was the way Americans could manoeuvre, stall, cut back and trim across the face of the waves on their boards. A younger generation of Australian surfers watched them with as much interest as their forefathers had watched the Duke.

The Surf Life Saving Association didn't take to the new boards; they didn't improve the techniques of surf rescue, and they certainly weren't faster to paddle. But no sooner had the

1. *Dave Jackman conquers the Queenscliff Bombora!*

2. *Peter Thomas at Fairy Bower.*

3. *Surfboard rally at Narrabeen, 1960.*

4. *John Pennings at Bells Beach.*

5. *Manly Boys, 1958.*

RON PERROTT

RON PERROTT

EVANS FAMILY

SNOW McALISTER

American surf team departed than hundreds of younger surfboard riders were trying to buy fibreglass Malibu boards. It was almost as though, overnight, nobody wanted the old hollow paddle boards any longer. Some quick-thinking Sydney board men had been able to buy some of the visiting team's 'hot dog' boards; Bob Evans bought a narrow-tail 10-foot gun-style board from Greg Noll, Peter Clare one of the Quigg boards, and Gordon Woods a 10-foot wide-nose wide-tail Velzy/Jacobs board and Bob Pike purchased Tom Zahn's 9'6" Malibu. The established board builders at the time were Bill Wallace, Gordon Woods, Barry Bennett, Norm Casey and Bill Clymer, a boat builder from Victoria who had moved to Sydney, where all the surfboard manufacturing was taking place. By the summer of 1956 these manufacturers were inundated with orders for Malibus — a somewhat frustrating situation, because the balsa needed for the new boards was virtually unavailable.

The only way the orders could be filled was by building the boards in the established manner with plywood covering a light timber frame, then sealing it all with coats of varnish. At the same time they began working on finding a source of balsa wood. The builders knew balsa was used in the making of model aeroplanes, but this was milled in short, thin sticks; balsa planks had been used as life preservers lining the bulkheads of ships during the war, but this proved to be unavailable. Some balsa was also used as packing cases for ammunition and supplies dropped to the allied forces in New Guinea during World War II.

The first person to actually build a balsa board in Australia was Roger 'The Duck' Keiran, nephew of Barney Keiran, of boxing fame. 'The Duck' was a keen surfboard rider but not an experienced surfboard shaper. The board he built was crude by manufacturers' standards, but it worked. He had acquired enough balsa to build three boards from Arthur Milner, a timber merchant in Melbourne, who supplied the trade builders for the war supplies mentioned earlier. The fibreglass and resin he had seen on the visitors' boards was now easy to come by, but it took much trial and error to cover the whole of one side of a board before the coating began to go hard. The Duck surfed all over Sydney, from Bondi to Freshwater, on his Australian-made balsa Malibu with just about all the manufacturers looking on with envy.

Several of the manufacturers wrote to companies in Equador requesting information as to how to import the precious wood. They were instructed to contact Arthur Milner, who came to Sydney to discuss exactly what size timber was required for the expected boom. Business arrangements took a long time in those days and it wasn't until the summer of '58 that their first shipment arrived. The board builders tore into it with sharp planes and a keen eye, discovering the properties of balsa which makes it unique. The lightest planks were the whitest, with flecks of dark grey grain running through them; the hardest, but heaviest, were the greener, darker ones. Selection of the planks was an intricate part of the process; you used the lighter ones down the centre, the heavier, more durable ones towards the rails. A scarf joint to give lift was the same as Simmons had devised 10 years earlier. As most of South America's good quality balsa was going to the USA, Australia was sent some pretty scratchy shipments. By 1958 the established manufacturers had moved out of Sydney's densely-populated eastern suburbs to the northside and the recently opened in-

6. *L to R: Midge Farrelly, Sugar Ray Robinson, Peter Thomas, Bob 'Surge' Evans, Jack 'Bluey' Mayes.*

7. *Australia's first surfboard competition, 1958.*

8. *Jack 'Bluey' Mayes in action.*

9. *Midget Farrelly in perfect quasimodo at North Narrabeen, Sydney.*

6

SNOW McALISTER

7

SNOW McALISTER

8

EVANS FAMILY

9

RON PERROTT

dustrial suburb of Brookvale. At one end of Brookvale was Barry Bennett; at the other end, Gordon Woods; and in the middle, Bill Wallace. Bill Clymer was in a garage in Manly where he and Joe Larkin did some beautiful work, using stringers, nose blocks and tail blocks made from cedar and redwood to set off the blond balsa.

Gordon Woods remembers the days of the bad balsa shipments only too well; he made it a rule to always inspect the load on the truck. On one occasion he found it all to be greenish, heavier style. He turned the shipment straight around, realising that one heavy board could ruin his reputation.

In 1959 more than 1500 Malibu balsas were produced in Australia. By now there were other manufacturers in Brookvale. Greg McDonagh was building some light boards with styrofoam and Scott Dillon and Noel Ward were having some success with the same material. Competition between the manufacturers was getting more intense as surfing gained in popularity. Every Saturday morning each manufacturer would set out to deliver his orders to the prospective board riders who waited anxiously at surf clubs all over the Sydney metropolitan area. Surfboard building developed into a lucrative business in which agents could order a quantity

of boards for their area and come to Sydney once a week to pick up a truckload. Mark Richards' father, Ray, started in the surfboard business in this manner, taking thousands of boards to Newcastle in the late 50s and early 60s.

In 1958 Bud Browne, the American surf-film maker, heard about what was happening in Australia and filmed the start of the explosion down under. One of the surfers he met was Bob Evans; he and Evans developed a rapport and Bob agreed to show Bud's surf movies in Australia. The movies gave Australians a window on the surfing world overseas and showed them what had been happening just a few months ago in California and Hawaii; soon local riders were making every attempt to emulate the action they saw in the movies.

Jack 'Bluey' Mayes stands out in this period as one of the best early hot doggers. Bluey grew up in Bondi and had been involved in surfboards right from the 16-foot 'toothpick' days. His style reflected the changing design of his boards and he soon adjusted to the manoeuvreability of the Malibus, or 'Okanui boards' as they were called in those days. On the north side a couple of younger board riders, Nipper Williams and Mick Dooley, were performing well on the new Malibus. As was to be expected,

their styles were a bit looser than Bluey's but still a little stiff, especially in the front leg, which was kept bent and in approximately the same place for the entire ride. Mick and Nipper had learnt to stand up on 'toothpicks', where keeping the feet close together and concentrating on balance was so important. Like many other surfers of this period they made the transition by tucking the back leg in behind the other to turn. This drop-knee style of turn was a characteristic of all such surfers throughout the late '50s and early '60s. Posssibly the early Australian Malibu surfers misinterpreted the poise and grace of Phil Edwards' backside turns which came running across our silver screens in the early days. What was really happening was that the turn was being loaded up with the power of the surfer, who was bending his knees and pushing the board through the turn. It had taken years for Phil and a handful of Californian surfers to develop this power through their turns, and it was not going to happen overnight in Australia.

The film Bud Browne shot in Sydney was included in his new movie of '59 and it was inevitable that some of the more adventurous American surfers would see it and be turned on to Australia as a new frontier where a pure surfer could stay one jump ahead of the masses. Bob Cooper was virtually the first American surfer to do

GORDON WOODS

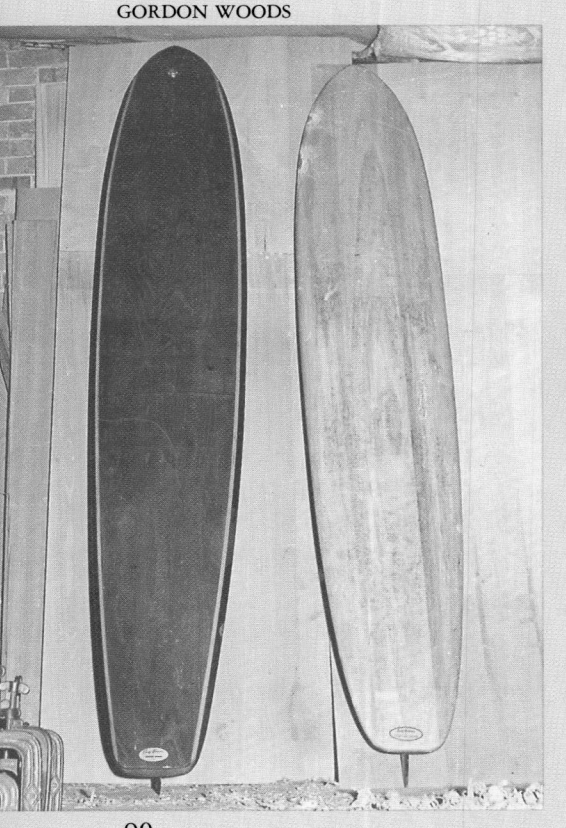

EVANS FAMILY

Above: *Bicycling to the beach — before boards got lighter.*

Left: *The Malibu board Gordon Woods bought from the visiting American team in '56. Wood's first hollow plywood copy (left).*

GORDON WOODS

Gordon Woods and Ross Renwick (centre) with two visiting American surfers.

this. He came in late 1960, just as the lid was about to blow; in fact, just in time to see the premiere of John Severson's latest surf movie at Anzac House. For Cooper it was a flashback to all the very worst things about the surf scene he had just left. It seemed it was almost surfer instinct to go wild over the screaming of surf guitars and the pounding of huge waves at Sunset. As in California, the theatre proprietors and the public could not understand or tolerate this behaviour, especially when a glass mural depicting the Anzacs in battle was smashed and seats were ripped out of the auditorium; the surfers were ushered out by numerous police. Many theatres still have closed doors to surfing movies as a legacy of the early 60s' larrikinism.

Some time earlier Sydney board-builder Barry Bennett had sent a letter to the American manufacturer Dale Velzy asking for information about blowing foam, so Cooper, who blew foam for Velzy, knew there would be a job for him when he arrived in Australia. He stayed a couple of nights with Bennett before settling into the Manly surf scene in a flat with Mick Dooley and Wheels Williams. He had seen Bud Brown's movies of local surfers at Manly and thought he knew what to expect, but there was one young surfer around who was head and shoulders above the rest: Bernard 'Midget' Farrelly.

Cooper was astounded at his natural ability and go-for-it attitude, and recognized that Midget was already mastering the Californian (Dora and Edwards) style of surfing. Cooper encouraged the young surfer and kept him informed of what was happening in the United States; Midget and his mates even began wearing American-style board shorts and adapting themselves to the American surf image. Cooper also kept pumping Midget on how good the waves were over in the Islands. So in 1961 Midget and a group of other surfers . . . Charlie Cardiff, Dave Jackman, Bob Pike Owen Pillon, Mike Hickey, Mick McMann, Tank Henry, Gordon Simpson, Nipper Williams and Graham Treloar . . . booked passages on the *Oriana* and, for the first time, Australians set out to ride the waves of Hawaii. Bob Evans went along too, to film the action for his first surf movie and to take a few pictures for the first issue of *Surfing World*.

That first year was a barrel of laughs. It was whispered by Californians and Hawaiians that in Hawaii in 1961 you could spot the Aussie by his cozzy, and in the ninth international surfing championships at Makaha that was true. Australia didn't do too well in the contest, but the experience gained from the first year was invaluable. With more and more Californians coming to the Islands, two distinct factions had become ap-

parent: small wave riders were the majority, made up of newly arrived Californians and local kids who only surfed in town; and then there were the prestigious big-wave riders, made up of older Hawaiians and the very best of the Californians. Some Hawaiians and Californians could perform in both big and small surf, and these were the real heroes: Buffalo Keaulana, Conrad Cunha, Paul Gebauer, Pat Curren, Mike Doyle, Phil Edwards, Joey Cabell, L. J. Richards, Mickey Dora, Ricky Grigg and Paul Strauch. The real test for this elite group was to ride Waimea Bay, the place where the biggest waves broke, representing a challenge that had not been attempted before. Waves of this size provided another dimension for surfing, one of drama and sensationalism, and this attracted film and TV producers and hordes of spectators.

As luck would have it, however, there was a lack of big waves for the 10th international surfing championship in 1962. That suited the Australian contingent, which included Midget Farrelly; they also had an extra year of competitive surfing behind them. Because of the small waves the judges extended the time limit. At first the waves were breaking on the outside, dribbling through to the inside, but eventually all the surfing was being done on the inside shore break. All the contestants were

JOHN ARNOLD

Left: John Arnold and his mates in South Australia.

Below: Jim Fordham — still the best day I have seen at Narrabeen, Sydney. April 26th, 1963.

JOHN PENNINGS

ROBERT KENNERSON

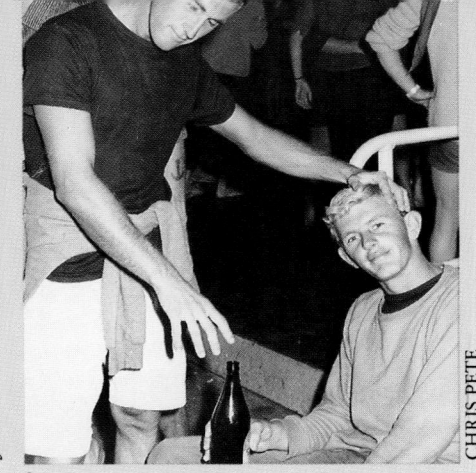

JOHN SEVERSON

CHRIS PETE

1. *Our Woody.*

2. *Bob Cooper in Australia, 1961.*

3. *Kenno and Bab-Louie after a few drinks.*

4. *Bob Evans who played a key part in introducing modern surfing to Australia.*

5. *The stomp! Two stomps on one foot, two stomps on the other and watch the surf club crumble.*

EVANS FAMILY

RON PERROTT

fairly evenly placed, with Californians John Peck and Chuck Linnen trying to keep up with Midget Farrelly. When the results were announced Midget had won — the first Australian to ever take out a major surf title! But, more important, Midget's victory indicated that Australia had at last caught up with California and Hawaii in modern surfing.

As a youngster Farrelly had lived for short periods in Canada and New Zealand before his folks decided to settle in Sydney. He nickname came when people saw him riding a plywood board at Manly; he was mighty small for his age. His uncle, Bondi boardman Ray Hookham, encouraged him in the early days, and he learnt by watching Nipper Williams and Mick Dooley as well. When he returned to Australia as the accepted world champion he became a symbol of a new generation of surfers who were more interested in surfing than surf clubs. Patrol duty and training for the bronze medallion began to conflict with chasing waves (and girls) and doing the stomp.

What was happening in Australia was almost precisely what had happened in California earlier on. Surfing had become a cult. In September, 1962 Bob Evans put out his first issue of *Surfing World*. Dave Jackman was taking on Australia's biggest waves and conquered the much-feared

Queenscliff bombora. The Atlantics had a smash hit with a number they called *Bombora*; soon surf music took over the local charts, the Australian group the Joy Boys recorded six surfing hits, and the Chantays and the Beach Boys invaded the record stores. Robert Helpmann, the ballet dancer, released *Surfer Doll* and *Surf Dance*; Barry Crocker recorded *I Can't Do The Stomp'* and who could ever forget Little Patti and *My Blonde Headed Stompy Wompie Real Gone Surfer Boy?* In the national stomping championships 45,000 kids stomped the afternoon away. Stomps were held at most surf clubs on Saturday and Sunday nights and Sunday afternoons until some of the club foundations actually crumpled under the pressure, and an old picture theatre was hurriedly converted into Surf City for stompers.

Yet the authorities still looked on surfing with scepticism. The conflict between surf club members and surfboard riders was intensified by the introduction of a system which allotted different parts of each beach to the different surfers. The local municipal councils had strong connections with the surf lifesaving movement and forced board riders to register their boards and pay a fee; the lifesavers were instructed to police the system. Surfers who rode waves in the 'wrong' area ran the risk of having their boards confiscated; this led to real

confrontation when some riders refused to let surf club members take their boards. There were also a few isolated brawls between surfies and 'rockers', who were basically bike riders from the landlocked western suburbs; media publicity about the conflicts helped give surfies a bad name. This got even worse when two of Australia's finest surfers, Bob McTavish and David Chidgy, stowed away on the *Orsova* while saying goodbye to some other Hawaiian-bound surfers. With so much flak hitting them the surfers decided to form their own association, and in 1963 clubs were created all along the east coast and banded together in the Australian Surfriders' Association.

About this time I was surfing down at Collaroy beach, on the north side of Sydney harbour, and getting into more trouble than I managed to keep out of. My mother bought my board registration sticker for me (it cost 10 shillings) because, like most surfers, I thought the registration system was a rip-off; getting my board confiscated for two weeks didn't help. A few friends and I formed the Collaroy Surfing Association, which had 17 paid-up members, about 10 hangers-on, and about the same number of girls who just hung around the beach looking beautiful at weekends or before the bus left for school on weekdays. The 'association' had its clubhouse on the beach or in

Above left: *Bobby Brown — an intricate part of the inside of the curl style which was to take Australia to the front of world surfing.*

Left: *Bernard 'Midget' Farrelly. 1962 Makaha International Champion.*

Above: *Bob McTavish and FJ Holden at an empty Noosa Heads line-up.*

Below: *Bob Pike at Pipeline.*

my bedroom; we also had our own social club which held parties and organised fund-raising activities. At school all we thought about was the latest surf equipment and what pigment we'd use on our new boards, and to further establish our identity we carried our board shorts hanging out of the back pocket of our jeans. And we thought about sex. Most of the girl surfers we knew were into the sun and stomp, and some of them became serious boardriders later on, but very few of them engaged in sex. So sexual intercourse became a group activity, involving several surfers and one of the more promiscuous girls who hung around the scene: Grunter, Brenda the Benda, Sally Apple Bowels, and others. These girls weren't well-respected in the normal sense of the word, but some strong ties did develop between them and the surfer dogs who chased after them. At the same time the local gremmies were busy peroxiding their hair to make it look as bleached as possible, tuning up on American slang, and trying to get enough cash together to buy a surfer van.

Two older members of the Collaroy crew, Robert 'Kenno' Kennerson and Ian 'Wally' Wallace, managed to purchase an old bread wagon. They had the artist of the mob, Denis '10 foot' Anderson, paint their favourite character all over the wagon: his name was 'Murphy the Surfie' and he

came via *Surfer Magazine*, the surfers' bible that came out of California four times a year (someone's 'with-it' mum would get one for her son at Christmas, or for his birthday, and the magazine would end up in pieces on his bedroom wall.) When the wagon was finished it looked fantastic and now, by sharing the petrol money and arriving before dawn at Kenno's, the crew could chase waves all up and down the coast. No longer would they have to build trolleys to carry the boards behind their bikes over the hill to Long Reef. Finally they were free.

This was the era of discovery in Australia, just as the '50s had been in California. Australian surfers were starting to head north and south from Sydney to realise the potential of

Australia's waves. Victoria's Bells Beach had already been discovered in 1961 by board-riding members of the Torquay boat crew. Surfers began riding the perfect, little rhythmical tubes of northern NSW and southern Queensland, which Roger Keiran had first ridden on a Malibu, and which were to play such an important part in the development of Australian surfing. The search for the perfect wave was full-on in this period. Bruce Brown and Phil Edwards cruised through NZ and Australia shooting for Brown's epic surf movie '*The Endless Summer*'. And I must have been doing a bit of surfing, as well as everything else, because I managed to win the Australian junior surfriding championship and began to be looked upon as a rival of Midget Farrelly. The competition was hotting up. ●

WORLD CHAMPIONSHIPS

In the early and mid-sixties surfing took off all over the world. Surfing films and magazines spread the good word about Baja in Mexico, Jeffrey's Bay in South Africa, Rincon and Steamer Lane in California, Waimea and Sunset in Hawaii, Bells Beach and Byron Bay in Australia. Two Australian surfers, Bob Pike and Mike Hickey, happened to be in Hawaii one winter and with a host of Californians and Hawaiians were invited to compete in the first surfing contest in Peru. After the contest Bob returned to Australia but Mike, who had met two French surfers in Peru and had heard about the waves of Biarritz, on the French coast, went off to Europe. The next thing everyone knew Mike Hickey had become the first European surfing champion. Surfing had reached Britain, where a small band of dedicated boardmen rode summertime waves in Cornwall and the Channel Isles. South Africans had taken up surfing and had picked up on the country's amazing wave potential; a few years later they were to produce a world champion.

Surfing contests were really happening. The east and gulf coasts of the U.S. were well into the second year of serious competition, with two major events and numerous small inter-club competitions. In California the West Coast Surfboard Championships had been held annually since 1960 at Huntington Beach, where shooting the pier was an important manoeuvre to qualify for the final. The surfing clubs were very big; some surfers would travel hundreds of miles to be a member of a particular club with an impressive stable of good surfers. The Windansea Surf Club and the Long Beach Surf Club were the two strongest clubs in California; they were involved in competition every weekend, either between clubs or with surfers competing against one another. Most of the talented surfers to bounce off this platform went on to win the prestigious Huntington contest: Mike Doyle, Corky Carrol, David Nuuheiwa, Ricky Irons and Rusty Miller. All these surfers were also sponsored by surfboard manufacturers; what with their club contests

and competition between rival companies they had very little time for anything else. If you were too young to surf you probably rode a skate board, and the competition associated with this craze was just as fanatical as in surfing.

In Hawaii a controversy over the judging system used at the international surfing championships erupted. The judging system allotted points mainly for the size of wave and length of ride; the manoeuvres were taken into account, but they were overshadowed by whether a surfer could take off at the point, ride through the bowl and through to the beach. The real crux of the problem was the all-Hawaiian judging panel. The year before in 1962 they had tried some outside judges and Midget Farrelly had won. This was regarded as an error which would not happen again, because the judges responsible, namely Dick Brewer and Buzzy Trent, had been removed. The contest was organised by the Outrigger Canoe Club, which was mainly a social club with strong surfing affiliations; the members were involved in traditional paddle boards, outrigger canoes and, to a lesser degree, board riding. To the Outrigger's contest committee the senior men's was the most important part of the competition, but the tandem, girls, and paddle board races were of significance also.

There was a nasty feeling on Makaha Beach in December 1963. Many talented Californians and Australians had failed to qualify and a showdown was avoided only because the contest was won by the well-respected caucasian Hawaiian, Joey Cabell, who rode the biggest waves in a hot dog fashion to go on to win what was then considered the world championship. One of the problems was that the Outrigger was not aware of the importance attached to the contest in the rest of the world. They were doing their best to make it a good function; they were excellent hosts, extending guest privileges in their luxurious club to all international competitors, and any judging bias that may have taken place was unin-

1

3   SURFER MAGAZINE

5   RON PERROTT

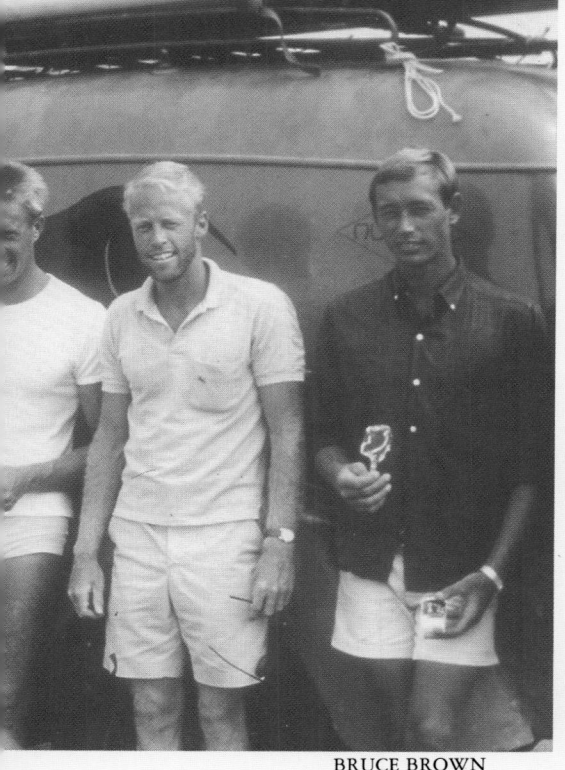
BRUCE BROWN

BRUCE BROWN

2

MARCEL

4
STUDIO COMMERCIAL

PETER RAE

6

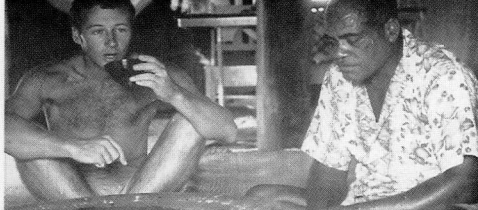
7

1. *One of the first Malibu surfboards in South Africa. L to R Robert August, Terrence, Mike Hynson, Jack Wilson, Bruce Brown and Max Wetteland.*

2. *Japanese discover surfboards and wax. 1962.*

3. *Line up for 1965 World Contest in Peru.*

4. *The French surfers of the early 60s.*

5. *Dairy Beach, South Africa — mid-60s.*

6. *Surf movies were happening!*

7. *Peter Rae in Fiji. Surfers were great travellers.*

tentional. But the Hawaiians were somewhat over-protective about outside talent excelling in their inherited sport, especially as they had only a few outstanding surfers right then in senior men's competition. Fred Hemmings was still a junior and Barry Kanaiaupuni was still surfing in town, lacking the experience to excell in big waves.

With so many talented Californians moving to Hawaii permanently, change was inevitable. At one particular surf break on the north shore this change was seen more vividly than anywhere else. The Banzai Pipeline was originally called Banzai by Flippy Hoffman because it seemed an impossible wave to ride; the Pipeline was added by Phil Edwards (the first surfer to ride it for the movie Endless Summer) because the waves looked like a pipe when they broke. It represented a new frontier. Butch van Artsdalen from San Diego, and John Peck were the first to meet the challenge continuously. In the winter of '63 both these surfers broke down the barriers by surfing so deep inside the curl that on rare occasions they actually disappeared. The Australian contingent was really impressed by and wary of the Pipeline. Midget told the rest of the team that surfing the Pipeline was like committing suicide, because of the way the waves pounded onto shallow live coral heads. When Peter Troy had to be rushed to a hospital for numerous stitches, the Australians made sure they took off a long way outside Peck and van Artsdalen.

I took Troy off to hospital; I was 16 years old, didn't even have a driving licence, and was in Hawaii for the first time. I was getting psyched up over the Pipeline, but after I rode it I didn't think it much different to, or more formidable than, the rest of the waves on the north shore of Oahu.

My being in Hawaii was the result of taking off first prize in an Australian open men's contest at Bondi in November, 1963. The prize, presented to me by Duke Kahanamoku himself, was a first-class air fare to Hawaii and California. The ticket and expenses were provided by Ampol Petroleum and the Sunday Telegraph newspaper, and the man who organised such impressive sponsorship was none other than Bob Evans. As well as his movies and surf magazines Bob found time, together with John Witzig, Ross Kelly and Ray Young, to put the Australian Surfriders' Association on a firm footing. Me, I was just pleased to get to Hawaii for the

95

Right: *Manly Beach, Australia. Scene of 1964 World Contest.*

Below: *Midget executing a copybook Phil Edward's drop knee turn.*

Below right: *Many spectators thought Joey Cabell had won the 1964 World Championships at Manly. But the final placings were: Midge Farrelly 1st, Mike Doyle 2nd and Joey Cabell 3rd.*

RON PERROTT

WAL HARRISON

RON PERROTT

BUD BROWNE

BRUCE BROWN

JOHN SEVERSON

Left: *The two memorable photos from early Pipeline: John Peck (top) and Butch van Artsdalen.*

Above: *Rick Grigg: equally unforgettable Waimea Bay.*

JACK EDEN

Left: *Farrelly at Dee Why point —
Australia's finest surfer in '61, '62 and '63.*

Below left: US Surfing Championships
Huntington Beach: Mark Martinson 1st,
Mickey Munoz 2nd, Robert August 3rd.

Below: *A perfect Paul Strauch crouch by the
man himself.*

SURFER MAGAZINE

SURFER MAGAZINE

first time in my life and to have a chance of copying my heroes, Phil Edwards and Midget Farrelly, on the best waves in the world.

Next year, 1964, marked the start of the first official world surfing championships. Bob Evans was the organiser, Ampol the sponsor, and the location was Manly beach. Because of the judging problems which had been experienced in Hawaii a judge was flown in from each participating country, and this helped make the contest a fantastic success. On the first day there was a crowd of 65,000 watching, the biggest crowd ever assembled in the history of surfing. The organisation was excellent, and Manly turned on a few well-shaped little waves for the heats and final. Midget Farrelly won, proving that what had happened in Hawaii two years earlier was no fluke.

After the contest most of the international guests went home, but some stayed on to explore Australia's waves. Max Wetteland, the South African champion, and Gordon Burgess, who represented Great Britain, stayed on in Sydney for a few weeks. Others

decided to head for less familiar surfing breaks. Linda Benson, undisputably the best girl surfer in the world, and Joey Cabell took a safari north. What Joey did with the waves at Angourie for the witnessing entourage of Australian surfers was the most significant input into local surfing up to that time; he really showed us the possibilities of what could be done on Australian waves. For the first time we saw how to make turns by bending the knees and pushing the board to make it jump around a section. He showed us how to shoot the curl and opened up the gate to riding it instead of shutting our eyes and putting our head in it.

Joey was often called the 'gazelle'. His soft touch on the board coupled with very direct movements gave plenty of reason for the nickname. Growing up in Hawaii, he had travelled like a free spirit from there to California, always showing up at just the right time with a new board and all the heart and talent needed to ride anything from two to 20 feet. Joey could see that surfing would be big, but realised that his future was not in the surfboard industry. In-

stead, he ploughed headlong into the restaurant business and with some partners developed the Chart House chain; he eventually sold out his interest except for the Hawaiian restaurant, which he still maintains.

Having got some financial independence he turned from surfing to skiing and attacked the snow slopes with the same enthusiasm he had given to surfing. Joey and Mike Doyle were together when Doyle developed the single snow ski. The two of them had some great adventures in the surf as well. Once when Joey was living in Kauai, in the Hawaiian Islands, Mike came over for a visit and the two of them decided to take off on a 30-mile swim around the Napali coast. They swam all day, coming in at night when they were exhausted. Joey Cabell made a success of almost everything he tackled; he is a single-minded, adventurous sort of man. That single-mindedness epitomises surfing for me; it's a self-indulgent sport, and demands that you put it ahead of everything else.

Below: *Kevin Platt at Angourie, New South Wales.*

Centre left: *Bobby Brown.*

Centre right: *Ted Spencer on "Little Red" at Lahaina, Maui.*

Bottom left & centre: *Kevin Brennan — 1965 Junior & Senior Australian Champion.*

Top right: *Mike Doyle at Sunset Beach.*

Below right: *(L to R) Rodney Sumpter, John Peck, Corky Carroll and Mike Doyle.*

Bottom right: *Russell Hughes in California.*

RON PERROTT

SURFING MAGAZINE

JOHN WITZIG

JOHN WITZIG

EVANS FAMILY

98

ART BREWER

BEV MORGEN

ART BREWER

THE NEW ERA

The new era? Looking back on it, I wonder how much was hype and how much was real progress. But for a while there surfing styles and surfboard design changed radically, and for someone like me, who was in the middle of it, being an Australian surf star was quite something: you seemed to be out in front of the world which was accelerating with incredible speed into the 20th century.

The new era started quietly enough. The year was 1964, and Mike Doyle, from Oceanside, California was the man to watch: he had won top place on the newly-introduced *Surfer* magazine opinion poll and he certainly cleaned up all the Californian contests. A big man with an open face and a quick smile, he was star material, equally at home on the beach or in the boardroom; later on he became the public relations man for a big swimwear corporation and then designed a line of soft foam-rubber surfboards, recently opening a high class retail store in Encinitas California. Doyle was fantastically competitive; even when he was just playing around he would stake everything on whether he could body surf a wave further than anyone else, or win any other on-the-spot contest. I was his biggest fan; I'd seen him surf in the first world championships in Australia and after that I had Gordon Woods build 10'6" soft railed 22-inch wide boards and coloured them just like Doyle's, with deep maroons and blues and competition stripes across the deck in club colours. I also learnt to surf in the Doyle style, emphasizing balance and stance, a style which Doyle had probably picked up from Phil Edwards. This stall style of surfing, which involved applying weight to the back foot and lifting the nose of the board till the wave caught up, didn't suit Sydney waves but in the longer, glassier waves of northern New South Wales, Queensland and Victoria it was great.

By the end of 1964 a group of younger surfers who had previously been juniors began to challenge Midget Farrelly's surf crown. I had

beaten Midget in the final at Bells Beach by surfing in the so-called 'functional' style with all the old tricks thrown in: big, powerful forehand turns, driving cutbacks, and hanging five or ten whenever possible. Then there was Robert Conneely, who had beaten me in the finals of the Juniors at the world championship; Kevin Platt, a fine exponent of the functional style, Richard Harvey. Kevin Brennan; Butch Cooney; Tony Raper; Bobby Brown; and a strong Queensland group with Bob McTavish, Russell Hughes, Keith Paul, Paul Neilsen and Peter Drouyn. The only exception to this NSW and Queensland domination of Australian local scene was a kid from Victoria called Wayne Lynch.

Bobby Brown was really the first of these to topple Midget, when he beat him in the 1964 NSW championship. Bobby came from Cronulla on the south side of Sydney, where he had developed by watching the smooth, flowing style of goofyfoot Gary Birdsall. At weekends he would come to the northside with the Cronulla crew and because he and I were both too young to get into pubs we spent plenty of nights in the back seats of our mates' cars sucking on a bottle of Barossa Pearl and talking surf. He and I made lots of safaris up the coast with Bob Evans in the early '60s. He was small in stature, which helped him fit neatly inside those little north coast tubes; with arms stretched out artistically he would tear along the inside of crystal-clear, backlit curls as though he were perpetually being filmed. Unfortunately he didn't make it overseas, even though he reached the final of the 1964 world championship; he was content to surf for his own enjoyment and more or less stay in his own backyard, shaping boards for Brian Jackson, right up until his death in a pub brawl in 1967, when he was the victim of a drunken brawl.

Bobby Brown played a significant part in the inside-the-curl style which was to take Australia to the front in world surfing. Like a dog at a bone, Australian surfers were diligently searching for the curl at Crescent

99

ART BREWER

SURFER MAGAZINE

Far left: *Corky Carrol.*

Left: *Gary Propper — heels over.*

RON DAHLQUIST

RON STONER

Far left: *David Nuuhiwa classic arch.*

Left: *Mike Hynson at Malibu.*

Head, Angourie, Byron Bay, the Gold Coast and Noosa. Some were chasing it overseas, like Rodney 'The Gopher' Sumpter, the 1963 Australian junior champion, who won a one-way ticket to Hawaii and California, knocked them dead in the U.S. by winning the national junior surfing title at Huntington Beach, and then went off to his native England, where he remained the local champion until 1969. In 1965 a 15-year-old midget (but not *the* Midget) from Bondi, Kevin 'The Head' Brennan, won both the junior and senior Australian titles in a dazzling display of tube rides, turning, and toes-and-heels on the nose at Manly; none of the other surf stars could keep up with him. Unfortunately his career came to an abrupt end a few years later when he died from an overdose of heroin.

In a final attempt to bring the surf clubs and the unaligned board riders together a long-distance paddleboard event was organised by the associations of both factions. The prize, a return ticket to Peru for the forthcoming world championships, was attractive bait; I entered for it and won easily, proving that boardriders could be just as fit as clubbies.

In Peru the second world championships were held in February, 1965. Hawaiians had introduced surfing there years before; when we got there for the contest we found the Club Waikiki, just outside Lima, ready to

100

look after us with beautiful food and excellent service. The contest was won by Felipe Pomar, of Peru, with me just half a point behind. The judging trend was becoming a bit too obvious; Midget had won in Australia, Pomar in Peru, and Hawaiians at Makaha . . . all winning in their home country. The system needed to change, mainly by accepting international judges.

In the U.S. surfing was gliding along in typical Californian style, much the same as it had been in the 1950s. The surfboards hadn't changed, and the names of the top surfers hadn't changed much either; along with Doyle, Weber, Dora and Skip Frye there were newcomers such as Corky Carroll, David Nuuhiwa and Dru Harrison, but their styles were basically an extension of their peers' — though David Nuuhiwa came from Hawaii. Because California was the hub of the surfboard industry it had attracted quite a few young Hawaiians; Harold Iggy was head shaper for Weber and Donald Takayama for Bing. And then there was David the surf star. He and the others had become close surfing brothers on the south shore of Oahu; Takayama was the finest talent of all on Ala Moana's scorching lefts, but it wasn't long before David Nuuhiwa was turning just as hard and standing on the nose longer. Who could nose ride for the most time and in the most critical part of the wave determined who was at the top in Califor-

nian surfing, and by 1966 David could outperform anyone else in that department.

The nose riding era reached its pinnacle in 1965 when Tom Morey organised a nose-riding contest at Ventura in California. All the manufacturers entered their teams and great secrecy was observed by the board designers. The eventual winner was Corky Carroll, the vanguard of the powerful Hobie team. Phil Edwards, Hobie's designer, would not allow Corky to see what he would be riding until a few hours before the event. Phil's winning design was based on a Quigg nose-riding shape with no nose lift, a concave, and heaps of kick in the tail in order to create drag. Ironically this contest was to produce a design concept that in years to come would affect every other surfboard made. The idea of low rails had been kicked around by Simmons and Quigg in the mid-'forties but it wasn't until Tom Morey brought out his nose-rider with low soft rails all the way around that the surfing world saw the first rail of that sort tucked under to an edge. The surfers this most impressed were the San Diego crew, namely Mike Hynson, Mike Haley and Skip Frye. After a few refinements they had this concept really working and it was to go on to become accepted good design right up into the 'eighties.

In Australia, however, a new movement was getting under way. In

JOHN WITZIG

JOHN WITZIG

FRANK GRANNIS

Left: *McTavish at Honolua Bay, Maui, 1967.*

Below left: *Headless Bob McTavish at Point Cartwright, Queensland.*

Below: *McTavish in California building 'Trackers' for Morey/Pope Co.*

chasing the curl we had begun to experiment with the power of the wave, getting involved in it as a means of self-expression. The key figure here was Bob McTavish, a flamboyant, highly individual character who was born in the inland town of Toowoomba, worked as a DJ on the local radio station, got involved in rhythm-and-blues, and then moved to Noosa. McTavish was an innovator; he made boards for Hayden Kenny and then Cord and soon became a much-admired figure among Queensland surfers. He had been on the beach at Angourie that day in 1964 when Joey Cabell showed us all how to surf the curl, and he began experimenting with shorter boards. He cut the tail off them first of all, and then started cutting the thickness out of them to make them float lower in the water. And he began using the manoeuvrability of the short board to perfect radical manoeuvres on the wave face.

By this time I'd headed north for the 1966 Australian championships, which were to be held in Queensland. I was looking for something new to relate to; it turned out to be McTavish, and together we designed a board for me to ride in the forthcoming contest. We did a lot of surfing together and at Greenmount beach I won the title with McTavish my greatest rival. Midget was knocked off his throne by this new approach to surfing; the 'new era' surfers were going for blatant changes

of direction, radical manoeuvres, looking for the most intense areas of the wave, chasing the curl without too much thought for aesthetics. I was nicknamed The Animal because I "ripped the shit out of the waves". Then some of us headed off for the world championship at San Diego, in California. Nobody took us very seriously when we arrived but George Greenough, the kneeboard rider, had become a good friend and he invited us to his home. Fortunately I found good waves at the 'Ranch' near Santa Barbara to tune up for the world contest. But the main factor was my board. Compared to what nearly everyone else in the world was riding it was small: 9'4" long, 2½" thick, and 22" wide, whereas someone of my size from California or Hawaii would have ridden a board 10 to 11 feet long and at least 4 inches thick. This style of board was the result of striving to attain perfect board control in any position on the wave under all conditions experienced in Australia and was influenced by two people: Bob McTavish and George Greenough.

Ironically Greenough was from California, but virtually no Americans outside of his home town of Santa Barbara had ever heard of him at that stage. In 1966 most of the Santa Barbara locals considered him a crazy kneeboard rider who surfed by himself most of the time and disappeared for days on end in a strange-looking boat he had built himself.

George first came to Australia in 1964, after his local fishing season had ended. He had gathered up his toys, including a weird surfing spoon, an air mattress, numerous shaped fins, a sleeping bag full of camera equipment, fishing gear, one pair of jeans and a T shirt, and instead of staying in Australia for just a few weeks he came for months. He bought an old car that he hurriedly converted into living quarters which he could sleep, surf and fish out of. His highly technical approach to surfing was evident in his flex-tail board which would store energy as it was weighted through a turn; combined with his flex-fins, the acceleration on a good wave was incredible. Towards the end of that trip George helped McTavish build a fullsize flex-tail surfboard. He also took me aside and explained, with a lot of technical jargon, why I was breaking the fin off my board at the base in driving turns. He became the guru of the short board era.

Anyhow, using my radical short board and the 'power' style of surfing a group of us had been developing on the Australian east coast, I won the world championship. It was a great credit to California that it had been able to discard the 'home boy' prejudices which had distorted the two previous world championships. The Americans were flabbergasted when I won the title, but they had to take notice of what we were doing. They were still busy nose-riding, whereas

1

ART BREWER

2

RON STONER

4

ALBERT FALZON

6

ALBERT FALZON

JOHN WITZIG

7

The figures of Australian surfing in the mid '60s.

1. *Keith Paul.*

2-5 *Nat Young.*

6-8 *George Greenough.*

9-10 *Wayne Lynch.*

11. *Midget Farrelly.*

ALBERT FALZON

9

ALBERT FALZON

10

JOHN WITZIG

3

5   JOHN WITZIG

8   JOHN WITZIG

EVANS FAMILY

11

in Australia the old Phil Edwards style had almost disappeared.

After that the new era really gathered momentum. Movies like *Evolution* and *The Hot Generation*, which concentrated on the new style, were shown all over the world. The Australian surf magazines argued that a new generation of surfers had made a real breakthrough in surfing by developing their own styles and boards instead of following the lead of the United States. There was a certain amount of parochialism in all this; up till then Australia had basically been a mimic of America, and it was an exciting moment when Australian surfers found they could suddenly leap ahead of their American counterparts. It took Bob McTavish and I some time to realise that we weren't standing on Greenough-inspired kneeboards, with their typical low centre of gravity, but on surfboards with their own built-in demands and gravity centre; this in turn affected the design of the boards. In 1967 Bob and I took off for Hawaii to compete in the Duke contest with modified 'stubbie' boards which were smaller than those we had been riding up and down the coast and which incorporated a V in the bottom shape as a means of getting the board up on its rail and keeping the board in the water. These 'fantastic plastic machines', as Bob called them, were not that successful in the waves at Sunset beach and in the contest. However, on Maui at Honolulu Bay tracks were taken out of the curl in a way which had never been done before. The Californians and Hawaiians who were there couldn't fail to be impressed; it was a bit like a reverse repeat of that time when the Californians brought their new Malibu boards to Australia.

One of Australia's finest surfers, Keith Paul, was in the U.S. at this time. He had been highly placed in contests in Australia, and in the States he acted as a publicist for the new approach. This was a period of very competitive sales between board manufacturers; the West Coast was only just maintaining its hold on the market over backyard East Coast manufacturers. Keith joined the already powerful Bing organisation and toured the east coast, continually extolling the virtues of Bing surfboards and the Australian new era. Australian-inspired designs became very sought after in the U.S. and one particularly opportunist American even opened a company called 'Surfboards Australia'.

By this time Australian surfing had become the new standard to judge surfing by, and no-one else personified this better than Wayne Lynch, one of those rare people who seems to have unlimited natural talent in the sport he takes up. From Lorne, in Victoria, Wayne grew up having to handle coldwater surf and spent hours in the water every day; no surfing session was real to him unless he had stayed in for at least a couple of hours, or preferably four or five. The amount of time he and Ted Spencer together with George Greenough spent in the water in Victoria in 1966, tuning up their technique, helped them greatly; Wayne was still making mistakes, but he was prepared to stay in the water all day if necessary to perfect a single manoeuvre and then learn to link it with others. He came of age in France while filming the movie *Evolution* and on one wave he rode deeper in the tube than anyone I had ever seen. Certainly when he arrived in Mauritius (it was the month the Beatles released *Let It Be*) he was surfing brilliantly. In Africa he built new boards. In France they were running smoothly for him, and he beat me in the French titles. And then, in Puerto Rico for the fourth world championships, Wayne Lynch the surfer was complete. He was an inspiration to watch.

Wayne didn't win the contest. He hadn't developed the sort of temperament you need to win under those types of competitive conditions. Also, most of the waves were slow, with long faces, and more suited to the older styles of surfing. Fred Hemmings won, and Midget Farrelly came second; given the waves at the contest, the results were justified. But Wayne Lynch, Ted Spencer, Skip Frye and I surfed all around Puerto Rico and confirmed that the new era was where the real development in surfing was taking place.

We didn't realise it at the time, of course, but we were already about to be overtaken.

●

103

JOHN WITZIG

BRAD BARRETT

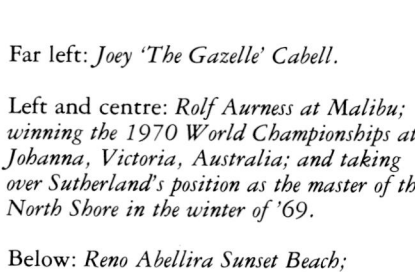

JOHN WITZIG

ART BREWER

ART BREWER

ART BREWER

JEFF DIVINE

Far left: *Joey 'The Gazelle' Cabell.*

Left and centre: *Rolf Aurness at Malibu; winning the 1970 World Championships at Johanna, Victoria, Australia; and taking over Sutherland's position as the master of the North Shore in the winter of '69.*

Below: *Reno Abellira Sunset Beach; Huntington Beach; Talented no matter what the size.*

Right: *Late takeoff at Sunset.*

Insets (L-R): *Jock Sutherland; Bill Hamilton; Angie Reno.*

POCKET ROCKETS AND TWIN FINS

In the late 1960s and early 1970s surfing took off in several different directions. The 'new era' surfing in Australia had broken down the old tradition, but nobody was too sure where to take it. So it was a time of experiment with surfers trying all sorts of new equipment: pocket rockets, twin fins, legropes . . . anything which would help push the limits a little further out.

In Hawaii Dick Brewer was designing a new style of board with soft, low rails which was dubbed a pocket rocket because it performed so well in the pocket of the wave. These boards worked extremely well in the Hawaiian waves they were designed for. Reno Abellira, Joey Cabell and several other members of the Hawaiian team took them to the world championships in Puerto Rico, but they were better on big, hollow Hawaiian barrels than the surf there 80% of the time. For the Australians in Puerto Rico the most noticeable

104

thing about the new boards was their rail shapes; they couldn't wait to get home and try something different to the Greenough-style high-in-front low-in-the-tail rail used all over Australia in the mid-sixties. But maybe the Aussies were too stoned to realise the full significance of the new rail shape; they scurried home to continue surfing deep in the tube on shorter and shorter boards, experimenting with both hard and soft low rails; in a way they'd become prisoners of their own innovations.

In the Islands, however, surfers continued to refine their own approach. The most consistent place for big, hollow waves between November and February is the north shore of Hawaii, and it was here that in 1967/68 a young Caucasian Hawaiian surfer, Jock Sutherland, won the annual Duke Kahanamoku contest with an unmatched combination of rides. Jock was the first totally 'ambidextrous' surfer, someone who could surf

goofyfoot or natural with equal skill. He was lovely to watch; always surfing where the vectors of power met, tight and dangerous, a poised and reflective surfer who somehow always seemed apart from the crass commercial scene yet the envy of those who would have given their eye teeth to surf as well as he did in the winters of 1967 and 1968. As it turned out they all had a chance to catch up because of the war in Vietnam; Jock joined the armed services and never did get a chance to surf to that incredible level of ability again.

Another fine young surfer, and the product of a completely different world, was 18-year old Rolf Aurness, son of James Aurness, star of the TV series *Gunsmoke*. Aurness senior was a dedicated water man and was wealthy enough to take his son to Hawaii or to their northern ranch in California whenever he had a break from filming or the waves were up; in order to give Rolf a chance to tune up for the

RON STONER

ART BREWER

STEVE WILKINGS

JEFF DIVINE

69/70 world championship, to be held in Victoria, he took him to Australia a month early to adjust to the local conditions and check out what the competition was like. Rolf brought a whole quiver of boards with him, all sensible sizes, 6ft 6in to 7ft 4in long, mainly narrow pintails with soft, low rails. They were perfect for beating the sections ahead of you in normal Victorian conditions. And he was surfing well; no-one else was even close to him in performance and consistency.

When Rolf returned to California he naturally checked in with his surfboard sponsor, Bing Copeland. Bing's surfboards were very trend setting in this period. The head shaper Mike Eaton (who was responsible for building most of the Bonzer tri fins in the early seventies) couldn't wait to put his latest creation under the new world champ. It was only 5'10" long by 22½" wide. Eaton had taken the length from the Aussie boards of that period and combined that with an idea that had been around since Simmons and Quigg: twin fins. They had never been tried on a short board and the combination was to prove a complete breakthrough in modern surfing. Rolf grabbed the new stick and

took off for Cottons Point in San Clemente where his good friend Corky Carroll had reported good 3' to 4' lefts running down the beach. Rolf could feel something completely different in the little twin. Corky and Rolf switched boards and Corky was amazed at the board's loose drifting turns, just right for the typical Californian summer waves they were experiencing.

Corky left the water and went right around to Hobie's and shaped a similar board, getting it out in the water the very next day. He made a few changes to the fin set-up. The fins were more straight up and down and with a lot less tow-in so a little more distance could be gained from the turn. That board worked incredibly well; as U.S. men's champion in 1966, 1967 and 1969 as well as over-all champ from 1966 through to 1970, Corky knew a winner when he saw one. He did a tremendous amount of travelling in those days promoting Hobie boards and the twin fin slotted right in, giving Hobie and the surfboard industry a new product.

The Australians had obviously gone too far in that '69 world contest in their search for shorter and shorter

boards. Wayne Lynch surfed a 5ft 8in, Ted Spencer a 5ft 6in, and I was on a 5ft 10in. They worked beautifully powering around the curl, driving off their large single fins, but they failed miserably whenever a wave broke ahead of them or the surfer needed to follow through and coast over long flat sections of the wave. Not the ideal competition board, to say the least; it's just a fact that small, displacement-hull surfboards are not suited to contests where the type of surf usually varies a great deal throughout the competition.

The one Australian surfer who seemed to be able to measure up on the small boards was Ted Spencer. He grew up in Manly, surfed around the world with film-maker Paul Witzig for *Evolution*, and developed a unique, smooth style of surfing. He was an innovative designer with lots of surfing talent. However, he abandoned competitive surfing in 1969 leaving Victoria just as the world championship circus was about to get under way. He later told me "what a lot of people call perfection, I call stagnation. What they see as perfection, in my eyes is the stroke of death for the spirit of progress. Refining your surfing does not simply mean refining

JOHN WITZIG

TRACKS

TRACKS

ART BREWER

TRACKS

Above (L-R): *Tom Hoye from California who made the first twin fin in Australia; Mark Warren; Grant 'Dappa' Oliver; Bunker Spreckels, flower child with space stick.*

Left: *Ted Spencer (right) and Shane Stedman — mid 60s.*

Right: *Robert Conneeley at Angourie, NSW.*

different manouvres, in a deeper sense it means refining your very self; then everything you do will be refined. A refined person understands that he is not the body or the mind, but the sustaining energy, the spark of life force within the body."

Back in Sydney, Shane Stedman, Spencer's boss and benefactor, was understanding but somewhat bewildered by Ted's aboutface. He saw the leading light of his impressive stable of fine surfers suddenly setting off on a tangent that could destroy his successful surfboard business. The Ted Spencer 'White Kite' was one of the most popular model surfboards ever to be made in Australia and certainly the most successful for Shane, who sold thousands of them even after Ted abandoned competition. By listening to and reading the teachings of A C Bhaktivedanta Swami Prabhupad, Ted Spencer gained guidance for his life. He is adamant that this is not to be taken as an endorsement of the Hare Krishna movement, but rather a demonstration of how he came to understand that the momentary pleasure derived from riding a wave could be achieved consistently in everyday life. In the early days of Ted's spiritual

development he had a shaven head and took on the saffron robes of a devotee of Krishna. Around the same time Bob McTavish became a Seventh-day adventist and was busy door-knocking in Byron Bay to enlighten the world about Armageddon. Many surfers have used different methods to come to a realisation of God, and their conversions have not been a fad; today quite a few have settled down to living happy lives beyond the material world.

Sceptics maintained that changing board size was just a fashion like mini and maxi lengths in dresses, but in fact by taking surfboard design to extremes we made many discoveries. No longer was the overall length the only relevant factor in speed; rail and bottom shape as well as the outside plan shape were also important. In 1969 it was a bitter pill for the Australian surf stars to swallow — they had gone off on a particular tangent and blown the world contest. From that moment on, the boards grew and by 1971 the average size of a board in Australia was 6ft 6in to 7ft, a full foot to a foot-and-a-half longer.

Coming a very close third in the

world championship was another Australian surfer that had been knocking on the door for years, Peter Drouyn, who had already had two trips to the Islands and had established himself as the junior Australian champion. His style was flamboyant and colourful; he had grown up with Mickey Dora as his hero and liked to compare his homebreak of Burleigh Heads to Malibu. In November of 1970 Peter set out for Hawaii. He gave a respectable showing in the three big contests, the Smirnoff, the Duke and Makaha. Then he kept the Aussie flag flying by competing in Peru, but became rather disillusioned by two things. First, he was a world class surfer who followed the contest scene diligently but still failed to make a living from his winnings; and second, his hero Mickey Dora had pulled a classic stunt by dropping his pants for National Television while executing a perfect 'el spontano' on a clean 6-footer in the first Malibu Invitational! Also Mickey had made the statement about how the system had turned his once beautiful sport into a 'soggy cartoon'.

This period was difficult for the so called pro surfers; the very most they could expect was an airfare and expenses, and this Peter had in 1971 for the Durban 500 in South Africa. After fulfilling his commitment to the contest in South Africa he continued onto London. Right from the start, Peter had always been a good actor; his race commentary had always been a crowd pleaser at contest presentation nights. In London he gained an entrance to the Royal Academy of Dramatic Art; then he went to The National Institute of Dramatic Art in Sydney in 1972. The similarity between surfing and acting was easily rationalised by Peter.

JOHN WITZIG

Surfing and acting were both art forms, he would explain, but surfing was the reflection of a lifestyle, of a sub-culture, whereas acting was a respectable profession which you could earn a living from. He scored a part in 'Tom Jones', which helped prove his point.

Surfing in the late '60s and early '70s was identified with long hair and smoking pot. Peter did not believe it should be limited in that way. He endorsed the belief that every young surfer had to go through a learning period, closely following someone better so that he could build on his basic skills. Some surfers remained at that stage, continuing to wrestle with the basics, but others went on to become artists of their sport like Peter. But in 1972 he lost his competitive drive, due to the fact that he was not earning enough money from his winnings, and at 23 he decided that acting would be a far more profitable direction.

If you run into Peter Drouyn today in his pocket he'll be carrying the plans for his latest scheme — a Surfertorium. His idea is based on the waterways inland from Surfers

Paradise, on which he wants to build a mechanical wavemaker which would create waves over an artificial reef. It would cost millions of dollars to construct, but at last, according to Drouyn, the sport would have consistent, quality, contestable waves which would eliminate the luck factor associated with contests, and which would be available at the press of a button!

When Ted Spencer pulled out of the Australian team for the 1969 world titles in Torquay the reserve was a 19-year old Sydney surfer named Terry Fitzgerald. Terry started surfing at Maroubra, drifting in and out of peer groups from Palm Beach to Dee Why before his family settled in Collaroy Plateau, right above the same beach where both Mark Warren and I had started surfing. He was taught to shape while on the Gold Coast in the early '60s by none other than Joe Larkin, one of the fathers of surfing in Queensland. He dropped out of 2nd year university on the grounds that he could always go back, and in the winter of 1971 he made it to Hawaii, where he ran into Dick Brewer. Brewer taught him the finishing touches of how to shape and

introduced him to mini-guns with cosmic sprays, which Terry took back to Australia to turn on the masses.

The basic principle with these boards was that you no longer needed physical power to turn; instead of overpowering the fin, as was done with the Greenough-inspired hull-shaped boards of the late '60s, you let the board cruise more. This principle worked well on the more powerful waves of Hawaii with their ever-present tubes. On that first trip Terry met Bunker Spreckels, who was the son of the movie star Clark Gable. Early in life at Malibu Bunker discovered surfing; together with his cosmic friends in Hawaii they took surfing into another dimension, riding further back inside the curl on smaller and smaller boards until on their 'spacesticks' they finally disappeared. Terry couldn't help but notice Bunker's vertical fins on the rails and couldn't wait to go back to Narrabeen and try a wing on his own pintails.

Narrabeen had come alive in the early 1970s. Everyone was pushing, with kooks and good surfers in the water at the same time. As well as Terry there

ART BREWER

DREW KAMPION

JEFF DIVINE

Far left: *Peter Drouyn surfed Sunset Beach with amazing talent in the early 70s.*

Left: *Mike Eaton of California; responsible for reviving the twin fin. Seen here with The Bonzer. Designed by Malcolm and Duncan Campbell of Oxnard, California.*

Below: *Brother Owl Chapman's unique style at Sunset.*

Right: *Barry Kanaiaupuni. Supreme master at Sunset in the 70s.*

were Mark Warren, Simon Anderson, 'Dapper', Gordon Barnes and the slightly older Colin Smith, plus many more who were just as hot on their particular day. Col Smith was a goofyfoot and in the vanguard of the Narrabeen crew. A natural athlete, he looked as if he could have excelled at any sport. He was responsible for opening everyone's eyes to what was possible on shorter, lighter and looser boards; surfing with incredible flexibility and timing, he led the way into the '70s with vertical off-the-lips time after time all the way down the line at Narrabeen.

These short boards with twin fins were introduced to Australia by Santa Cruz surfer/shaper Tom Hoye, who had been turned on to the concept in California by Corky Carrol. He built the first one at Barry Bennett's board shop in Brookvale. A local surfer, Geoff McCoy, left Keyo surfboards and began building twin fins under his own label for the Narrabeen crew. This really put McCoy on the map and these boards were responsible for Narrabeen becoming the focal point of Australian surfing in the early 'seventies.

Narrabeen lies just north of Sydney

before you get to Broken Bay or Pittwater, and consists of a series of long, shallow lakes which interconnect and meet at the sea through a common entrance at North Narrabeen. It is a suburban area, first settled in 1854, but the lakes have retained much of their natural beauty, especially since power boats were banned in 1980. When it rains the lake level rises, large volumes of water pass through the narrow gap in the sand at the lakes' entrance, and much sand is deposited further out to sea. It's an irregular cycle but over the years some sort of balance has been reached and the sandbank which is formed is more or less permanent, although it varies from time to time in shape and in size. At its best it is the shape of a right-angled triangle with the right angle next to the lakes' entrance. When the north or east swell is running or any wind except a southerly is blowing you get long, hollow lefts winding down the beach for a couple of hundred yards. It doesn't get that good too often but it has a rideable wave most of the time. Narrabeen surfers formed a club in the early '60s and kept having competitions against other clubs for the next 10 years, until the other clubs faded away. And then they turned

against each other in friendly contests between themselves. Out of this tremendously competitive attitude evolved the whole Narrabeen scene.

About this time in California we saw the emergence of a cord tied to the surfer's ankle and attached at the other end to the surfboard, and the leg rope was born! Meanwhile the surfing scene was getting itself organised. The American Broadcasting Company, through the program *Wide World of Sport*, had covered the Duke and the Smirnoff contests since their inception, taking surfing into the living rooms of middle-class America in prime-time television. On the advice of Ronald Sorrel, a Honolulu stockbroker, the International Professional Surfing Association was formed in 1971 to liaise between the surfers and companies. The go-between was Fred Hemmings Junior, a caucasian Hawaiian surfer of considerable ability who very early on could see a career for himself in promoting professional contests. Fred was the 1968 world surfing champion and had the imagination to use his crown to get into the boardrooms of some of New York's most prestigious companies. He also had a talent for translating surfing parlance for television audi-

PHOTOS ART BREWER

ences and to do this Smirnoff employed Hemmings with a fee of 35% of the total contest budget. As the front man for professional surfing in the early 'seventies he was largely responsible for the rapid increase of commercial interest in the sport and for sowing the seeds of an international pro circuit.

Yet all over Hawaii and the U.S. surfers were looking for something more. There was a general movement away from competition because the uniform concept of judging was producing a final of six surfers who surfed more *like* each other than they surfed *unlike* each other. Boring. What everyone was looking for was a contest that accentuated the differences rather than the similarities. Finally an 'expression session' was put together in the winter of 1971 in Hawaii and the recognised 20 best surfers in the world were invited to surf without being judged. They were Jock Sutherland, Jeff Hakman, David Nuuhiwa, Reno Abellira, Rusty Starr, Tommy Stone, Brad McCaul, Barry Kanaiaupuni, Tiger Espera, Jacky Baxter, Keith Paul, Booby Jones, Ryan Dotson, Jimmy Blears, Mike Tabeling, Ben Aipa, Bill Hamilton, Owl Chapman, Gerry

Lopez and me. The contest was organised by the directors of Golden Breed Sports wear. However the session didn't live up to expectations. The exclusion of some of the Hawaiian brothers brought about physical violence to one of the organisers, and by Hawaiian standards the surf for the exhibition was fairly ordinary. The idea died a slow death a few years later.

A few weeks after the doomed Expression Session the second Smirnoff Pro-am contest got under way, offering the largest stakes ever in the history of surfing contests. The first Smirnoff was held in Santa Cruz in California, but the venue didn't live up to expectations so it was moved to Hawaii. The writing was already on the wall; the age of the professional surfer was not far off. I won the contest in good 15ft waves at Makaha, but the first place prizemoney of $3,000 barely covered expenses and the airfares from Australia.

The sixth world championships were held once again in San Diego, California in 1972. Giving no thought to professional or amateur status, the contest organisers ran into financial difficulty when the televi-

sion rights were not picked up. A week before the Australian team was about to leave no tickets had arrived, and after communication with the International Surfing president, Eduardo Arena, it was learnt that the competitors had to pay their own way. The contest was plagued with poor surf and lack of organisation, which is the sort of thing which happens when too much is left to too few people who are not getting paid for their efforts. (The 1966 world contest had been hosted by San Diego City Council, and officials who were good at organising took care of all the problems.) So the 1972 world contest was a bummer for the competitors, but it produced an interesting final; Peter Townend from Australia, David Nuuhiwa from California, and Michael Ho, Larry Bertlemann and Jimmy Blears from Hawaii. Jimmy Blears won the contest, a decision the other competitors did not agree with. Jimmy was quoted as saying he didn't agree with surfing competitions at all because surfing was an individual thing which could not be evaluated with a stop-watch. This championship signalled the end of surfing contests until some far-reaching changes could be made.

•

SOUL SURFING

The feeling of disenchantment with competitions spread among surfers throughout the world. The media began debating the question: is surfing a sport, or an art form? I supported the idea of an 'expression session' because I genuinely felt there was more to surfing than competition. Many young surfers today, I feel, are missing out on the possibility of expressing themselves through their surfing, or of getting closer in tune with nature, because their lives are dominated by contests. According to four times world champion Mark Richards: "Surfing is anything you want it to be".

So in the early '70s 'soul surfing' became the fashion. The longhaired, back-to-nature surf stars of the time were heavily involved in meditation, astrology, health foods, the self, the striving for physical perfection . . . and drugs. Taking psychedelic drugs and smoking marijuana became the norm. Surfers began dropping out and experimenting with communal living; everyone was trying to leave the city. I went to Byron Bay. Some surfers had young families and weren't into the communal style of things, but they agreed with the general philosophy. As for smoking pot: I found it helped me to centre my concentration, but I never smoked it just before competing in a contest. In fact as far as I'm aware no-one was successful in competition while high, because being high doesn't induce the aggressiveness you need for competition. Smoking pot was a sign of the times; it was the 'look inward' era of flower power, mysticism, the Maharishi and the popularisation of eastern cults, which affected everyone from the Beatles and Rolling Stones to surfers.

California was the centre of this new drug cult, so naturally there was a tremendous demand there for psychedelic drugs and marijuana. Because of California's close proximity to Mexico a flood of marijuana started coming over the border into the U.S. It's difficult to estimate the extent of surfers' involvement in smuggling, but they were involved to a certain degree. Most Californian surfers spent some time in Mexico due to the quality of the waves there and the totally different lifestyle. Although marijuana was not used by the Mexicans themselves they proved to be very astute farmers and opportunists who were only too keen to develop stronger and stronger strains of marijuana. A lot of surfers were in the right place (or wrong place) at the right time and became involved in smuggling. In the early '70s they used hollow surfboards and false bottoms in cars and campers to bring back enough to support their own use and make enough dollars to ride waves for a few months more. Some became greedier or more involved than others and in order to elude the authorities banded together to form a group called the 'Brotherhood' from Laguna Beach, or Dodge City as it became affectionately known.

The Brotherhood was not an organised body of criminals; rather it was a bunch of friends who found they could pool their money to use more sophisticated means of smuggling, employing the use of planes, fast boats and decoys. The business advantages were obvious and many families made small fortunes from the profits. Some members of the Brotherhood had higher ideals; through the intake of quality marijuana, sesemea from the Oaxaca in deep Mexico and LSD from San Francisco, they aspired to be associated with people who were heading towards a 'higher plane of consciousness'. Ken Kesey stopped at Malibu in the Psychedelic Bus on his way from San Francisco to Los Angeles and distributed oranges that were laced with LSD. Timothy Leary was the most notable exponent of acid to be connected with surfing during this period; he came to them as a guiding light, giving faith to converts and helping drug casualties.

The accumulated profits by some of the members of the Brotherhood were enormous. They had the very best of everything; beautiful cars, expensive houses in many parts of the world, and just about every toy that was available. To some the amount of accumulated wealth was insignificant.

Above: *Michael and Melinda Hynson.*

Below left: *"It's a cake walk once you know how" . . . Gerry Lopez mid '70s.*

Below: *Jackie Dunn, Pipeline.*

SCOTT PREISS

Above: *From the inside looking out.*

Below: *Country soul.*

JOHN WITZIG

They were involved in the lifestyle; turning people onto a better life through drugs was the rationale. Several travelled the world every few weeks, setting up deals and expanding their business. In those days hash from Afganistan, Nepal, Lebanon and Morocco was very much in demand by the American smoking public and the Brotherhood tried to supply the demand. Which led to this sort of story:

Tom and Diane were typical young travelling Australians. They had married just before setting out for Europe in search of waves and adventure. In France they came into contact with the blond hash of Morocco which had the unique quality of being able to keep everybody laughing. And they watched with wide-open eyes as a group of Newport surfers boarded a plane from Portugal to Los Angeles with one of the boys nursing a broken leg; unknown to the authorities, the cast and one of the boards was made of keif (hash).

As the winter crept into Europe in 1969 they motored south into warmer waters, surfing through Spain, Portugal and finally Morocco. That winter was spent surfing the Moroccan coast from Casablanca to Kenitra and eating the blond hash mixed with dates. Upon leaving Morocco they decided to smuggle a quantity of hash, or keif, in order to

DANA FISHER

ALBERT FALZON

JEFF DIVINE

JOHN LYMAN

Top: *From the outside looking in.*

Above: *Nat Young (Back to Nature 70s).*

Above right: *Locals only.*

Right: *Going with the flow.*

PETER CRAWFORD

sustain the lifestyle they were becoming increasingly fond of. Their
beat-up old Bedford van, containing a
few kilos of dope, was driven back to
England and the hash readily dis-
posed of, giving Tom and Diane
enough money to buy a better car and
head out for Afghanistan where the
legendary black hash comes from. By
welding false bottoms under the body
of the car they sent a cargo to the
United States. In California the
Brotherhood took charge of selling
the hash for a modest fee. In this way
Tom and Diane made many trips fi-
nanced by the Brotherhood and accumulated a modest fortune.

JEFF DIVINE

The Brotherhood had hundreds of
Toms and Dianes from all different
nationalities who were employed in
this manner. They became so expert
at pulling motors out of VW buses
and stuffing the compartment behind
the motor with hash that they knew
exactly what shape to have the blocks
pressed into and how much to the
gram to expect when the vehicle arrived in the U.S. The entire operation
was now run in a most businesslike
fashion.

STEVE WILKINGS

Perhaps the most incredible scam was
pulled between Columbia and
California and came quite late in the
1970s, after the authorities had
busted cars, surfboards, false-bottom
suitcases and bodyruns. Smugglers,
and in particular the Brotherhood,

GUY MOTIL

HOOLE/McCOY

JEFF HORNBAKER

had been forced to become pretty clever to beat the authorities. All but the diehards who were in it for the challenge had long since quit or were serving time in U.S. and foreign jails. In this case an advertisement was placed in a local U.S. newspaper stating that the first person who wrote in with the correct answer to a simple question would be given an all-expenses-paid trip to South America. Naturally the response was overwhelming and after some scrutiny into the backgrounds of the contestants the winning couple was picked out. Basically they were chosen because they were older, ordinary looking people who would qualify as typical tourists, the type who had saved diligently for the trip of a lifetime. After making contact with the organisers the couple went off to South America with plenty of spending money, stopping everywhere at first-class hotels and finally visiting a pre-selected artifact shop where they were invited to choose as much as they liked. Unbeknown to the tourists the artifacts were hollow and had perfect duplicates. Those they carried home in their personal baggage were laced with cocaine; the others were sent directly to the organisers in California that night. Upon their arrival back in The States the mastermind of this plan told the tourists it was necessary to pose for pictures with the artifacts. They naturally saw this as payment for a beautiful trip and were de-

115

Sweet dreams are made of these: the Ranch '73, and Blacks in the mid '60s.

lighted to do so. At the rented photographic studios the artifacts were switched with the copies that had arrived earlier while the couple had their faces made up for the session. The shots were taken, the smiling couple returned to their homes, and another brilliant scam had been pulled off.

Surfers, drugs and rock 'n' roll sometimes went together. Jimi Hendrix discovered surfing while on Maui in the late '60s and put together a free concert on the grassy slopes of Haleakala crater which was announced only one day in advance. There were only a couple of hundred people there. The sun was shining, the trade winds blowing, and the sky was filled with incredible Hendrix music. People were gathered on the grass, under their sun zodiac sign; 50 Capricorns together, next to 25 Aries. Elizabethan banners and colours rippled and snapped in the wind. The stage was decorated in pastel materials. Colour, motion, smiles, sound, energy . . . but according to people who were there, the only ones that crossed the rainbow bridge that afternoon were Hendrix and his band. And when Hendrix shouted to everyone to "stand up and let's get together, this is the last one", he may have had some premonition of what was in store. A week later he was dead. The movie *Rainbow Bridge* is the only record we have of it all.

The surfers who were directly involved with Jimi Hendrix were Mike Hynson, Leslie Potts, David Nuuhiwa and Chris Green. Jimi considered surfers to be a chosen race on earth, and certainly David, Mike and many of their friends displayed great style in their lives. David was the reigning surfing superstar in 1972, riding in a chauffeur-driven white Rolls Royce, wearing pop star clothes, living a full social life. Soul surfing even had its effect upon surfboard design; surfers wanted to get deeper and deeper into the tube, so they needed narrower, sleeker boards. As a reaction against the sense of competition which had previously come to dominate surfing it helped restore a sense of balance to the sport, but it was followed by a new and very different stage; the development of the professional surfer.

THE BIRTH OF PROFESSIONALISM

PETER CRAWFORD

Surfing was becoming big business. So many people all over the world had taken up the sport that it had begun to attract advertisers, manufacturers, sponsors, franchise merchants, publicists and, finally, the professional surfer. In a way it was inevitable; the question was, how would surfers handle it?

A good example of the answer was Gerry Lopez. Gerry never won a major surfing contest, but he was undoubtedly an incredible surfer. Of Japanese-Hawaiian descent, he became known as 'Mr Pipeline' because of his ability to surf there; it's arguable whether he was the *first* to surf as far back in the curl there as he did, but he did it consistently and the name stuck. He made the classic comment: "It's a cakewalk once you know how." Together with Barry Kanaiaupuni, Reno Abellira and Jeff Hackman, all of them Hawaiians, he intensified the trend towards tube riding on longer, narrower boards.

But Lopez also proved to be a good businessman. He adopted the Lightning Bolt as his insignia and that, plus his reputation and his acumen in business, made him quite wealthy. Originally Lopez sold his boards through a single shop outlet owned by Jack Shipley in Honolulu. Then he and Shipley joined with marketing man Duke Boyd and Richard Graham to form the Bolt Corporation which, based in California, set up a franchise arrangement that gave manufacturing rights to companies in all the major surfing countries. Boyd was an experienced marketing man; he had been instrumental in getting the Hang Ten products off the ground. He pulled in all the top surfers of the day, including myself, to promote its products. It was Boyd who dreamed up the original two-foot symbol which became Hang Ten's logo. The Bolt Corporation didn't just franchise surfboards; it licensed companies to manufacture clothing, jewellery, thongs, board shorts, everything. It was a great success.

The same commercialism was invading surfing contests. In Australia, May Day of 1974 saw the start of the

JEFF DIVINE

WARREN BOLSTER

STEVE WILKINGS

world's richest surfing contest. The beaches of Sydney's north shore were to play host to the first 2SM-Coke Surfabout, and all the international stars came to compete against Australia's best. The contest was blessed with good waves, as is often the case with Sydney in May; the points start breaking when the swell gets big from the south. Media coverage was fantastic, and when the sports commentators and announcers told the city to rush out, take a seat on a rock and watch the finest surfers in the world, Fairy Bower became a perfect amphitheatre.

Both the Coke and the Bells Beach contest had changed their judging systems to the very latest 'Hang Ten'

objective system. It differs from the older subjective system in that instead of the whole ride being assessed and allocated points by a judge, the judge only declares each manoeuvre performed, and each manoeuvre is allocated predetermined points. These points vary as to the difficulty of the manoeuvre and the size of the wave. The rider's score is the overall total of all the manoeuvres he performs. The advantage of the objective system is that it provides competitors with a definite framework to work in and removes any bias regarding style. However, like all judging systems, it collapses in poor surf, where the range of manoeuvres is severely restricted and the luck factor is greatly increased. These inadequacies were

Reno Abellira — 'little big man' at Sunset Beach, with his '75 quiver and his wife Joanne in 1976.

underlined at Bells in 1974, where competitors in different heats of the same round encountered radically varying conditions and wave size. It was useless to blame the judging system for the results. The only solution was to hold the contest in good surfing conditions so that each competitor was allowed the opportunity to surf at his full capacity, but that was outside anyone's control.

Bells Beach was the perfect venue for a pro contest because the high cliffs

PETER CRAWFORD

JOHN WITZIG

LEROY GRANNIS

Above: (L to R): *The late Jim Freeman (talented cinematographer). Fred Hemmings Junior (President of I.P.S.). Larry Lindburg (American Broadcasting Company executive).*

Top and centre: *Bells Beach — the site of Australia's first professional contest and annual Easter pilgrimage for most professionals.*

surrounding the beach gave good viewing points for spectators. Because the contest was held over the Easter holidays a large crowd from Melbourne could be guaranteed. Sponsors for the contest were easy to find, the major one being the Victorian-based Rip Curl Wetsuit Company. The company's two directors, Doug Warbrick and Brian Singer, were both active surfers who had watched with interest the development of pro surfing in Hawaii. They saw the annual amateur Bells Beach contest as the ideal pro meet, and virtually turned it into one.

In 1973, 1974, and 1975 Michael Peterson from Queensland's Gold Coast burst upon the scene, winning every major event he entered including the Coke, Bells and Stubbies. Peterson had picked up on my power style of surfing; he showed that he knew the judging method and could surf to it. In 1976 something went wrong. After dominating Australian competition for three years, his winning streak came to a sudden end when he failed to place in any of the professional events. It seemed he had lost that rapid-fire machine-like quality and the psychological edge that went with it. The fact that Michael had been experimenting with drugs was probably the reason, but he guarded his privacy closely and gave only rare interviews so no-one knew for sure what had gone wrong. When in 1974 he was asked why he was winning he answered; "I could say, but I won't."

There were a lot of changes taking place in Australia at that time. In 1974 the Labor Party was campaigning to get re-elected and was giving a lot of prominence to environmental issues. When I came third in the Surfabout contest I gave the prize-money of $600 to the Labor Party. At a rally at the new Sydney Opera House, which had just been opened, I gave my reasons; I felt the party took the right attitude by opposing beach mining, racism, foreign ownership, uncontrolled development and trade with South Africa, and by promoting care for the environment. Perhaps the issue that affected surfers most directly was the sandmining of beaches in northern NSW and southern Queensland for zircon and rutile. After the sandminers had flattened the dunes the developers tried to move in with proposals for tourist complexes and housing. Some of the most environmentally damaging of these proposals were stopped by the

PETER CRAWFORD

Above: *Col Smith*

Right and Below: *Michael Peterson. In 1973-4-5 he won every contest in Australia.*

HOOLE/McCOY

PETER CRAWFORD

ALBERT FALZON

Terry Fitzgerald. The sultan of speed, at Sunset. With cosmic quiver of winged pins.

JEFF DIVINE

PETER CRAWFORD

PETER CRAWFORD

ART BREWER

Top: *Reno at Waimea Bay.*

Above and Above right: *Peter Townend.*
Always the bridesmaid never the bride until
he won the world championship in 1976.

Right: *East Coast's masked bandit — Mike*
Tabeling.

work of the various conservation movements and by the voices of people like myself, Midget Farrelly and *Tracks* surfing newspaper.

By 1975 most of the surf stars in Hawaii had cut their hair, the highly artistic designs on surfboards had begun to fade away, and surfers were seeking sponsorship from companies which had not previously been interested in the sport. Highly colourful, special effects in surf movies and magazines had become 'old hat'. Surfing articles began to forget the exploration of the cosmic vibration. Surfers were out to project a new image of clean-cut sportsmen. The person most responsible for this turn-about was Fred Hemmings Jr. He had a vested interest in surfing's new image, being the world's No. 1 contest promoter as well as being a clean-cut college type himself. Meanwhile the east and Gulf coast of the U.S. were beginning their struggle for recognition. Mike Tabeling, Bruce Valuzzi, Claude Codgen, Yancy Spencer, Gary Propper, Fred Grossgruetz and Jeff Crawford, all from the east and Gulf coasts, were doing well in the west coast contests. Because of the small, choppy surf they normally encountered in the Atlantic Ocean they really appreciated a good wave. Both Mike Tabeling and Bruce Valuzzi had spent a number of months in Australia in 1969, soaking up everything possible. In 1975, Ricky Rassmussen, a 20-year old surfer from New York, won the U.S.A. Open Championships by using Puerto Rico as his training ground, just as Californians used Hawaii. Rick came to Australia to compete in the Coke Contest and came back again for the contests in 1976. But probably the most impressive surfer to emerge from the East Coast at this time was Jeff Crawford. In the 1974-75 Hawaiian contest season Geoff definitely had someone smiling on him. ABC TV crews covered the Pipeline Masters event for American national television; Geoff won, giving enormous prestige to the East Coast.

The age of professional surfing was just about getting to the stage where the winners could make a living from their prize money. But invitations to the pro contests were basically on the buddy system, and it became increasingly difficult for any newcomer to get into the professional contests. In order to change this a contest called the Pro Class Trials were held annually in Hawaii before the winter

Mark Richards at Waimea Bay — '74 Smirnoff Contest.

JEFF DIVINE

season began. The first six place getters in this contest were given invitations to the Smirnoff contest and, with luck, a chance to join the professional ranks.

The Smirnoff and Duke contests had been offering prize money since 1970, and in 1974 the total prize money for the Smirnoff was $11,000. The finals of that contest were held in 20ft to 30ft waves at Waimea Bay. It was the first time a major contest had been lucky enough to be held under such intense conditions and the prestige of surfing increased immensely, which in turn increased the viability of professionalism. For the first time ever the monster wave faces of Waimea Bay were not only ridden but carved upon. Late takeoffs, bottom turns and cutbacks were added to the long-established do-or-die repertoire of big wave riding. Most of the surfers in the final had never seen anything like it in their lives, and few could believe that they were actually going out under those conditions. Reno Abellira emerged from the water the winner with Jeff Hackman second. The only Australian in the final was Peter Townend. Not being big in stature, he made the enormous wave look even bigger.

The feeling of taking off on one of

those waves is both incredibly fast and incredibly slow at the same time. You go for just one wave; you can't hesitate or you will get flattened by the wave behind. When you think you have it and you are about to stand up, give one more paddle. On the takeoff you must almost burst through the wave on top of the real wave and freefall for the first 6ft. Your board just drops away beneath you. You are actually tipped over a bit beyond vertical. Looking down you are reminded of how far it is to the bottom! On the bottom turn you don't crank it, you just lean until you feel the rail bite. The force is tremendous, you feel you are riding on a moving mountain of water; it's an amazing sensation that very few surfers ever get to experience.

Waimea is unique surfing, it makes you a member of an exclusive club; but surfing really big waves anywhere is a heart-in-mouth experience and, if you're up to it, really rewarding.

●

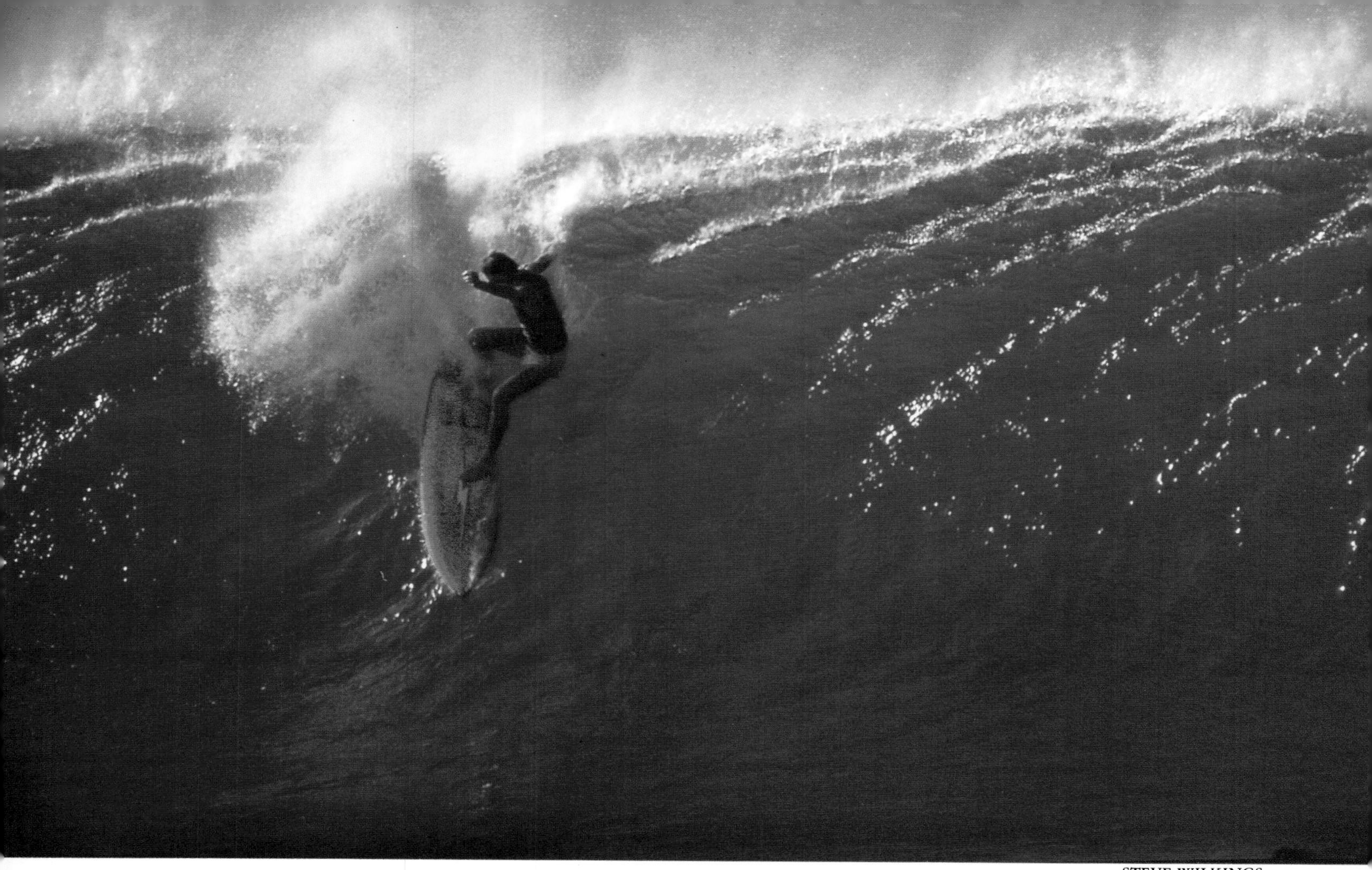

STEVE WILKINGS

HOOLE/McCOY

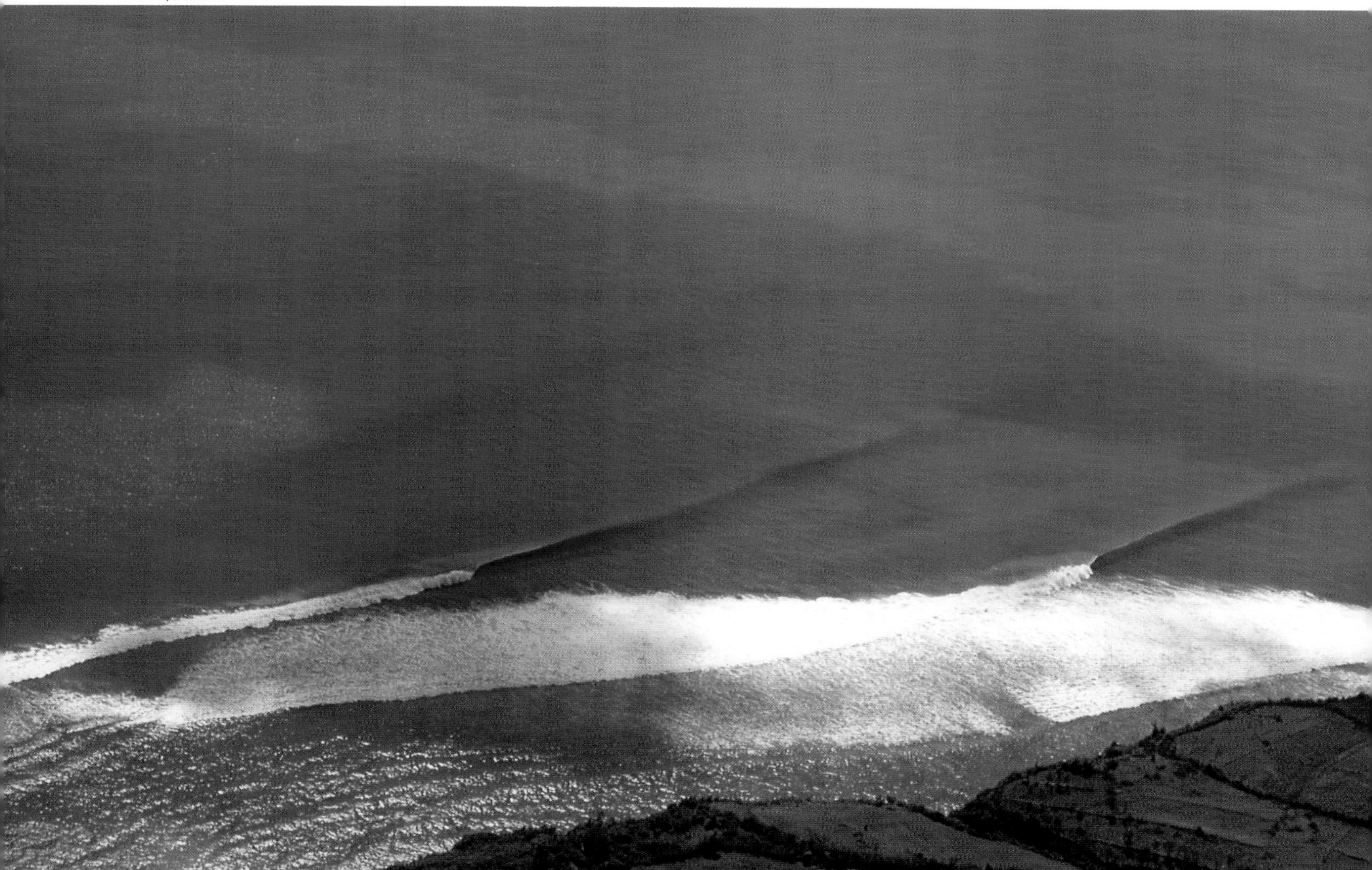

BUSTIN' DOWN THE DOOR

Mid-seventies. The international pro circuit was under way. New surfers were emerging from Australia, Hawaii and the United States. Surfers were discovering waves in places like Bali which had virtually never been surfed before. New board designs were coming out of Hawaii. It was a time of expansion.

In 1975 the Smirnoff final was held at Waimea Bay and the Australians scooped the pool. Australian surfing had 'come of age', and it was time for the new generation to show their stuff, which they did. Australians came first, second and third; Mark Richards, Ian Cairns and Wayne 'Rabbit' Bartholemew, in that order. The media went mad; whatever had happened to the Hawaiians? In fact one caucasian Hawaiian, 20-year-old Rory Russell, really stood out in this period. Rory managed to manoeuvre himself into the 'Mr Pipeline' slot by the winter of 1975 and became a real surf star. He visited Australia for the first time the year before on his way to the new surfing mecca, Bali.

When Alby Falzon took Rusty Miller and Steve Cooney to Bali in 1970 to make a surfing film, no other surfers had ever been on the island. No Balinese surfed; it was forbidden because the elders believed that evil spirits lived in the ocean. Religion played a big part in the lives of the Balinese, and religious taboos carried a great deal of power. For instance, one of the newly discovered surfing spots in Bali was Uluwatu, which means 'the place of the living dead'. There is a legend that thousands of islanders plunged to their death from the cliff face at Uluwatu and there is a temple on the headland which overlooks the surfing take-off point. Looking around at the sheer cliffs you can see the waves disappearing down the bay, which is where the real surf is.

In those early days it was a real adventure to get to Uluwatu. Only a handful of guides knew the way through the steaming heat, across paddy fields and paddocks of thorn bushes, down narrow muddy paths, through villages, and finally down to a waterfall which takes you to a huge sand-filled cavern. Once beyond the

ISLAND STYLE

HOOLE/McCOY

Top left: *Tricky take-off at Pipeline for Rabbit.*

Left: *Line-up at Uluwatu; which means in Balinese, 'The place of the living dead'.*

Above: *Conflict — one must learn respect to surf in the islands.*

Above right: *The eye of the tiger — Uluwatu.*

Right: *Girls will always flock to Bali.*

TERRY WILLCOCKS

Mark Warren 1976 Smirnoff Champion.

ART BREWER

PETER CRAWFORD

JEFF DIVINE

cave the waves were great. Only a handful of Australians and Americans had surfed Bali by the mid '70s including Gerry Lopez, Rory Russell, Wayne Lynch and I. The Balinese were entranced with surfers and surfing, and it was only a matter of time before the locals in this dreamland woke up and started surfing themselves.

In Hawaii, the locals had already woken up. Animosity between the Haoles (whites) and the natives of Hawaii was at an all-time high; so many Haoles had moved to Hawaii there was not enough room for the brothers to get any waves, so the Hawaiians reacted. Angrily. Some Hawaiian surfers were making it extremely difficult for the visiting Caucasians to surf. I know of an instance when one such surfer berated a Hawaiian for dropping in on him. Later the Hawaiian, with ample support, chased him to his car. He was dragged out and badly beaten. There were many such examples, and even today the Hawaiians make no bones about this dislike of outsiders coming to surf their turf.

In the late '70s Ben Aipa was the undisputed lord of a whole new push in Hawaiian surfing. It started on the south shore of Oahu with a bunch of young kids. Ben Aipa was advisor and surfboard builder to these hot-ties. Both the swallow tail and the stinger (a 'step' in the outside rail of the board) had their birth through the hands of Ben Aipa. A big man by any country's standards, Ben bridged the gap from long boards to short. His 220 pounds could generate more power in a turn than anyone else. Ben was an excellent master; he could see the skateboarding-type manoeuvres that surfers like Larry Bertlemann, 'Buttons', Mark Liddell, Michael Ho, Dane Kealoha, and Mark Foo were trying for and so he designed and built boards for acceleration and control.

Skateboarding was responsible for the first three-hundred and sixty degree loop being executed on a surfboard. Exactly who was first out of the group mentioned above to pull off this manoeuvre is a moot point, but no-one did it more consistently than Montgomery 'Buttons' Kaluhiokalani. He was all-Hawaiian with not much care for tomorrow. Instead of going to school he went surfing; in a way he was a new breed of Hawaiian beachboy. spending all his time on the breaks between Ala Moana and his Mum's apartment behind Waikiki. In his constant search for more responsive equipment he moved away from Ben Aipa to other surfboard manufacturers. Buttons never really considered the consequences of his actions, he just moved spontane-ously with no real thought of making a career in prosurfing. He liked to compete, having done it since he was twelve, but he always had such a terrible state of nerves that he never did well in pro competition, where control and performance are so important. The only pro contest he won was in Japan in 1978, where he picked up $1,800 for his trouble. He and Mark Liddell were sponsored by a Japanese businessman living in Hawaii. For most young surfers a win like that would have been the impetus needed to launch a full-on assault on pro surfing, but Buttons came home unchanged and took up where he left off, just cruising Hawaiian style. Without a sponsor and faced with the problem of having to support himself, he took a job as kitchen hand in a local restaurant, which meant he faced a tough time qualifying for the north shore contest season or making the pro circuit. Even in those early years it was imperative that a pro surfer go surfing and do nothing else.

Skateboarding had expanded all over the world in the mid '70s; it was the surfers' other sport. California was the centre. It was where all the finest skateboard parts were made, plus what to wear to protect yourself — gloves, hat, kneeguards, and all the rest. Most of the pro skaters were surfers and it seemed that the new

WARREN BOLSTER

Top left: *Buttons in full drift.*

Above: *Ben Aipa — Mr Power.*

Right: *A skateboard style manoeuvre.*

Below: *Ian 'Kanga' Cairns successfully jockeying Buzzy Kerbox out of the slot.*

Below right: *The Bronzed Aussies.*

WARREN BOLSTER

McCORMACK

PETER CRAWFORD

JEFF DIVINE

ART BREWER

Above: *Brian Keaulana in the infamous Makaha back-wash.*

Left: *Rory Russell as Mr Pipeline.*

Below left and top right: *Mark Liddell tucked away and powering off the top in inimitable style.*

skateboarding craze was to be even bigger than the old one in the early '60s because of the development of the trick skateboard parks. However, due to the amount of claims, no insurance company would underwrite the parks and the sport went into a decline which will persist until the problem is worked out.

Back in Australia, Peter Townend was an excellent skater — and — surfer, consistently placing second in the Australian championships between 1971 and 1974 and in the Queensland titles 1970-75. He was the Aussie who made that classic comment in the finals of the Smirnoff about the force of the turn "either breaking your leg or pushing you right through the board" and how he was going to practice for the following years by "jumping off a three storey building into a garbage can of water". The next winter, after the inspiration of Waimea, he was surfing a little more aggressively and it looked like he would be the Aussie to beat.

PETER CRAWFORD

SURFING MAGAZINE

Peter had grown up on the Gold Coast and started surfing in 1967 along with Michael Peterson and 'Rabbit' Bartholomew. PT, as he was known in the surfing world, had had eight trips to the Islands by the age of 22, and made his living from the sale of surfboards carrying his endorsement. In 1976, with the advent of the pro circuit, Peter was crowned the new world champion with his stable mate in the surfboard industry, Ian Cairns, coming a very close second. Upon returning to Australia they had discussions with journalist/promoter Mike Hurst and together with Mark Warren, formed the promotional team of the 'Bronzed Aussies'. By pooling their talents they hoped to offer a new and more attractive promotion deal to prospective sponsors. Whether it worked or not is debatable. The media did give a little more attention to the team in the beginning, especially when they were joined by other prominent surfers, namely Cheyne Horan and Jim Banks. But within the surfing fraternity the general feeling was that the sport was worthy of more than managers and press releases and posing in matching jump suits.

Ian Cairns, the second Bronzed Aussie, came from Western Australia, where his reputation was justifiably strong; he had won 11 State titles. In 1972 'Kanga', as he is nicknamed,

went to Hawaii for the first time. The following year he won the coveted Smirnoff contest and in 1975 The Duke. A big man whose presence makes itself felt, Ian was what professional surfing was all about. His talent took him around the world constantly and enabled him to become one of the few surfers who could live off their ability.

In 1976 Mark Warren, the third Bronzed Aussie, won the Smirnoff contest, which was held at Sunset Beach. For Mark it was his finest hour; after years of consistently making the finals he had at last won a major professional contest. Mark was one of Australia's finest surfers, displaying clean, clear, tight, decisive surfing that simply had to take him to the top. He began his career as a trainee teacher in a teachers' college, then went to work as a salesman for McCoy surfboards, and in 1975 made the commitment not to continue in college but to become a professional surfer. He is still rating high in pro contests into the late '70s.

The winter of 1976 in Hawaii saw the end of surfing competitions at Waimea Bay. The local residents brought a lot of pressure to bear on the contest organisers because they were tired of giving access through their property to a never-ending procession of tents, cameras, surfboards,

surfers and spectators. It was clear by now that professional surfing needed a permanent association. The International Professional Surfers' Association was set up in 1976; previous attempts had been made in both Australia and Hawaii at such an association but had failed because the surfers involved neglected to give it real support. Pro contests were springing up everywhere. In South Africa the Durban 500 had started giving cash prizes. There were pro contests in Brazil and Japan as well as Australia, Hawaii and the east and west coasts of America. What was needed was some method of packaging these contests into a world-wide tour. Fred Hemmings, together with another fine Hawaiian surfer and shaper, Randy Rarick, set about organising this, combined with an international ratings system where each place in a rated event was worth a certain number of points. This would produce a real world champion. By the end of 1977 Randy had worked out a series of thirteen contests all over the world with a total prize money of $150,000. Sponsorship for these contests was immediately picked up by a Californian footwear company, Beachcomber Bill!'s. This, together with the internationally adopted I.P.S. rating system, made 1976-77 something of a breakthrough. •

A stoked Rabbit and Toni.

*Under cyclonic conditions the Gold Coast
comes alive with the energy of swells.*

SURFING GOLD

Gold Coast, gold business, gold contests; they took a long time to arrive, but as the commercialism of surfing increased the rewards became greater. Some liked that, some didn't. For the pro surfers sponsorship was becoming important; the prizemoney in the major contests was climbing but it was rarely big enough to cover expenses, so surfers had to lend their names and glamour to board shorts and wetsuit manufacturers. Surfing was being transformed. And along the Queensland coast a different sort of transformation was taking place; the beaches, headlands and waterways of Queensland's southern coast were being turned into the Gold Coast, and from that influx of people emerged a new group of surfers.

So 1976 saw some changes on the surfing front. For the first time since its inception in 1961 a non-Australian won the Bells Beach Classic; Jeff Hackman, who for so long had been regarded as one of the world's finest big wave surfers, with numerous wins and places in every major pro and amateur meet held in Hawaii, romped home to win the Victorian crown. Hackman had been a star since he first learnt to stand up and cut back in the early '60s. Growing up in Hawaii in the era when big wave riders reigned supreme, he was the youngest man to surf big waves at Sunset and Waimea; at the age of thirteen he rode them with a style never seen before. His acute sense of timing, coupled with a unique style of carving and bending long arcs down any face, made him one of the first well-respected pros. Not being tall everything was magnified when it came to Jeff. If the wave was twenty foot it looked like thirty, yet because he handled it with such ease you never really knew just how big it was.

His style adapted well to the short board era but he never really had the aggression to excel in small, sloppy surf, needing a real wave to perform. In 1976, after finishing ninth on the I.P.S. pro ratings, he decided to quit the circuit and together with two Californian surfing businessmen set about organising an American connection for the already highly successful Australian-based Quiksilver Boardshorts. That it developed into such a success surprised Jeff and his partners as much as it did the rest of the swimwear manufacturing industry around the world. Surfers are a fickle lot; they had always demanded quality material, a good loose cut, and double-stitched seams that could take abuse. They did not mind spending a little more but wanted quality. In California this formula had been proven before by Nancy Katin, who had successfully made surfers' boardshorts for years. Jeff brought Quiksilver to America just at the right time. The pro phenomenon was about to explode and Australia was synonymous with the pro movement, having ten names in the rated top twenty. The colours were bright and new; almost without exception all the best Australian surfers wore them. With that formula Quiksilver became the name and logo on everyone's thigh from Sweden to Tahiti.

This same formula for success was applied to another Australian surfing product, Rip Curl wetsuits. Coming from the same small town of Torquay, in south-western Victoria, their success is a phenomenon over which businessmen still scratch their heads, especially when in 1980 Rip Curl received the export award for the most rapid expansion of any Australian company and moved into a giant complex of 20,000 square feet. Here thousands of wetsuits are manufactured every week and exported all over the world. Rip Curl mounted a vigorous magazine advertising campaign based on giving free suits to all the top surfers, from the respected oldies down to the hot young grommets, which resulted in hundreds of surf shots of guys wearing Rip Curl. They were also the major sponsor of the Bells Beach contest. Rip Curl's two principal owners, Doug 'Claw' Warbrick and Brian Singer, are both veteran surfers. In the early days they saw very little reason to actually have to pay the pro surfers for endorsement. Their only indulgence was Victoria's own Wayne Lynch. Wayne was to Victorian surfing what a pig is to mud and Rip Curl found in him the perfect medium for promoting their products: a '60s cult hero with a heavy underground following. They turned the surfboard part of their operation over to him to give further credibility to their involvement in surfing and to provide Wayne with a steady income from the sale of his personally shaped surfboards. After constantly diving in and out of competition since the first came to prominence in the mid '60s, Lynch finally developed a temperament to win and had a close victory over Mark Richards to take first place in the 1975 Coke contest.

The hefty size of the cash prizes was attracting many old pros into competition, including Paul Neilson, another Australian, who had won the Smirnoff contest in the early '70s. Paul grew up on the Gold Coast, Queensland; his early surfing was encouraged by his elder brother, Rick, and by Peter Drouyn. The Gold Coast is a unique place for surfing: a densely populated but dispersed metropolitan area surrounding four of the finest point breaks in the world. In the early '50s the Gold Coast's real estate potential was realised by a small band of southern businessmen who drove around the numerous headlands and decided to go headlong into tourist development. Naturally many other aspiring investors arrived.

Surfers Paradise developed into a skyscraper-and-canal complex which ended up rivalling Waikiki as a trap for the tourist dollar. Families moved into the area from all over Australia; small businesses catering to the residents and tourists came to life; and the 22 kilometres of the Gold Coast became one of Australia's major cities.

For surfers who came to live on the Gold Coast the main attraction was waves, and that was exactly what the coast had plenty of . . . especially under cyclonic weather conditions. Surfers are avid cyclone watchers and the bottom line about cyclones is that they are unpredictable — no matter how much time you give to studying weather maps you just can't predict exactly what they will do. There is only one choice — be there or regret it. The cyclone season starts in December and goes through to April and for this reason alone the first Stubbies Classic was held at Burleigh Heads in March, 1977. As well as being the first professional event to be held on the Gold Coast, it was unique in that the Stubbies was the first of a new generation of surfing contests dreamt up by that flamboyant Gold Coaster, Peter Drouyn. Out of disenchantment with the subjective and objective methods of judging Peter devised the 'man on man' system, on which only two sur-

1

2

TERRY WILLCOCKS

5

ART BREWER

1. *March '75; A young Shaun Thomson learning the subtleties of riding the tube.*

2. *Joe Engle; wide eyed in the Burleigh burrow.*

3. *Shaun; deep in the tube and turning into position.*

4. *June '83; Stay aware — they are still out there.*

5. *Shaun putting in the miles on the north shore.*

SATO

3

JAMES H. METYKO

4

PETER CRAWFORD

Sequence above: *The Rabbit running through a tight Burleigh barrel.*

Below: *Open door for 'the Beaver' at Burleigh.*

fers are in the water at the one time. The resulting competition produced intense high-pressure surfing. Apparently the basic idea came from gymnastics and tennis; each surfer is judged in ten categories, each having a minimum score of .5 and a maximum of 1.0, and the surfer with the highest overall total by the five judges wins. Certainly it still has the problem of subjective assessment by a particular judge but it comes very close to eliminating personal bias, or at least closer than ever before. The main reason is that because there are only two surfers, the winner is usually clear, even if by the smallest margin.

In the man-on-man method of judging, the first man to his feet gets the wave. If the two contestants get up simultaneously, the surfer farthest from the curl is obliged to give way. That's the basic law. However, while the man-on-man method always produces a winner it has also produced some unethical practices, especially

the practice of engineering your opponent to drop in on you so that he then faces elimination. The man-on-man system has never been used in Hawaii because the Hawaiians maintain that they have consistently good surf which obviates the need for such a judging method. Up until 1977 Hawaii used the objective method, but then changed to the subjective system using 20-point marking for their six-man heats. Now that's been changed to 10-points and four-man heats following a meeting of the top professionals in December, 1981. This method was to be adopted for all rated events that make up the world championship.

With the fundamental ingredient of perfect 6-foot Burleigh waves the first Stubbies was a tremendous success. Michael Peterson came back for one last big bite at the apple and took the $5,000 purse, just ahead of Mark Richards, a hot young kid from Newcastle nicknamed 'the wounded seagull'. The Australian leg of the cir-

SEQUENCE PETER CRAWFORD

JEFF DIVINE

Right: *The young Rabbit with semi gun. December '76.*

Below: *Guy Ormerod with a clean lay-back at 'Lenny the Ox'. (Lennox Head north coast N.S.W.)*

PETER CRAWFORD

cuit was now worth $40,000. As the pros moved south for the Bells and Coke contests everyone was full of praise for the new system. However, both the Coke and Bells had been organised months before on the basis of the old six-man final with points for manoeuvres, and to change systems at this stage was impossible. Anyway, both surfers and organisers were a little apprehensive as to whether the new system would work in anything less than perfect waves. The old system proved itself consistent in that both the contests were won by a big powerhouse named Simon Anderson from Narrabeen.

That 1977 season in Hawaii saw some changes to the Aussies' domination of the big three contests, with Hawaiians coming back with a vengeance. Reno won the Smirnoff, Rory Russell the Pipeline Masters and Eddie Aikau The Duke. Still, the Australians were there in force. Mark Richards came second in the Smirnoff, with Terry Fitzgerald third. Col

SURFER MAGAZINE

PETER CRAWFORD

PETER CRAWFORD

Top: *Roll up, roll up! The circus is in town.*

Above: *Silver trails off clean curves left by America's east coast master Jeff Crawford.*

Right: *The well respected Allan Byrne with his channeled thruster.*

Far top: *Wayne 'Rabbit' Bartholomew; looking for it.*

Far centre of bottom: *Gold Coaster Paul Neilson; always a tough competitor both on and off the court.*

PETER CRAWFORD

Smith took first place in the pro class trials on a revolutionary new board which Jim Pollard and Phil Fraser had just built for him. The board had a new bottom shape which incorporated channels running parallel to the stringer. These channels can vary in number from two to six; they begin at the tail and run for about two to three feet, then fade out. Their depth is from ¼ to ½ an inch. They produce lift in the tail and work well with single fins; the effect achieved is similar to that of the multi-fins. Some of the top surfers are using them today and it is one of the design developments which has stayed with us.

With such a mixed bag of winners all over the world and a few problems concerning rated and non-rated contests still to be ironed out with the I.P.S., it was proving to be a question of consistency and dedication as to who would be the official world champion after the circuit was completed in Hawaii. Not that there was much monetary gain, in fact only $2,000 cash, but the prestige and the sponsorship which followed made the crown a worthwhile goal. Ironically it was not a Hawaiian or an Australian who showed this consistency, nor someone riding a channel bottom or a twin fin, but a surfer who rode a single fin conventional surfboard. The

best surfer in the world in 1977 was a South African, Shaun Thompson. Shaun was born and raised in Durban. His father was of Jewish descent and one of South Africa's best swimmers until a shark ripped out his biceps and destroyed his competitive career. It seems strange that his father should have encouraged Shaun's interest in surfing after the shark attack; Shaun is terrified of sharks to this day. (Perhaps there is something in the theory that sharks can sense this terror because while Shaun was surfing in the quarter finals of the 1981 Surfabout, a pack of six sharks was attracted into the line-up where Shaun was doing battle.) When Shaun was still quite young he got hot in the shark-meshed breaks around Durban and developed a strong aggressive style not unlike the Australians of his age. Shaun first came to Australia in 1969 for the world championships in Victoria and also spent a couple of months in the Islands. He watched the Aussies' domination of the competition scene in the early '70s and learnt how to apply that same power through his board, but because of the long periods of time he spent in Hawaii he also learnt to relax in the power — a characteristic of Hawaiian surfing that was personified in Gerry Lopez.

Lopez had geared his whole surfing to

Right: *Shaun Tomson; Burleigh Heads, Queensland.*

Below: *Jeff Hakman; carving clean tracks from 2-20 feet.*

Bottom: *Rabbit at 'Off the Wall' with the door wide open.*

Below right: *Michael Peterson at Sunset Beach, Hawaii.*

DAN MERKLE

JEFF DIVINE

JEFF DIVINE

SURFING MAGAZINE

COURTESY QUIKSILVER

PETER CRAWFORD

PETER CRAWFORD

Top: *The name on everyones' thighs.*

Centre: *Bill Bolman at the '77 Stubbies clearing up a few rules for Mark Richards and Michael Peterson.*

Above: *6' hot and glassy. Burleigh Heads, Queensland.*

setting himself up and getting in the tube, and that had come about through riding the Pipeline. Shaun took tube riding one step further by riding every wave he could in the tube, not just the Pipeline. Anywhere from Sunset to Jeffries Bay he might be seen only on takeoff and then after he popped out way down the line at the end of the ride. Shaun remembers those long tubes as being the places which demanded the most intense concentration; the turns inside a critical barrel were primarily carves into position. What was the secret? "It's being able to slow down and accept the reality of the situation you are in, when natural instinct is telling you to trim up tight and get the hell out of there," he says. This slowing down of the whole situation makes it seem as if time is suspended; you are actually breathing inside the tube when from outside it looks like a wagon wheel which is running backwards. The tube had been discovered beforehand but no-one rode it really consistently until Shaun Tomson.

In 1977, as the reigning World Champion, Shaun was somewhat disillusioned. He had spent $20,000 to earn a total of $20,000 in winnings, and he was the biggest money-earner by a margin of about $5,000. Most of the pros had gone heavily into debt to follow the circuit around the world.

Still, everyone wanted to go on and see the international circuit grow. The 1978 Australian season got off to a bang with local boy Wayne 'Rabbit' Bartholomew winning the Stubbies from Mark Richards in surf which was not nearly as good as in the first year. The positions were reversed in the Bells and then a newcomer to the pro ranks, Larry Blair, romped home in the Coke from Wayne Lynch. The Australian leg of the world circuit was worth $64,000, mainly due to the involvement of a national television station which made a six-part TV series of the Coke contest.

In South Africa, Shaun won the Gunstan for the sixth year in a row and was refused a Brazilian visa on political grounds. Cheyne Horan had his first win in Rio with 'Rabbit' second. In Florida Jeff Crawford won ahead of Bobby Owens and Dane Kealoha. The Hawaiian contests were worth a total of only $30,000 in prizemoney but everyone was so aware of the ratings game that competition was fierce. Michael Ho won The Duke but the contest was not rated. Shaun won the Cuervo Classic,

which used to be called the Smirnoff, and that same unknown Australian, Larry Blair, did just what he bragged he would and won the Pipeline Masters. But none of this made any difference to the fact that Wayne 'Rabbit' Bartholomew became the new world champion, leading right from the start of the year with his win in the Stubbies.

'Rabbit' had grown up on the Gold Coast where his Dad taught school. When his family split up Bugs moved with his mother and sisters to a beach house where he started going surfing. At first it didn't interfere with his schooling but slowly the disease got hold of him and he wagged school to ride waves. After a few successes in school surfing competition he was smart enough to explain his truancy to the headmaster, who could understand that Wayne was not going to be an academic and that the school might as well do all it could to help him. One day a year all the students were allowed to discard their school uniforms and wear anything they liked to school, for which they paid the modest sum of 20 cents. Somehow all these 20 cents added up to $250 and Rabbit's high school became his first sponsor! The money was used to send him to California for the 1972 world championships, where he was a reserve, and on the way home it let him visit Hawaii, where he took more than his share of wipeouts. Rabbit came home to lick his wounds and did not go back to the Islands until 1974, when he still failed to earn a start in any of the professional meets. The following year Rabbit competed with a fury — without any success, other than a win in the eating contest for the Surfabout, where he put away five pounds of vegetables! As a radical young man in 1976 he surfed naked for *Tracks* newspaper and made some outrageous comments. In Hawaii he felt the repercussions to a particularly provocative article; after being beaten up and receiving nine stitches from a flying ashtray Rabbit started to settle down a little and thought before he spoke. In 1977 Rabbit came second on the pro circuit with consistent radical surfing on a single fin board, and in 1978 he became world champion.

●

Above: *Hawaii's well respected surfing family: The Aikau's.*

Right: *Louie Ferreira backdoor, Pipeline.*

THE
ISLANDS

The Hawaiian islands provide surfing which is intrinsically different to anywhere else in the world. It isn't just the big waves, though of course they come into it. It has to do with the fact that surfing has been going on there for centuries, and this creates a different feeling to anywhere else. Surfing isn't just a sport, it's a tradition. Whole families get caught up in it; skills are passed down from one generation to another, fathers teach their sons all their knowledge of the water, and this comes out in everything from surfing styles to board design.

In the late '70s a whole series of Hawaiians emerged from the islands and made their mark on world surfing. Yet 1978 started badly when, in April, Eddie Aikau, the eldest son of the most respected Hawaiian surfing family, lost his life in a tragedy at sea. Eddie and fifteen other crewmen had set out in the 42ft sailing canoe, Hokule'a, in a traditional re-enactment of the spread of the Polynesian people across the Pacific. Exactly what happened no-one knows. Eddie was a fantastic waterman and in the midst of a furious Pacific storm, when the canoe had a serious list, he continually made requests to the captain to let him paddle his board for help. The next morning the captain finally granted his request and that was the last anyone saw of him. The Aikau family, his surfing friends and the Hawaiian people went into mourning.

Eddie's death, sad though it was, didn't halt the growing number of local surfers who moved into the professional ranks. They included some very talented surfers, such as Buzzy Kerbox, Bobby Owens, Dane Kealoha, Keone Downing, and of course Michael Ho. Right from the start Michael Ho was very serious about doing well in professional competition and he proved it by winning The Duke contest in 1978. An energetic, tightly compressed ball of surf energy constantly looking for somewhere to explode, his style is typically Hawaiian — not aggressive and lip-hitting like an Australian of his age but rather flowing smoothly

from rail to rail, complementing the wave without trying to overpower it. It was not until the final showdown of the 1978 Stubbies that Australia had a chance to see Ho in action, when he really impressed everyone and came a very close second to Rabbit.

The only other contemporary Hawaiian surfers who earned that sort of respect in Australia at that stage were **Larry Bertlemann** and, a year or so later, his older cousin Dane Kealoha. When Larry was around the age of 11 the Bertlemann family moved from the big island of Hawaii to Honolulu on Oahu. Like David **Nuuhiwa** before him, he seemed to have that same natural Hawaiian charm — afro hair and deep chocolate skin and like so many other kids growing up in town, his surfing had graduated from Waikiki to Ala Moana. He improved on those scorching lefts until he was regarded as one of the best on the sough shore. While still in the juniors he decided to turn pro. His adviser, and surfboard benefactor, Ben Aipa, didn't want him to do it at such an early age, but after a taste of the money in the Pipeline Masters he was fully into it. Larry was always a smart kid, and he willingly took the advice of his elder counselor, Colonel Benson about sponsors. He approached serveral big companies in Hawaii and ended up with a pretty impressive array of sponsors, including Toyota, Ocean Pacific Sportswear and Town and Country Surfboards. With this security he could travel the world,

WARREN BOLSTER

following the pro circuit, and still have plenty of money to live on and plan a future. Larry didn't really fire in Australian contests, but it didn't seem to bother him. He was a true professional and accepted the losses, reasoning that if he complained or got mad his public would look on him as a bad sport, which would be bad for him and for pro surfing in general.

Larry's development in surfboards was unusual. After less than a month on a borrowed 9'6" log he had stepped straight down to 5'8". Like the other hot young crop of town locals, Aipa used him as a test pilot for swallow tails, stingers, and what Aipa called a fast rail — a little edge on the bottom of the soft low rail. The rail was incredibly sensitive, providing the powerful acceleration and radical direction changes which were needed to keep up with the skateboard-like manoeuvres the kids were trying for. Ben Aipa had been impressed by vees in the bottom shape right from the '60s when he had seen McTavish and I on the north shore. He used them continuously as a means of keeping the board in the water, and getting it to roll up on an edge. After years under the direction of Aipa, Larry learnt enough to shape his own boards. With the aid of Craig Sugihara of Town and Country he became an accurate shaper and was primarily responsible for the revival of twin fins in Hawaii and California. Not that he used them in big waves at that stage; he rode them only on slower, small waves where the wider twin fins allowed the board to ride over the flat spots. The wide tails were a definite advantage in small surf and a necessary part of the professional surfer's quiver for travelling the world circuit, where the types of surf encountered varied so much.

Larry's stable mate at Town and Country was his cousin, Dane Kealoha. In 1980, in the first two contests of the season in Australia, the 22-year-old Kealoha was ahead on the ratings because he had come second in both the Southside Open and the Stubbies. He had had a steady rise to the top with a win in the

JEFF DIVINE

SURFER MAGAZINE

PETER CRAWFORD

JEFF DIVINE

Left: *Rory Russell deep in the tube at Pipeline as seen from the tail of Wilkings' camera mounted surfboard.*

Top: *Tommy Carroll taking-off at 'Wave Rock' Pipeline on a particularly awesome wave.*

Above: *For beauty and power the Islands reign supreme.*

Above right: *Local boy Randy Rarick guts up and into one of the biggest waves I've ever seen at Waimea Bay.*

Right: *Buttons: sizzling hot even on a single fin.*

Kealoha projecting himself out of a big pipeline barrel.

Top right: *Bobby Owens: delicate dance in the green room.*

Bottom right: *Bill Barnfield over the top!*

amateur Smirnoff in 1976 and then consistent placings in the pro events after he entered them in 1977. In 1978 he won the Niijima Cup in Japan and ended up ninth on the ratings. 1979 was even better; he finished fourth and was the top-rated Hawaiian. On land Dane is a very rational man, prepared to rise to the top step by step, intent on not getting overamped and peaking out. In the water it's another matter; he puts great energy and aggression into his surfing. But the essence of his style is speed. Accelerating forehand turns, radical cutbacks (practically 360-degree loops, as the wave closes out), all put together with grace and precision. Perhaps his greatest asset, and the characteristic that sets him apart from his contemporaries on the south shore of Oahu, is his ability to ride big waves. His favourite size is 8 to 10 feet Hawaiian, which is 10 to 12 feet everywhere else in the world. He likes the fact that he can't go wild

like he can in small surf and has to take it easy, conquering fear first and making slower manoeuvres with more concentration. Dane first surfed the north shore when he was fifteen. With an elder brother and father who were both keen surfers, the transition from small to big waves was as natural as it was from amateur to professional competition. He is fully committed to being a pro surfer, spending the entire year travelling the circuit. Like Bertlemann, he has good sponsors who relieve the pressure of having to win dollars every time and who thus make it possible for him to live the surfer's dream of getting paid to go surfing.

Every surfer who has made it in the Islands has his or her tale to tell about the day they learnt how far to push. Back in 1977, Bobby Owens was a 17-year old caucasian Hawaiian who had just made the decision to turn pro. With a father in the ser-

vice, his family had moved from Florida to Hawaii in 1966 and Bobby took up surfing immediately. His lesson in respect for the ocean came at Waimea Bay where he and a friend were cleaned up and held down under the water for a long time. Like all surfers who have been placed in a position like that at the Bay, it had a sobering influence which only surfers who have gone through it themselves can appreciate! An experience like that tends to mould your style to one where you always surf within your limits, especially in big surf, and where you tend to slowly expand your repertoire of manoeuvres and don't really push beyond your ability. This makes for excellent big wave riders; Jeff Hackman is a perfect example of this and Bruce Raymond is his Australian counterpart.

BOB BARBOUR

STEVE WILKINGS

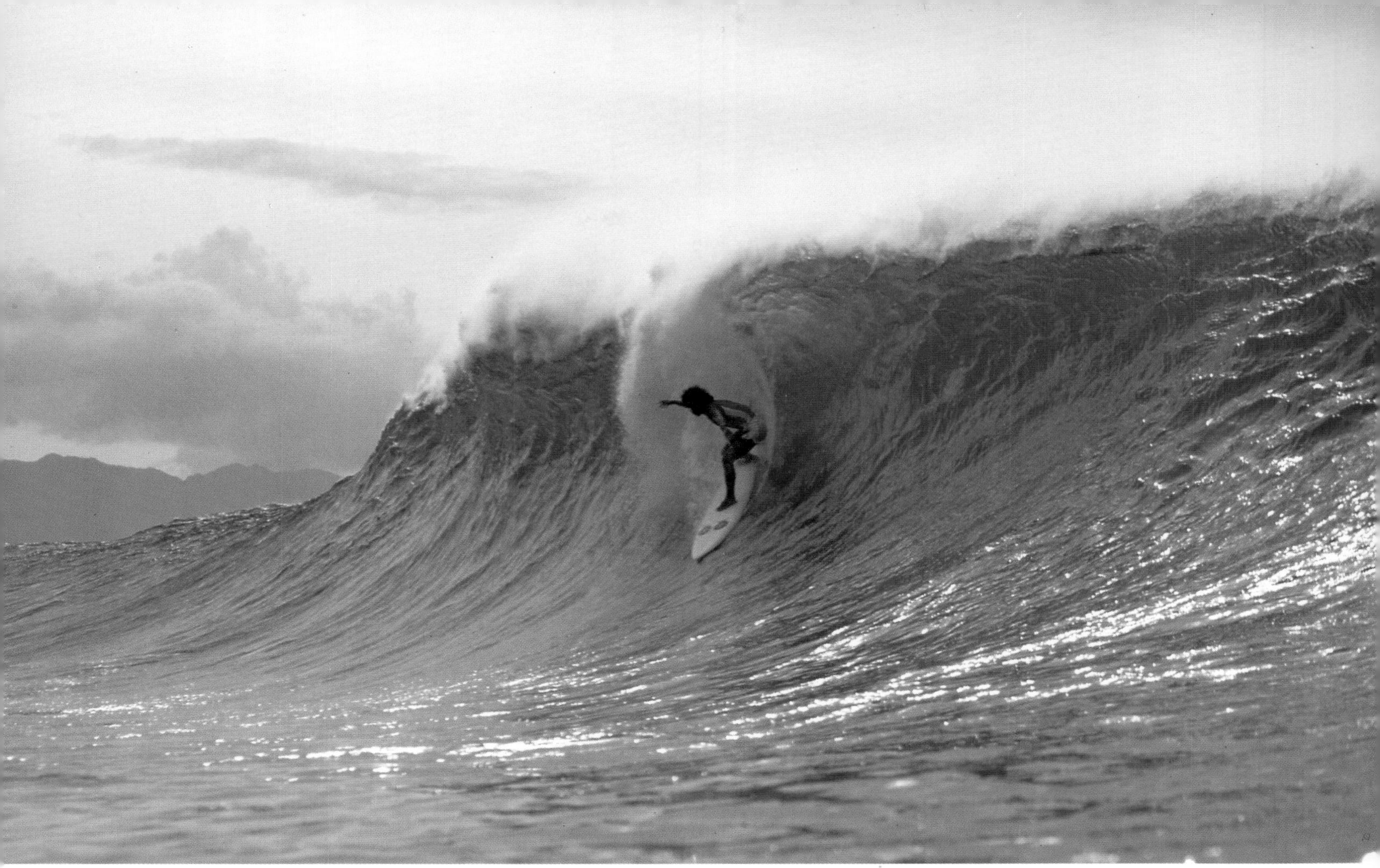

JEFF HORNBAKER

Left: *Honolua Bay, Maui: when the north shore of Oahu gets too big and stormy: perfection can be found at Honolua.*

Above: *Late drop from Michael Ho at the Pipeline.*

Below: *Derek Ho (Michael's little brother) cranking on the power at 'Ala-Mo' south shore, Oahu.*

SATO

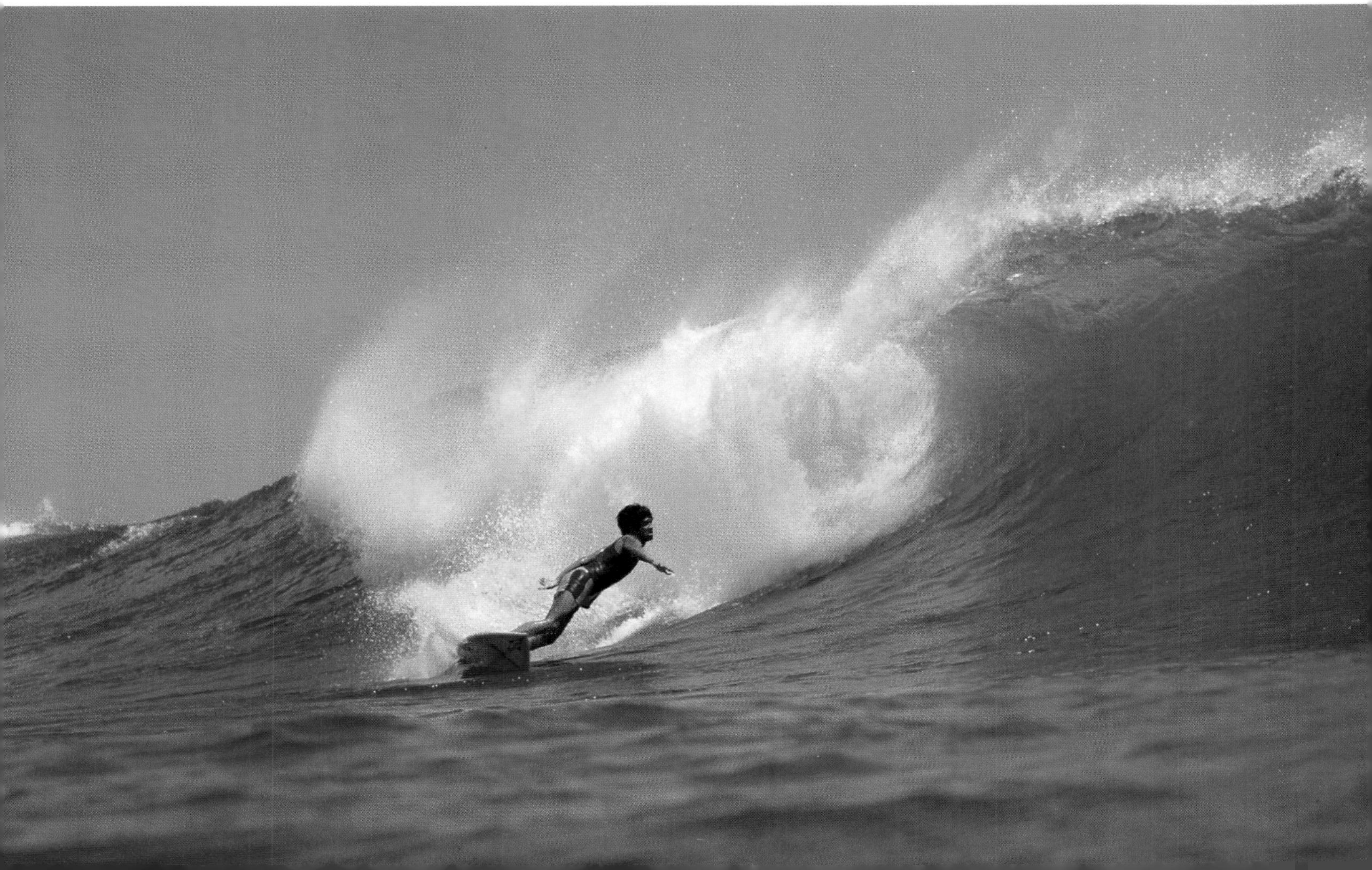

Top: *Larry Blair, Pipeline: with accelerator flat to the floor.*

Above: *The legendary Buffalo Keaulana and 'Teddy Bear' Davis going out for a little exercise at Makaha.*

Spread: *Lopez being propelled out of the tube at Pipeline by the spray, after the cannon has fired.*

Mark Richards high in the curl on his backhand.

THE WOUNDED SEAGULL ON A TWIN FIN

To win the world surfing championship once is hard enough; to win it four times is amazing. But that's exactly what Mark Richards has done . . . a record which may never be beaten in the history of surfing. He won the world title in 1979, 1980, 1981 and 1982. He's an extraordinary surfer who combines natural talent with real competitive drive . . . and a sense of humour. Most pro surfers make a living by shaping or selling or endorsing boards and products; Mark does all that but is unique in that he could easily live off his contest winnings alone.

His dominance of world surfing in the late '70s and early '80s is shown by the fact that in 1979 he won the world championship even though he decided to enter in only nine out of the possible 13 rated events in the championship series, which gave everyone else plenty of chance to catch up. Nobody did. Mark won four of the events he entered and picked up sizeable cheques for second and fourth places in the others. He also won the unrated Duke contest and his winnings for the season totalled more than $25,000.

Richards is identified with the popularity of the twin fin in surfing. He led the way in surfing not just small waves but sizeable Hawaiian faces with a twin fin board. But even someone like Richards, like all pro and amateur surfers, has to be wary of the sheer power of the sea, no matter what sort of equipment is being ridden. Mark has given a scarey account of how he was held down at Sunset a week before the 1981 north shore tournament was about to start. The world champion was caught inside by a series of pounding waves that gobbled him up and then dragged him down and along the bottom.

"There I was, ten feet below the surface with something like 100 tons of pressure on top of me and unable to do a thing," he said. "It was the scariest situation I have ever known. I was running out of air fast but couldn't penetrate the layers of foam. I thought I would eventually pop to the surface, but I was stuck down there like I was inside a cave, and the breaking of the next wave just made it worse. I kept saying to myself, just stay cool, you'll be alright, but with my air going fast I finally let go of the board and began scrambling for

The wounded seagull executing his own manouevre: the snap-back!

M.R.: off the top.

JEFF DIVINE

the surface. My lungs were really hurting — I didn't panic. You never panic in a situation like this. Better to let the turbulence take you and trust in fate. But I reckon another few seconds down there and I would have blacked out."

Mark was lucky. When he burst through the foam to daylight his board was bobbing right next to him. This ordeal is one that just about every good surfer has gone through or will go through. But in the world of professional sportsmen it puts them in a very elite group, facing more than their share of danger. Conquering your fear is a relevant part of competitive surfing and unless you do that you will never make a good pro. Here's Mark Richards again: "Sure, I get twinges of fear when I'm paddling out at say Waimea Bay with giant peaks thundering ahead of me, but that is before the heat starts. Once the event gets under way I don't think about anything other than catching the waves. The man in

the street can appreciate what top tennis players or golfers have to face in a tournament because most people have tried these sports themselves, but with surfing they have only seen big wave riding on TV. This is one major reason why the sport has not gathered the mass spectator following it deserves. People identify best with sports they understand or participate in themselves. This is probably why surfing will never reach the heights of cricket or football — not that I want to see the sport become like World Series Cricket anyway."

How Mark Richards came to the top is an interesting story of development through design, He was born in Newcastle in 1957; his father Ray had already become the steel city's surfboard baron, bringing the first production balsas and foam Malibus to Newcastle. Newcastle has always been big on surfing, all through the surf club era and more recently with their get-up-and-go attitude to kneeboards and wave skis. At ten years

SEQUENCE ART BREWER

Guess who?

PETER CRAWFORD

old, Ray gave Mark his first board. It was 6 foot long and made by Gordon Woods. By continually hassling his mother, Val, to take him to the beach after school, and by surfing Greenmont Point and Rainbow Bay on the Gold Coast during the family's annual jaunt to Queensland, he developed into a competent surfer by the age of fourteen. After interclub competition in Merewether Surfboard Club he entered the State junior titles where he finished third behind Mark Warren and Grant 'Dappa' Oliver, the junior stars of that time. He was already considering a future in surfing. Mark was only average at school; he says that he never cut class to surf unless the waves were *really* good, but of course the definition of good is a relative and constantly changing thing! In 1972 he had his first trip to the Islands. In 1973 he won both the State and Australian junior titles. His style was weird but effective; one leg bent and tucked in behind the other in skiing stance, arms outstretched, a totally individual approach, the per-

fect product of watching others but developing his own style. He was conscious of his uniqueness and felt comfortable about it even when his peers in the junior ranks christened him 'the wounded seagull'.

At this early stage Mark's equipment was more or less left up to his father. Owning a surf shop in such a surf oriented town meant that Ray had to be totally on top of the latest Australian designs. After Gordon Woods' Malibus, Mark rode 6'6" rounded pins by Midget — not exactly what Midget was into at that time, as that was Midget's side-slipper era. Following that I supplied the majority of the boards for the Richards' surf shop and Mark rode my smaller down-railers for a while. Terry Fitzgerald made two boards for him, but by then Geoff McCoy had moved to the central coast and had begun to grind out the very latest in Californian design, the twin fin. The first local twins were built at Barry Bennett's factory by Tom Hoye from Santa

AARON CHANG

Above: *The rewards of success.*

Below: *You can tell by the trail M.R.'s covering lots of ground.*

PETER CRAWFORD

Quiver of '83.

Reno Abellira on tiny fish-tail twin at Narrabeen in 1976.

Cruz. They had wide, round, diamond or square tails with ugly S decks putting the thickness towards the tail. They were only suited to small surf where they could be surfed flat in the water; as soon as they were used on wave faces they had the inherent problem of tracking. The straight up and down parallel fin placement often caused the early twins to stick rather than roll off the face and hold track down the line when it was time to change direction. After the initial development by Mike Eaton, the design was kept alive and kicking with a bunch of locals in the San Diego Sunset Cliffs area where Steve Lis built the first short 'fish'-style twins.

David Nuuhiwa adapted the design to suit the variable surf conditions of Huntington by working with shapers Terry Martin and Steve Brom and the result was a thicker, harder-edged twin, bearing a toed-in, tipped-out fin setup. Exactly who took it first to Hawaii is still a mystery; probably Nuuhiwa on one of his regular visits to his native island. Suffice to say they surfaced in the Islands underneath the hot young crop of town locals whose equipment was almost solely supplied by Ben Aipa. The surfer who first brought one of these fish-style twins to Australia was Reno Abellira. Reno's designs were made in Australia by McCoy and therefore it was perfectly natural for one to be slipped under the hottest up-and-coming McCoy boy, Mark Richards.

But they still didn't work in the Islands on bigger waves and Mark Richards rode Brewer's and Tom Parrish's guns and a few of Ben Aipa's stingers for smaller Hawaiian barrels. Almost just for reassurance he jumped back on single fins for a while, to see if his style of constant carving on the face would adjust back. The result was disappointing.

He then started building his own boards, twins that were not too different from those Reno had delivered through McCoy, but it wasn't long before he was making his own refinements. During 1978 the challenge to ride big waves on twin fins became an obsession. He went back to the Hawaiian north shore armed with three 6'10" twins and a burning ambition to ride them at Sunset. None of them worked and while the photos from the previous winter at "Off the Wall", a well-known Hawaiian break, were sending kids into raptures all over the world the king of the twin fins was having equipment problems, not being able to switch from twins to singles and back again as he had done in the past. He ended up giving all the singles away and surfing a 6'6" twin at Sunset, which was just ridiculous. In 1979 he planned his strategy well in advance. "I got back onto a single before I came," he said. "I made a 6'2" swallow and rode it solidly for two weeks, plugging back in. When I arrived on the north shore I had no problems adapting." He surfed 6'8"

159

Left: *Mark Richards four times World Champion, and stoked.*

PETER CRAWFORD

to 7'4" rounded pin single fins in all the contests and, as usual, did well. He won the world championship yet again.

Mark's twin fins were important not just because of what he performed on them but because of their effect on surfing. The big-name model surfboard had long been a joke among surfers who knew anything about the scene; the arrangement seemed to be simply one of cash for decals. Mark, however, was determined to put some credibility back into the 'designed by' label. The production of his model has become an increasingly profitable concern, and now his boards are available in Australia, Hawaii, USA, Britain, South Africa and Japan under franchise arrangements with local manufacturers. To further control the manufacture of the Mark Richards model he makes full templates and stipulates widths and thicknesses. Leaving nothing up to the shaper to interpret, he sends up-to-date sample boards and makes personal inspections of the factories at least once a year. The Mark Richards twin fins took off and spawned flocks of 'junior wounded seagulls,' arms flapping and Superman crests flying, all over the world. The boards had a major effect on the direction of surfing; they were designed for radical manoeuvres on the face with the main emphasis being on the snapback. For the first time quick, radical direction changes were being pulled off anywhere on the face of a wave, and it was this idea of surfing out on the face more than in the tube that inspired Mark to use his twin fins in all surf under 8 feet. Before long, most other surfers — especially the pros — were doing the same thing.

●

LOGAN MURRAY

Right: *Hot New Zealand surfer Kevin Jarret taking his lunch to the beach.*

Below: *A secret spot in New Zealand.*

LOGAN MURRAY

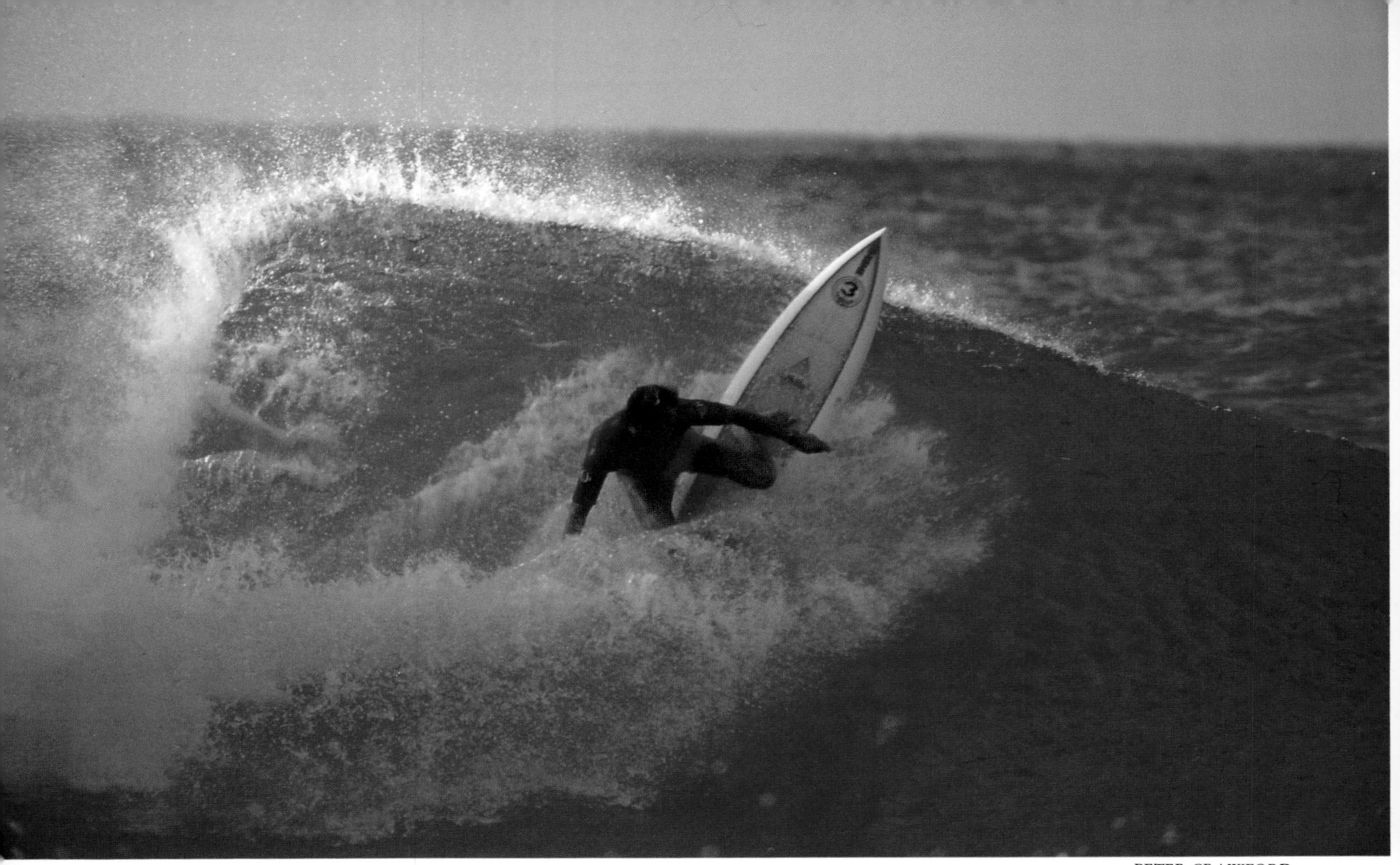

PETER CRAWFORD

Two angles on Simon Anderson (coming out of the barrel at Pipeline) that show the amazing versatility of the three fin (thruster).

Developing his surfing at Narrabeen on Sydney's north side has made Simon particularly strong on his backhand.

PETER CRAWFORD

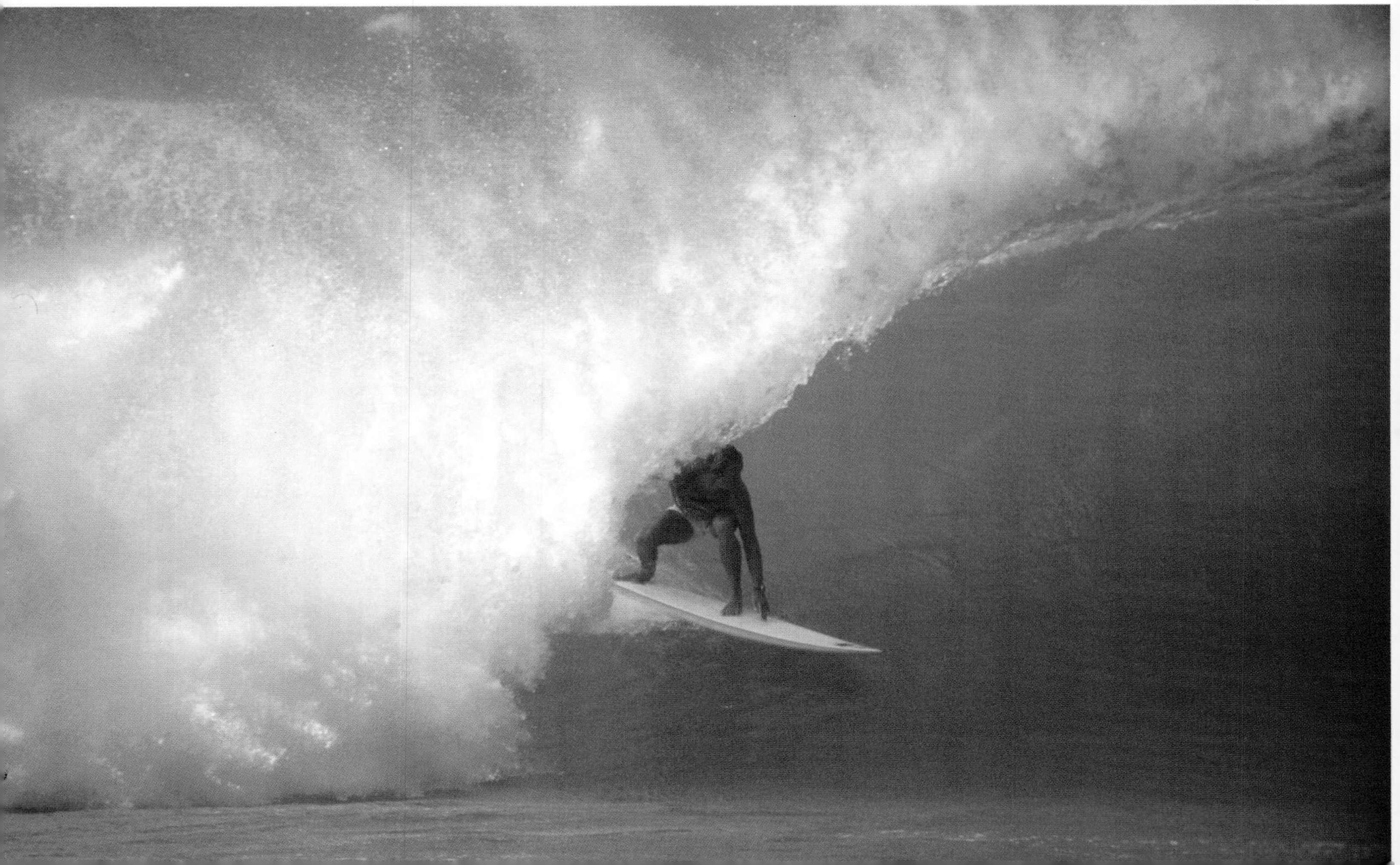

PETER CRAWFORD

TWO FINS ARE GOOD THREE ARE BETTER

There were many reasons why the surfing world took to the twin fin with such zeal — the main one being that it was fun to ride, especially in small waves. Compared to the old single fin the get-up-and-go of the twin fin was exhilarating and fresh. It helped women surfers tremendously because it needed less effort to turn. However, a lot of surfers couldn't handle the excessive looseness of the design, especially older surfers who were used to big forehand turns. Even some younger ones found the twin a problem on their backhand or in stronger surf.

One of those surfers was Simon Anderson, and in 1981 the Aussie giant designed the three fin 'thruster', which was a valid attempt at toning down the twin fin and giving the surfer more hard drive capabilities and more control in the pocket. The basic idea was not unique to Simon; designers and builders of boards had been trying the three-fin principle for years. Older surfers will have no trouble remembering the Bonzers designed by The Campbell Brothers for Bing Surfboards in America and produced by

Gordon & Smith in Australia. Then there were the tri-fins of McTavish, Midget, Brewer and others. After being disillusioned with twin fins myself I put a centre box in between two outside fins for the sole purpose of being able to gain more power in a turn yet still retain the manoeuvreability of the twin. Reflecting on this makes one conclude that no one person is ever responsible for a particular breakthrough, but rather that several people come independently to the same conclusion at the same time. In research for this book I have come up against that several times. For example: Tom Blake is credited as having been the first to put a fin on a surfboard, but Tom says his device was really a keel and gives credit to Joe Quigg for the first fin. George 'Peanuts' Larson put a fin on a board before he met Tom. Perhaps the piece of apple crate that George used was not as refined as Blake's carefully shaped redwood, but it had a fin. I am sure you get my drift. Perhaps the same happened with nose lift, vees, twin fins and triple fins.

Anyway, as I was considered the rider of the vees and Mark Richards the

rider of the twins, so Simon Anderson's name is synonymous with three fins. The concept did wonders for Simon's surfing, putting sting into his more rounded turns. Simon called his boards 'thrusters', partly as a marketing device but also because they were deliberately designed to give more thrust out of a turn. It's like adding twin 'carbies or radial tyres to a car. The constant squirt action of the water flowing between the fins, coupled with the increased planing area in the tail, gave his boards instant acceleration.

Simon was an excellent surfer before the thruster — so much so that in 1977 he pulled off the Coke and Bells contests, even though the Coke was run in the tiniest waves possible. What made that contest such a triumph for Simon is that he is a big man, a solid 6'2" with plenty of meat on his bones, which means that it usually takes a fair size wave to get him up and moving; but then again it was run on his home ground in "the Alley" (Narrabeen). He grew up there in a typical working class family whose first priority was to provide happiness and a healthy lifestyle for

DARRELL JONES

Above: *Devotee of the three fin principle, Hans Hedemann on the North Shore.*

Left: *Talented Californian Sam George cutting back on a thruster: 90% of the best surfers in the world are surfing three fins in '83.*

CHUCK SCHMID

The north shore of Oahu, from Velzyland on the right to Haleiwa on the left.

Simon and his two brothers. Simon's elder brother Mark excelled at swimming and represented Australia at the 1968 Olympics in Mexico. But Simon was not interested in training, he wanted to go surfing. In the beginning Simon and Mark shared an old Malibu log, but with Mark at the pool much of the time it was Simon who used it most. Reluctantly Mr and Mrs Anderson gave Simon a new board for his 13th birthday and that was it. Simon was hooked. Going to Narrabeen High School with Mark Warren and Grant 'Dappa' Oliver a year above, and hot to ride anything that tubed, he found it difficult to stay at school. Whenever he noticed the other two surfers absent or the wind blowing offshore he would slip out the school side gate and head over to 'the Alley'. His simple rationale was that if they could do it, then he could too. It came as no great surprise to Mr and Mrs Anderson when Simon's grades began to slip. Consequently when he was 16 he left school and went to work in Brookvale for Shane Steadman, fixing dings in boards.

This was Shane's 'popout' era. The big department stores, especially Waltons, had taken an interest in surfing because they could see surfers as a potential market, but they had never really got involved in it until Shane introduced them to his 'Standard', a tiny mass-produced surfboard

which retailed for under $100. People had tried to mass-produce Malibus before but they had never been successful. The latest in mass-produced boards are the Morey-Doyle soft foam boards which have been labelled 'big marshmallows'; they don't hurt you when they hit you on the head, and they don't bruise the hips of the lady surfer, but because they cost much the same as a conventional custom-made board they haven't found a lot of buyers. Shane's popouts did; at the height of the boom in the surf season of 1973-74 some 5000 boards were eaten up by the surfing public. Shane's head shaper during this period was Terry Fitzgerald; by that stage he hung about at 'Narra' exclusively and he was the surfer who got Simon the job fixing dings.

In 1971 Simon won the Sydney junior titles and amazed himself by coming first in the Junior nationals. Shane's had become quite a stable of young talent, including Butch Cooney, Chris Young, Terry Fitzgerald and Frank Latta. By watching Fitz handle the tools and Latta's polished, step-by-step method, Simon was carving out ten 'Shane Standards' a day — and surfing. In 1972 he won both the State and Australian junior titles. Simon was building quite a reputation for himself, so much so that other Narrabeen surfers were starting to come to him for advice on their surfboards and were asking him to shape custom boards for them. Naturally Simon was a part of the Australian team for the San Diego world contest in 1972, along with several other Narrabeen hotties: Grant 'Dappa' Oliver, Mark Warren, Tony Hardwick, Col Smith and Terry Fitzgerald. The home trip through Hawaii failed to impress him; all he could think of was getting back to Narrabeen, having a few tubes at the Alley and a few down at the pub on Friday afternoon and getting stuck into the first batch of blanks. With every board his accuracy was improving, and through constantly surfing his shapes he was eliminating the variables he found undesirable. He finally came down to a clean, simple, rounded tail that is his preference to this day. In the early days his boards were incredibly thin; although he defended the thinness by talking about the desirability for sensitive rails, it was only a matter of time before his boards grew a little thicker and their fineness came from their rail shape.

In 1975, Simon left Shane. He had had enough of working for other people and together with the glasser from Shane's, Garth Cooper, opened the Energy Factory. Simon was the shaper and principal investor and Garth the manager and glasser. With a steadily growing clientele of discriminating surfers, the business flourished. Then came Simon's success in the 1977 Coke and Bells contests. This was a breaking point, because Simon had become a successful professional surfer who should have been giving his full time to his surfing, but his shaping was demanding a lot of his time. One had to suffer. Realising that his pro days were limited, he hit the contest trail in earnest. His financial interest in the Energy Factory was taken over by Steve Zollar with Simon continuing to shape as his time would allow. Zollar is an expert craftsman in fibreglass and resin, as seems to be the case with most older surfers who are also kneeboarders. In the mid 1970s Zollar had developed something of a cult following on the north side of Sydney with his accurately foiled fins and meticulous glass jobs, put out under the Clean and Natural label. Even though some kneeboarders couldn't sand a fin, at least they had an eye for detail.

From there Simon Anderson went from success to success. He won Bells in the biggest surf ever experienced in Australia for a major contest — a phenomenal feat of surfing, in which he defeated world champion Mark Richards and the best surfers in Australia. And he refined the details of his three fin 'thruster' until it became the most widely acclaimed board in the world and, naturally, widely copied. Two fins are good, Simon argued; three are better. By combining the best features of the twin fin and the single fin, and by shaping his boards to make use of his fin configuration, Simon took the evolution of the surfboard a step further.

The question is: what next? ●

DAVE EPPERSON

SURFER MAGAZINE

Left: *Three fins combine the best of both the twins (loose quick movements) and the single fin (powerful decisive turns).*

Above: *Deep in Mexico: continually waves break in the correct form on every point and beach in the world at the right time: the trick is being there.*

Below: *Johnathan Paarman stretches out in the quality typical of Durban, South Africa.*

PAT FLANAGAN

Gavin Rudolph at Durban, South Africa: In '71 Rudolph opened everyone's eyes to South African surfers when he won the Smirnoff Contest in Hawaii.

Below: *Line-up at Jeffreys Bay.*

JEFF DIVINE

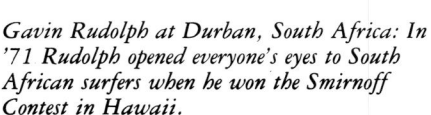

Left: *Paarman excells in big powerful waves similar to his home breaks in Cape Town, S.A.*

Below: *Powerful Wollongong, N.S.W., local Chris (Critta) Byrn momentarily taking his board out of trim in readiness for the oncoming Jeffrey's section.*

STEVE SAKAMOTO

Top: *Kneeboard riding has evolved as much as surfboard riding, as this photo of an unidentified Californian shows.*

Below: *Bruce Pemberton at Dee Why Point.*

PETER CRAWFORD

KNEEBOARDS & WAVE SKIS

Kneeboarders have always seemed to me to be the purest surfers of all. They hunt waves with a passion, avoid the competitive excesses of the board riders, and usually seem to surf purely for the joy of it. Board riders often get to know the kneeboarders in their area and grow to respect their grassroots enthusiasm. When a set comes it's always the board riders who jockey for take-off position and get the first waves; and then, inevitably, when you are paddling back out you'll come across a kneeboarder making the most of that one freak wave which came through after all the others! So, like a lot of other surfers, I've come to admire the kneeboard fraternity . . . or 'cripples', as we call them.

For some reason most people believe that George Greenough is the father of kneeboarding in Australia, but this is not true. For instance, there were competent surfers who rode waves on their knees in my district long before George ever came to Australia. In our group at Collaroy in the '60s there were always two kneeboard riders, Barry Stark and Rick Wright. 'Starky' was the first kneeboarder I knew of, and he turned Rick Wright on. And that image I mentioned of paddling back out comes from Long Reef's first bombora, where in my mind's eye I can see 'Starky' taking off on a wild six-footer, tucking his flippers underneath him, and digging his knees into a big bottom turn. Ricky Wright was big and gangly and a lot more free form, futuristic perhaps, as his style was in the direction both board and knee riders took. The only other person to my knowledge who rode waves on his knees in those days was Brian Tetstall from North Curl Curl. Like the other two, he had independently developed his style of surfing on his knees from lying down on coolites and belly-boards, or 'Paipo' boards as they were called in Hawaii. The Paipo is still very popular, and many 'pure' surfers use these short, exceptionally thin plywood slabs and a pair of fins for surfing everything from Sunset to Makapuu, which is a windward side surf break on Oahu, ideal for boogie boards and bodysurfing. The popu-

larity of the Morey boogie board is further evidence of how many people like this type of surfing. Some of the finest watermen in the Islands have preferred it; Wally Froiseth and Val Valentine are two names from the old days that spring to mind.

Kneeboards evolved much as surfboards did, by constant experimentation, testing, innovation. Barry Stark started off with the front half of a cut-off balsa log; by 1963 he was riding a three-stringer, six-foot stick shaped by Kenno. I remember telling him how good Brian Tetstall from Curl Curl was. Tetstall had an influence upon one of the finest kneeboarders of all, Peter Crawford. The Crawford family had lived at Bondi but when they moved to Dee Why it was natural that young Peter should copy the local kneeboarder, so Brian Tetstall was Peter's first hero. When the southerly came blasting through, all the 'Curly' surfers would climb over the hill to Dee Why. By watching Tetstall there on his thin balsa slab, Peter's interest was kindled beyond the rubber mat he had found on his way back from the beach once when he lived in Bondi; he became a kneeboarder.

Peter Crawford lost no time in graduating up to Dee Why point. He learnt respect for the ocean and earned the respect of his peers. When Greenough came along in 1966 he was an inspiration to Peter, who could see in George the way development came through design. He was impressed by George's refined fins and flexible spoons but could not get them to work in the mushy beach break encountered most of the time at Dee Why. For this reason he developed a wider board which would plane across flat spots, but kept it nice and thin in order to use the rail for turns.

The first contest for kneeboarders was held at Dee Why in 1970, when a bunch of forty to fifty 'cripples' gathered in order to battle it out for a new Shane 'shoe', which was Shane Steadman's answer to the Greenough spoon. Peter Crawford won the 'shoe', and that was the beginning of an in-

credible career. He won that first contest on the same sort of 'slab' (so named by Midget) that he rides today, an exceptionally wide 5'8'' glider. Like the early surfboard contests, the kneeboard competition was an excellent design forum where everyone compared each other's designs. Ross Warr and the Newcastle guys were down in full force and were so impressed with Peter Crawford's slabs that they ended up riding similar versions in Newcastle, where the surf was similar to Sydney's.

The first Duranbah kneeboard contest was held on the Gold Coast in 1971. Peter Crawford won and was to go on to win it six or seven times. It is still the most prestigious kneeboard contest held in Australia, and Peter Crawford's tale of the first one is a classic. The early '70s were the very beginning of the pro contest scene and the Duranbah kneeboard contest offered a purse of $200. Naturally this amount was worth a good deal more then than it is today and attracted the interest of the pro surfboard riders. Only one desperate ever seriously tried for the Duranbah bait, and that was Michael Peterson. With his excellent wave judgement he defeated everyone until he came up against Peter Crawford in the semi. Peter had developed kneeboard knowledge and cunning and successfully dusted Michael Peterson, with the result that Michael stomped angrily off the beach.

Around this time the Australian Surfriders' Association decided that kneeboards were growing so much in popularity that the State and Australian board riding titles should incorporate kneeboards. The first Aussie kneeboard titles were held on the Gold Coast in 1974. A talented and aggressive big wave rider from Manly, Graham 'Flip' Wilson, romped home. The next Australian championship, held at Victor Harbour in South Australia, was won by a transplant American, Kevin Barr. Things were hotting up for kneeboarders, with contests in all states plus pro meets in Victoria and NSW.

The Point Leo contest, in Victoria,

GARY MURANE

Peter Crawford moving fast through the 'suck up' at Dee Why Point.

was a major event; in 1975 Neil Luke was the leading southern entrant and came very close to snatching the $400 prize from Peter Crawford. Back in NSW the scene was set for an incredible duel for $1000 first prize between Peter Crawford and the rapidly rising talent of Steve Artis. As sometimes happens in competition Peter Crawford had the waves against him; right in the dying seconds of the final, just as the hooter was sounding the end, Steve took off on the wave of the day! He won. Steve's board design was a refinement of Peter Crawford's slab but had a narrower, rounded pin tail, similar to that of a conventional board. He has found this more suitable to the hard-driving turns and deep tubes that typify his style.

The next year, 1976, was an interesting year for kneeriders and will be remembered well by the finalists in the Australian championships. When they were all assembled they were told that the 360 degree turn was not a 'functional manoeuvre' and would not be judged. This didn't say much for the contest system and signified the end of Peter Crawford's involvement — he was the only one who, at that time, had perfected this stunning manoeuvre. Anyone who

has surfed Dee Why point to any degree is familiar with what the locals call the 'suck-up' — a shallow rock ledge that causes the wave to pitch. It was this which gave Peter the perfect situation for experimenting with his 360 degree turn. The actual track to take came to him in a dream, but then he had to put it into practice. This is how he describes it: "When the curl is throwing, you start your bottom turn and are heading up the face normally. Then things really happen quickly, it just clicks in your brain so you bury your rail and just keep burying it right around. It's a full turn, a bottom turn that just keeps on going on the rail all the way around. I really had to discipline myself to keep on turning. I'd see the situation all the time and go for a re-entry or something, but I could see it in my mind and just had to discipline myself to keep turning."

Kneeboard action was really brewing on the south side of Sydney, and Maroubra had a big mob of dedicated surfers on their knees as well as standing up. In the 1979 Australian kneeboard contest David Parks from Maroubra put it all together beautifully to take first prize. He had a good run until a North Narrabeen boy, Michael Novakoff, leapt into the

spotlight with his flashy, unique style of heavy weighting and unweighting of edges linked up with lightning fast turns and every manoeuvre in the book. Novakoff won the first world championship in 1982 at Duranbah and will probably go on to win for quite a while. His tri-fin boards, based on Peter Crawford's width and Steve Artis' templates, give him tons of drive and make him the boy to beat — if his knees hold out. Many kneeboard riders have had serious problems with their knees, especially with cartileges and constant fluid on the knees. This problem used to be associated with women polishing floors and was called 'housewives' knee', but now thousands of surfing kids run the risk of getting the same complaint.

Kneeboard riders have one great advantage over standup surfers; they are able to fit inside waves that others can't. I will always remember Peter Crawford's story of one wave he caught with his friend, Boyd Kellner, at Dee Why point. The two of them were locked in the tube, rail to rail, for the entire ride from first rock through the suck-up to the other side. Kneeboarders have always impressed me as dedicated surfers who surf for their own enjoyment —

PETER CRAWFORD

DANA EDMUNDS

PETER CRAWFORD

Above: *Knee riders can fit inside waves that stand up surfers can't.*

Above right: *Maui's Ray Pina up and flying in the islands.*

Right: *Peter Stanton at North Narrabeen making the most of that one freak wave.*

perhaps it was the Greenoughs, Crawfords, Zollars, Wilsons, Stantons and Ken Hortons who gave me this impression. They are all highly talented, individual surfers.

The surf ski is an Australian invention and most of its development has taken place on the Australian east coast. The first ski was fashioned back in the early 1930s by Dr G.A. 'Saxon' Crackenthorp, who found he couldn't manage a conventional surfboard and decided to create one which he could ride sitting down. It was a cedar plank about eight feet long, twenty-eight inches wide, and six inches deep. This gave it a low centre of gravity which made it easy to balance, and the use of a paddle made it easier to get out through the surf. Others began to take the ski up and slowly refined it; the first hollow skis were produced, and then Mickey Morris and Billy Langford of Maroubra built the first double ski. By 1937 the ski had been adopted as standard lifesaving equipment by the Surf Life Saving Association, and since then it has been used regularly for rescue work and as a competitive craft in surf carnivals.

Little thought was given to the problem of designing a ski which would be primarily a wave-rider until Hayden Kenny, from Maroochydore in Queensland, built one on the principles of a good friend of his from California, Merve Larson. Wave skis, as they were known, never did take off in California. Merve Larson appeared in early surf movies riding across the waves at Santa Cruz in his Kayak, but apart from him and a few close friends no-one seemed to be interested. In later years, Shane Steadman sent plenty of his hollow skis to both California and Hawaii but the interest was just not there. Only in South Africa, Australia and England, (where a few diehards braved the cold) did the movement flourish. In Australia, because Hayden Kenny lived on the Sunshine Coast, the popularity of the wave ski didn't extend far beyond the Sunshine and Gold Coasts. The Adler family put out a hollow ski on the Gold Coast called the 'Free and Easy'. A few of these and a few Hayden skis filtered down to Sydney but anyone who was interested had to do a lot of searching to find one. These skis were between 9'6" and 10'6" in length and 21" to 26" wide. They had the same thickness throughout their length and the footwells were wide apart. Most had deep seatwells and the outlines were blunt; some had square noses and

sides which were almost straight. They varied a lot in bottom curve, some being almost flat while others had lots of curve. This general size and shape gave them a somewhat limited performance which consisted either of coming straight into the beach or of taking off on the angle, pointing along the wave and riding it in a straight line. All the skis of this time were difficult to turn quickly and fin size was often reduced to gain manoeuvarability. While this meant that the skis were easier to turn it also meant that they would sideslip and become dangerous in crowded conditions.

In the early '70s Michael Petrie was a keen board rider who had been into surfing since he was 12 years old and who eventually landed a cushy job as a lifeguard on Queenscliff Beach in Sydney. Several times Mick was caught out by the head lifeguard for boardriding while on duty and was finally given a warning that if he did it again he would lose his job. So, sitting on the beach watching ski rider Max Lawson make big, slow turns on the wave face, Michael was inspired to go and get a ski — a couple of airline steward mates had one, an 8'6" moulded Byron Bay surf craft, and Mick convinced them to sell it to

Above: *Dan Gildea about to disappear in a clean envelope.*

Above right: *Ben Severson and one other boogie rider in the green room.*

Right: *Wally Froiseth with Flippers on at Makaha in the '40s: the balsa paipo board 4' long with twin fins was the forerunner of the present-day kneeboard.*

him. Naturally he wrote RESCUE in big bold letters on the bottom and everyone was happy. He spent many 8-hour shifts as paid lifeguard contentedly riding waves with Lawson and slowly began to realise the potential of the ski.

One day he and Lawson were sitting beyond the break waiting for the next set when up paddled another ski rider they had heard about, Roger Shackleton. Roger was riding one of Bill Wallace's skis, handshaped in the traditional surfboard method, and it had a seat belt. Roger explained how the seat belt would hold you on in a hard turn and when you got tipped upside down you could roll right back up. The trim young Englishman, who had migrated to Australia at the age of twenty, proceeded to roll over and show Lawson and Petrie how it was done. Roger had not really perfected the Eskimo roll at this stage and when bubbles and panic were obviously getting the better of him Michael Petrie leapt off his ski and righted him! Still, the theory sounded good to Mick and he agreed to meet Roger at his Brookvale factory, where Roger would hand-shape him a new ski and put on a seat belt. Mick Petrie went on to become the Australian ski champion. Lawson was

not so impressed with the new-fangled seat belt and continues to surf without one to this day. But the seat belt gained in popularity, just as the legrope did with surfboards, and today it is widely accepted by ski riders.

Roger Shackleton denies that he was the first rider to use a seat belt; he suggests that in different spots along the east coast many individuals put seat belts on their skis quite independently of each other. This sounds feasible, as we know the first fin was put on a surfboard in much the same way, with many surfers reaching the same solution at the same time. One breakthrough Roger will take credit for is the shape of the fin now accepted on all skis, which came about through trial and error. The early wave skis were finless; this made possible radical turns and manoeuvres like the 360-degree turn and backward surfing. However, the drawbacks to surfing without a fin became apparent as ski riders started to do manoeuvres like surfboard riders: cutbacks, re-entries and, most important of all, tube rides.

It was probably the desire to tube ride that caused the ultimate demise of the finless wave ski and brought

about the change to the surfboard-style finned ski we know today. The finless ski allowed the rider to position himself for tube rides but if any part of the lip landed on the ski or the rider the ski would slide uncontrollably. The riders were unable to develop their skills any further until some way could be found to maintain forward momentum and stop sideslip. The obvious answer was the fin, but the shape of the skis didn't suit the use of a conventional surfboard fin as they were too straight and too wide in the base. This sparked the development which resulted in today's designs.

The old-style skis lacked curve in almost every aspect of their shape and most turning was done by spinning the ski on its flat bottom until it pointed in the right direction. The standard fin made this difficult because all the fins were either too big and made the ski stiff or too short and allowed the ski to slide out unexpectedly. Shackleton's answer was to design the now universally accepted Raider surf ski fin. The principle is simple. "We needed a small area fin to allow the skis to turn but we also needed a deep fin, because the short fin allowed the skis to slide. By reversing the normal design and put-

Above & sequence: *Michael Petrie displaying clean decisive surfing. The modern wave ski is a far cry from Saxon Crackenthorp's invention of the '30s.*

PHOTOS PETER CRAWFORD

ting all the area at the bottom of the fin and not the top, we could achieve the desired effect." This fin design got performance moving along in the right direction and slowly skis started to look more like surfboards. There were major changes to plan shape and length, plus the introduction of a 45 degree chamfered rail with an edge instead of a soft egg profile.

These changes brought about another set of problems. As the body weight has to be wholly supported by the ski, buoyancy is of paramount importance. The new skis were getting shorter, narrower and thinner, and therefore less buoyant. This made them very difficult to paddle out through a break. The next step was to increase the width to maintain stability and buoyancy; this didn't improve performance much, and development would have slowed at this point if Doug Holliday hadn't built the Dart in Newcastle.

The Dart followed the general design ideas of the time except in one major area: the centre of the ski was built up while the sides were kept to normal thickness. This gave a tremendous increase in buoyancy, which assisted paddling but did not affect performance adversely. This proved

that the thickness of a ski could differ radically from surfboard design while still producing good performance. With wave skis becoming more popular, pressure could be applied to the blank manufacturers to increase the width and the thickness. The results can be seen in modern high-performance skis which are thick at the back and thin at the front — quite logical when you consider that most of the rider's weight is in the seat. This has allowed manufacturers to reduce the length still further and the average length would now be around 7'6". This will float a person of 14½ stone (or 92 kilos).

The smallest ski Shackleton has made is 6'4" which is being ridden by the 1982 Australian champion, John Christensen. In winning that championship John stopped an almost uninterrupted run of contest successes by Mike Petrie, who won the very first wave ski event back in 1978 at Long Reef. The 1980 Australian titles were held at Dee Why with the impressive sponsorship of Peter Stuyvesant, who put up a $5,000 purse and made a documentary of the event; Petrie won. However, a year later Stuyvesant was deterred from sponsoring the 1981 Australian championships by the interference of

Warringah and Manly Councils, who refused to grant permission to a promotion by a cigarette manufacturer on their beaches. Petrie failed to win that championship when the final was held in 2 foot waves at Fairy Bower; a talented Central Coast ski rider, Paul Wise, defeated him on a countback.

It seems logical that older surfboard riders should make exceptionally good ski riders. The contest results of Mal Saunders and John Payne, on Sydney's north side, are examples of this. However, the advent of wave skis has opened up surfing to a previously non-surfing section of the community which has a genuine desire to get fit and enjoy riding waves. The only problem is that a lot of them have little understanding of the ocean or waves or of accepted manners in the water. This means ski riders tend to be regarded by board riders as kooks on goat boats who constantly drop-in on other surfers. Ski riders will have to make a genuine effort to be more careful of the rights of other surfers if they are to achieve respect in the water.

●

175

PETER CRAWFORD

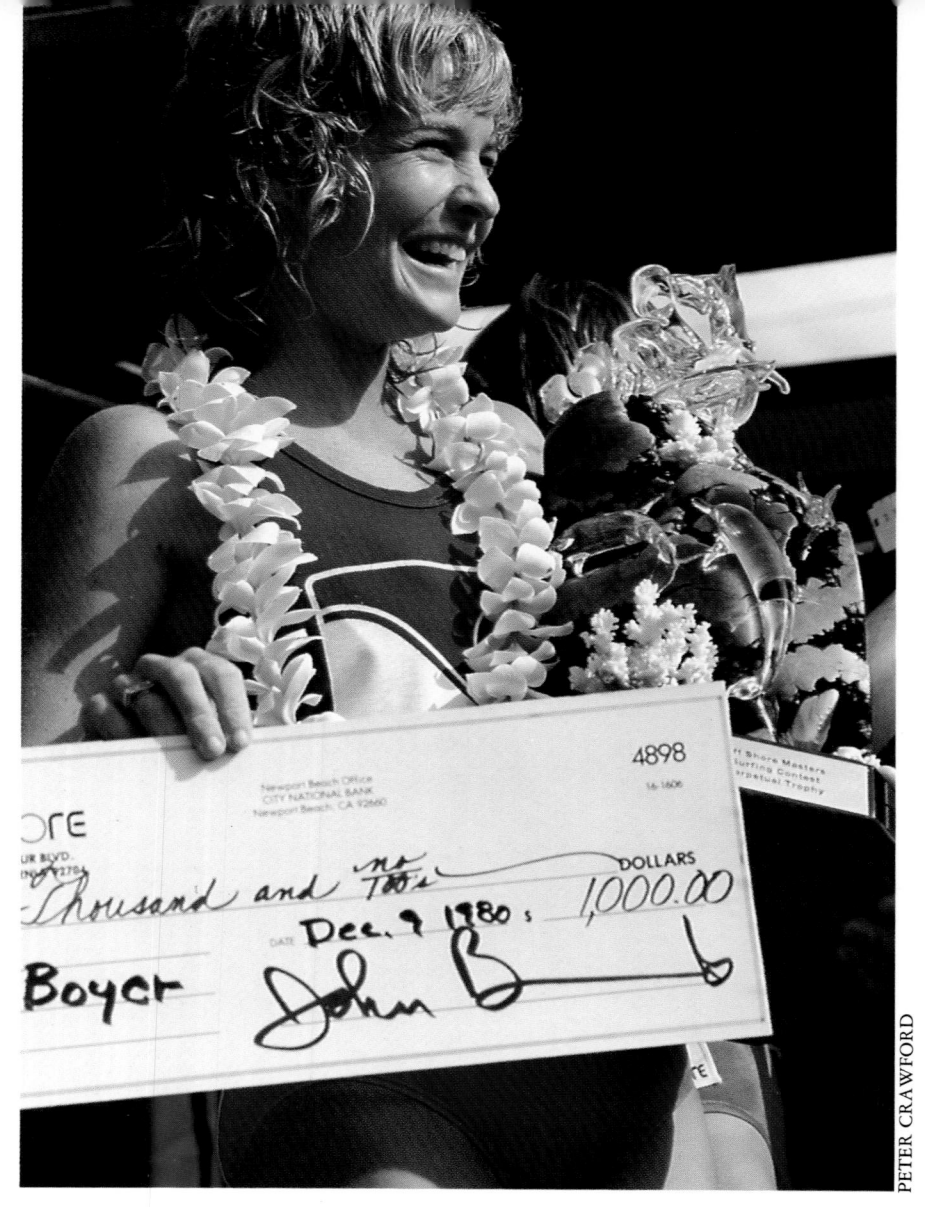

Above & below: *Lynne Boyer: professional surfer. A lady with tons of natural talent.*

JEFF DIVINE

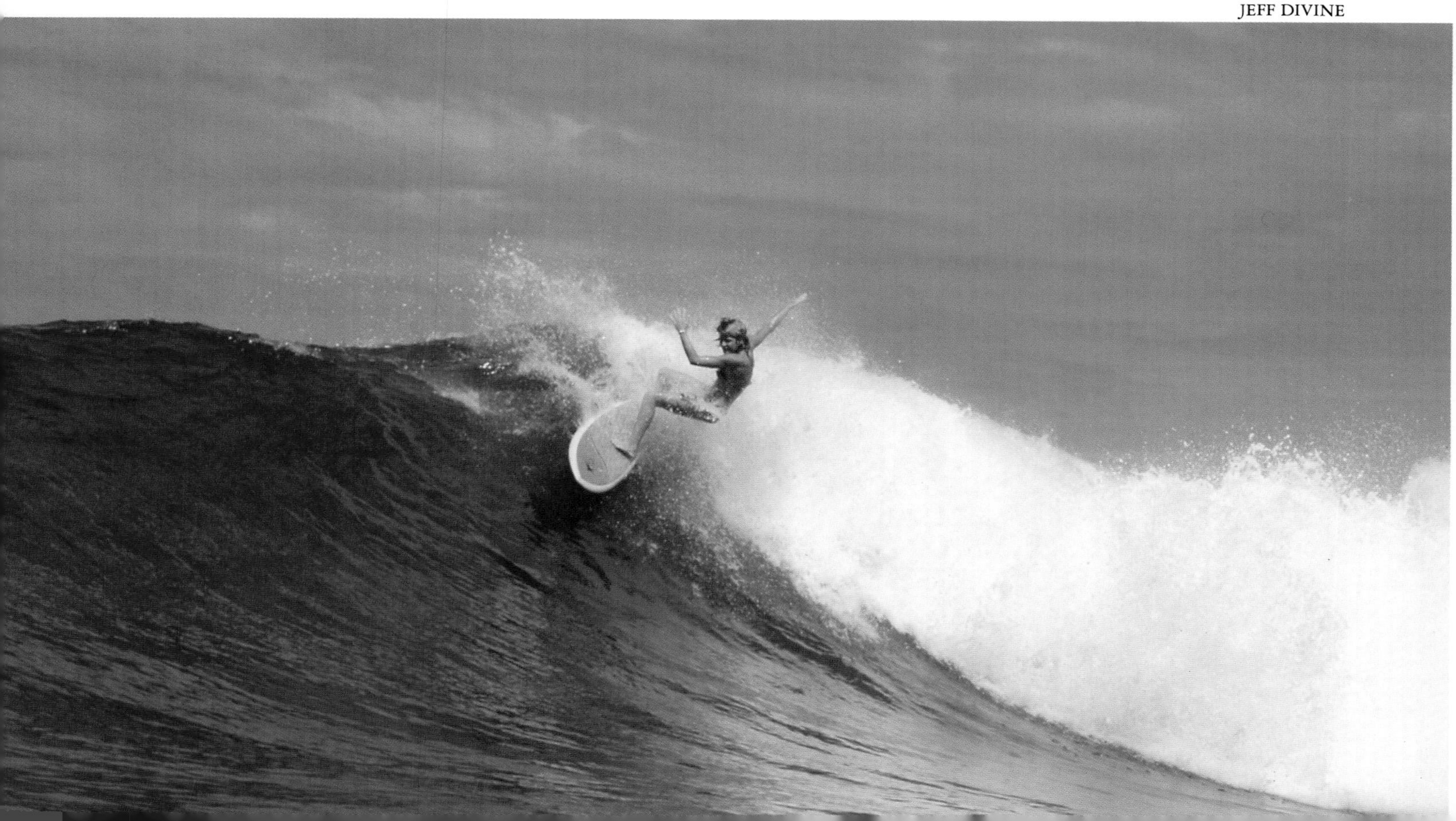

SURFER GIRLS

Surfing is often thought of as a male sport, but in fact women have been surfing in California since the early 1920s and today there are women surfers in every surfing country in the world. Like the men, they range from rank amateurs to gifted professionals. And though women may once have been included in surf contests in a somewhat patronising way, these days they compete because they have truly earned the right to.

One of the earliest women surfers was Mary Ann Hawkins, a Californian who showed very graceful form in the surf. She was the first of a long line which stretched down in the 'sixties, to Marge Calhoun and her daughters and of course Linda Benson, followed by some of the top professional surfers today. The first Australian to ride a surfboard was, in fact, a woman: Isabel Letham, who rode tandem with Duke Kahanamoku when the Duke introduced Australians to board riding at Freshwater in 1915. With the advent of the Gidget movies and films like *Puberty Blues* the popularisation of surfing among women was complete.

No-one would ever be able to say that the early surfer girls didn't have style, if lacking a little in ability. Linda Merrill was the classic example, displaying feminine ballet-like artistry as she danced from the tail to the nose on Californian and Hawaiian waves in the early 'sixties. In Australia there was Phyllis O'Donnell,

JOHN LYMAN

who played a lot of competitive squash and showed the same determined style to win in her surfing. Gail Couper was a quiet country girl from Lorne, near Torquay, who developed into a talented woman surfer. Gail gained a lot of confidence from her friendship with Joyce Hoffman, who was the 1966-67 world champion. Joyce grew up in an ideal environment to become a champion surfer, right on the beach in Capistrano, California; she had a father who was totally involved in surfing and an uncle who would go anywhere to ride a clean wave. Joyce and Joey Hamisaki, from Hawaii, were probably the first well-respected girl surfers. Joyce was finally dethroned by a younger lady, Margo Godfrey, also from southern California, surfing on a nine-foot plank. Little Margo did all the same things as Joyce but with more of a will to win, being the determined underdog. In 1968 she finally broke through and topped the Western Surfing Association's ratings by just beating Joyce Hoffman on several occasions.

The 1969 Puerto Rican world contest was an easy victory for Margo. Her

BEV MORGAN

WARREN BOLSTER

Top: *A real pleasure to go surfing with.*

Above: *Kim Mearig punching into a powerful cutback at V-land.*

Left: *Linda Merril displayed feminine ballet-like artistry dancing from the tail to the nose in the mid '60s.*

There are surfer girls and surfer girls.

ART BREWER

SURFER MAGAZINE

style was so similar to the other hot kids on the Californian team that everyone was talking about "the girl who surfed as good as a guy". In keeping with the general anti-contest feeling in the late 'sixties and early 'seventies, Margo stopped competing altogether and went surfing for her own enjoyment, developing more wave judgment and putting the finishing touches to her boyish style of riding. In 1975, after three years of married life on Kauai, professional contests started and Margo was the first pro woman surfer. She won the W.I.S.A. Hang Ten Championships at Malibu and also the women's event at the Smirnoff, in Hawaii. In 1976 she did it again and in 1977, when the I.P.S. circuit began and included girls' events, she was crowned women's world champion with a win in the Bells contest, the Coke, the Brazil International and the Women's Masters in Hawaii. In 1978 she won the Stubbies and the Bells, lost the Surfabout, but topped the overall Surfer magazine poll ten years after she had first topped it in 1968. It had been an illustrious career of complete domination of her sport unequalled by any male surfer.

In 1979 Margo decided not to go on the circuit and spent the full year with her husband on Kauai, building a new house. In 1980 the dollars were too attractive and she made another successful comeback to go on to win the Bells contest and still be rated No. 1 on the I.P.S. ratings. Margo has only a slight build, but she was a bit of a tomboy in her youth and perhaps that helped her to be 'one of the boys' and to develop a style similar to that of any other aspiring young surfer. After getting involved in health foods and yoga and all the normal diversities of the 'back to nature' surf stars of the early '70s, Margo discovered answers in the teachings of Christ. Living on the island of Kauai with her family, working hard, teaching surfing for the resort hotel, developing spiritually and mentally, she seems to have achieved real contentment and happiness. In the summer of 1982 she had a son, and Margo is now finding being a mother as satisfying as being world champion.

The reason women's events were included in the early professional meets was purely sexist. The American TV

networks required women to fill out the programme and serve up surfing as good mass entertainment. This media attitude, however, is slowly changing. There is no doubt that more and more young girls are being attracted to surfing, and their parents don't discourage them as much as they used to. The advent of professional surfing has helped this process; so has the twin-fin board, being small, light and easier to turn than the single-fin board. But perhaps the people who have been mainly responsible for this change in public attitude are the professional women surfers themselves. Two examples of this are Jericho Poppler and Rella Sunn, two ladies who have worked hard at producing this social change. Jericho grew up in a beach suburb in California, Rella in Hawaii. In the mid 'sixties they were both regarded as freaks in the almost totally male-dominated sport. But then, when the growth of professionalism enabled them to travel and give their views to the world, they had little trouble raising sponsors. They are both very dynamic ladies who see women who start surfing as much more honest than men. "Boys are out to prove

178

Below Right: *Place-getters in '60s US Surfing Championships. A few familiar faces. 2nd from left Margo Godfrey next to Joyce Hoffman and a bewildered Jericho Poppler (2nd from right).*

Below: *Rella Sunn. Driving forehand turn by the first lady of Hawaiian surfing.*

Below Right: *Linda Benson at Makaha. Queen of the '60 surfer girls.*

SURFER MAGAZINE

LEROY GRANNIS

JEFF DIVINE

they can conquer the waves and demonstrate their particular ability to their peer groups. But girls are more like artists who work their choreography to the waves and go out to dance routines set up by the situation the waves dictate," they say. This attitude is both poetic and interesting, especially when you consider the beating anyone takes to become a competent surfer. There is no question that women should have always been able to surf as well as men, but the simple fact that they didn't meant they were given a separate contest and treated as freaks just a few years ago. Perhaps if the contests had been open to both sexes we would have seen a greater number of talented women surfers before this. It's probably only speculation, but I believe the time will come in competitive surfing, as it has in other sports, when the person's sex will be interesting but no more. The real issue will be the amount of talent someone has, whether the person is female or male.

There are hundreds and probably thousands of these new-breed girl surfers around the world. Pam Burridge, for instance, lives on the north

side of Sydney and was one of the first pupils to enroll in my surf school at the end of the 'seventies. In 1982 I caught up with her again after a five-year break; she had just returned from the surf contests in Japan. She epitomises the new breed of stoked surf rat who, until she interrupted her schooling to go pro, could be found in the surf every morning, hungry for one last set before the school bell. Pam is now gaining an education through travel. She is a gifted surfer who has earned respect everywhere by surfing every wave as well as she can and by not expecting any special treatment because of her sex. The fact that she is the No. 1 Aussie girl surfer is great, but it does not impress the locals on the northside too much.

Pam started out like everyone else, on a rubber mat, enjoying the ocean for what it was. Her parents did not discourage her interest in surfing when she entered her 'teens but instead took advantage of the surf school, where she got advice on how to handle the tricky situations that crop up. She was a perfectly normal girl, but with tremendous enthusiasm; she

was determined to become a competent surfer and it came as no surprise to me when she won the women's events of her local club, or that she consistently made the finals of the men's Manly Pacific interclub contests. In 1979, 1980, and 1981 she won the NSW titles. In 1980 and 1981 she won the Australian titles, giving her the perfect foundation to build a career as a professional surfer.

The picture is looking pretty good for Pam Burridge. She has generous sponsors who take care of everything, including air travel and accommodation, and what she wins in prize money is all hers. It is a fantastic opportunity to learn from travelling the world and experiencing different cultures. I hope she will end up living in Australia, where the society can benefit from Pam, her education and her forward thinking.

●

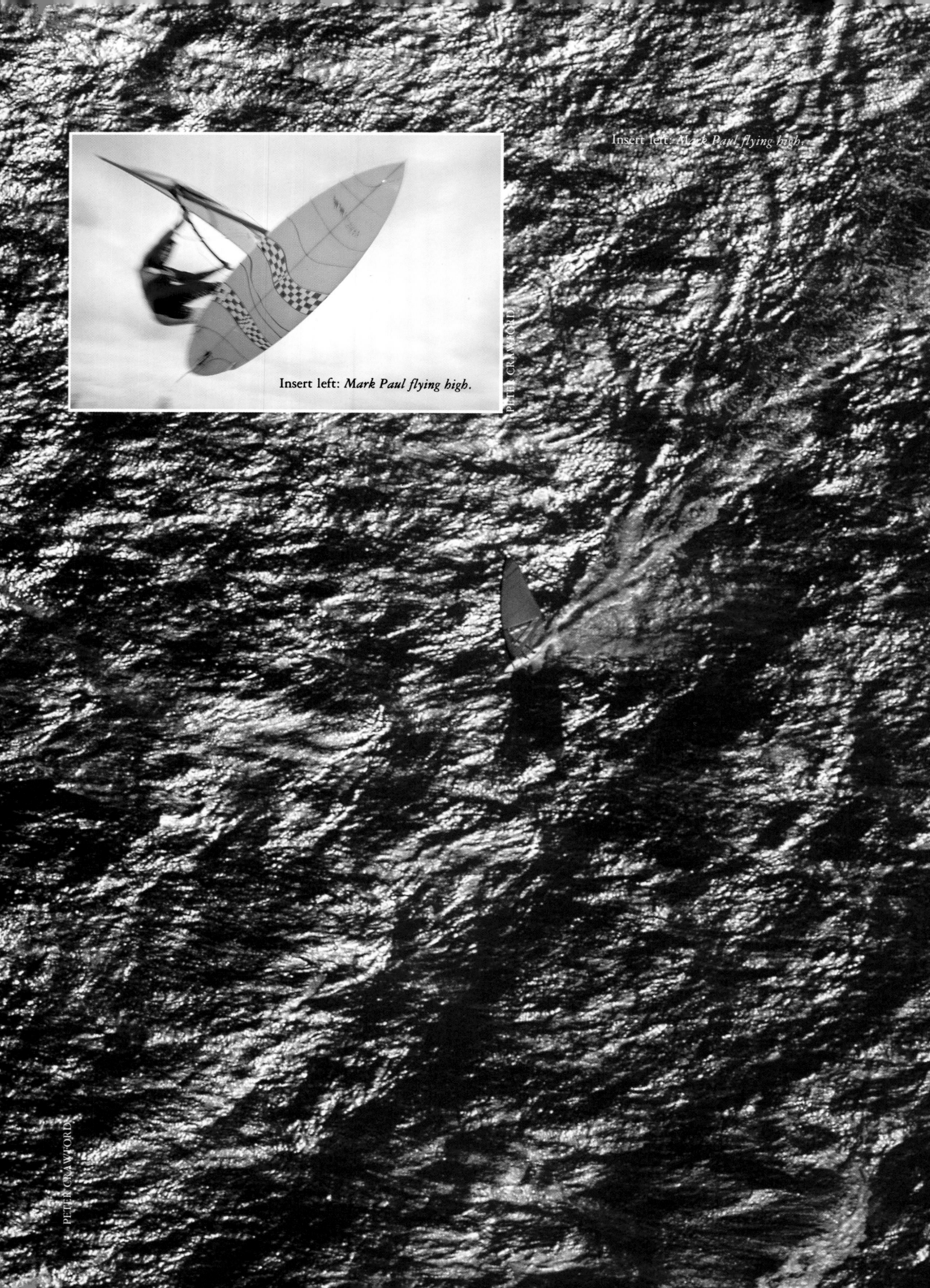

Insert left: *Mark Paul flying high.*

Insert left: *Mark Paul flying high.*

PETER CRAWFORD

PETER CRAWFORD

PETER CRAWFORD

SURFING WITH A SAIL

All surfers, at some stage of their involvement, have asked themselves why they go surfing, especially when the waves are bad for a month with the wind constantly onshore. Sometimes being a surfer is a frustrating bloody nightmare. It's important that we keep surfing in perspective. The main reason we all ride waves is because it's fun, but I feel that if we keep going in the direction we are headed this essential ingredient in surfing will be lost. In some places it has already happened. When you paddle out in some breaks, especially in densely populated areas like Hawaii or Sydney, you can feel the bad vibe. Not long ago at the Pipeline I started hooting with glee when another surfer got an incredibly good ride. A couple of hotties looked at me as though I was from another planet when really I was just from another era.

As the number of people surfing increases every year, so do the pressures. The development of surfboard design is allowing more and more people to reach a high level of competence, which leads them to search for better quality waves. The fact that they can now appreciate and ride waves which once might have been beyond them will eventually bring about a conflict situation where too many surfers are competing for the same number of quality waves.

This combination of factors would seem to indicate that surfing will eventually self-destruct unless we look at ways of avoiding the conflict which is approaching. As I see it, we have a choice between three things:
1. Making waves.
2. Building artificial reefs.
3. Sailboarding or windsurfing.

Let's take the first one, making waves. It's been tried for some 20

Right: Sails of nylon against the sails of Sydney's Opera House.

years now. In the heart of the desert in Arizona there is a machine that produces waves, and Japan has an indoor surf stadium, but to my knowledge man has not yet found a way to produce quality surfable waves. For some years now Peter Drouyn has been running around with plans for a surfatorium on the Gold Coast's inland waterways, and this looks interesting. But so far the cost has stopped it being feasible. We'll have to look at alternatives.

One possibility is artificial reefs. You only have to live in Sydney, as I have on and off for the past 30 years, to become aware of the real problem with the local surf: there is an abundance of good swell, but that does not get converted into quality waves because of the lack of acceptable ocean bottom shapes along the coast. The swells are there but the waves aren't. Artificial reefs would remedy that; they could be built at such a height and in such a direction so as to create a rideable wave whenever the swell was right. Extensive studies have been made in the United States, Hawaii and Australia of this idea and I feel confident that, one day, it will be converted into a reality. But once again the cost is a problem.

Then there is sailboarding. I personally think this is the most likely immediate answer. Sailboarding developed in the mid '70s, basically by adding a sail to a surfboard, an idea Tom Blake had been working on in the 1930s. Since then it has become much more sophisticated and has spread throughout the world.

What, precisely, is it? Bob McTavish has given an excellent description of it in an article he wrote for *Tracks:*

"OK. A definition of surfing. Well it's got to have something to do with the surf obviously. I mean, clubbies racing in and out through it is enough for the newspapers to call it surfing. Most tourist brochures call bobbing up and down between flags — 'surfing'. Obviously that's not good enough for us.

"How about 'The art of riding waves'. Fairly close. Gets us into the guts of it. 'Art' indicates the difficulty, the variety, the personalisation. 'Riding waves' zeroes it in on the part that counts, and cuts out all the racers and bobbers.

Let's go a bit further before seeing how windsurfing fits in. Let's try

PETER CRAWFORD

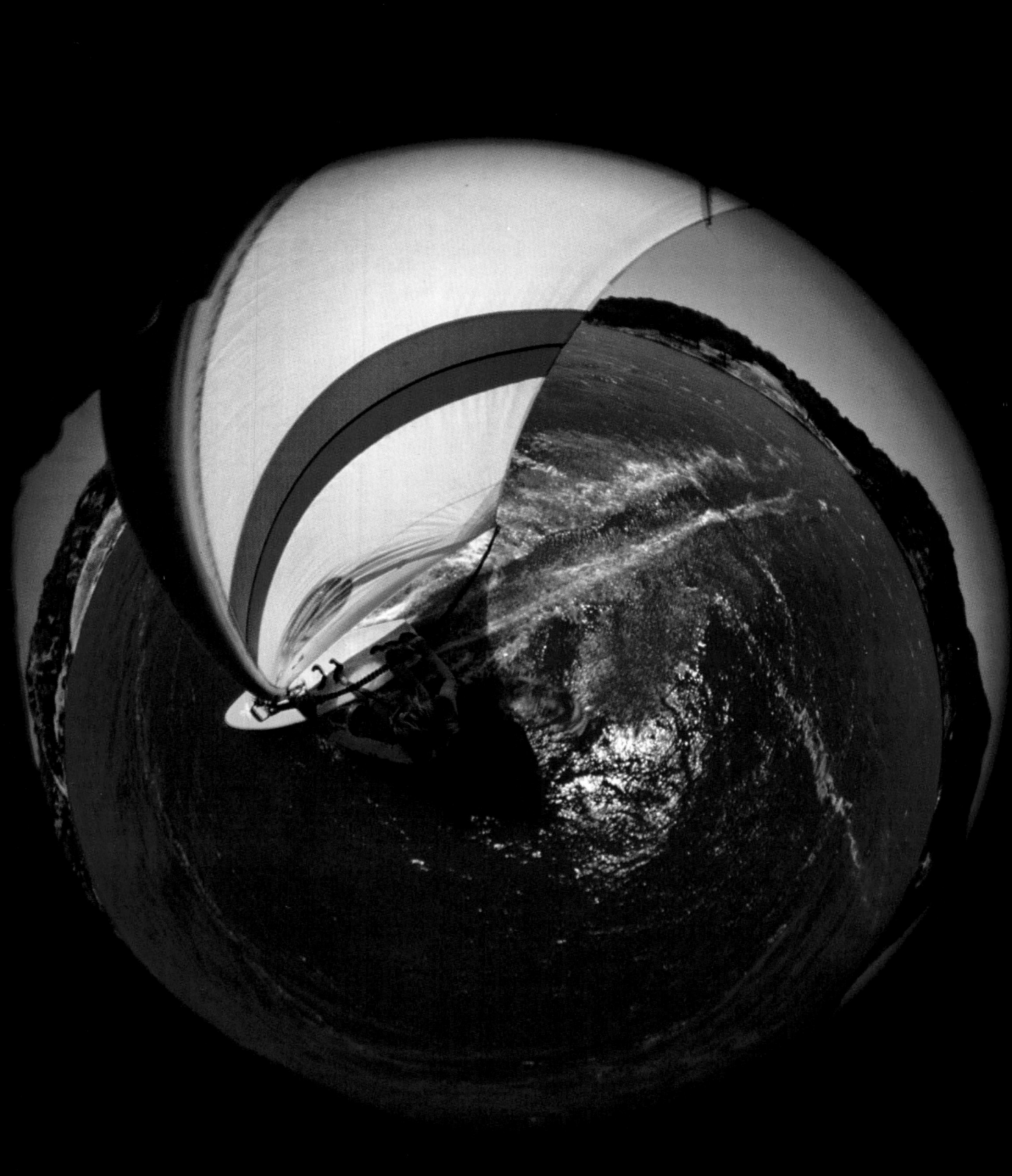

George Greenough's unique perspective from a camera mounted on top of his mast.

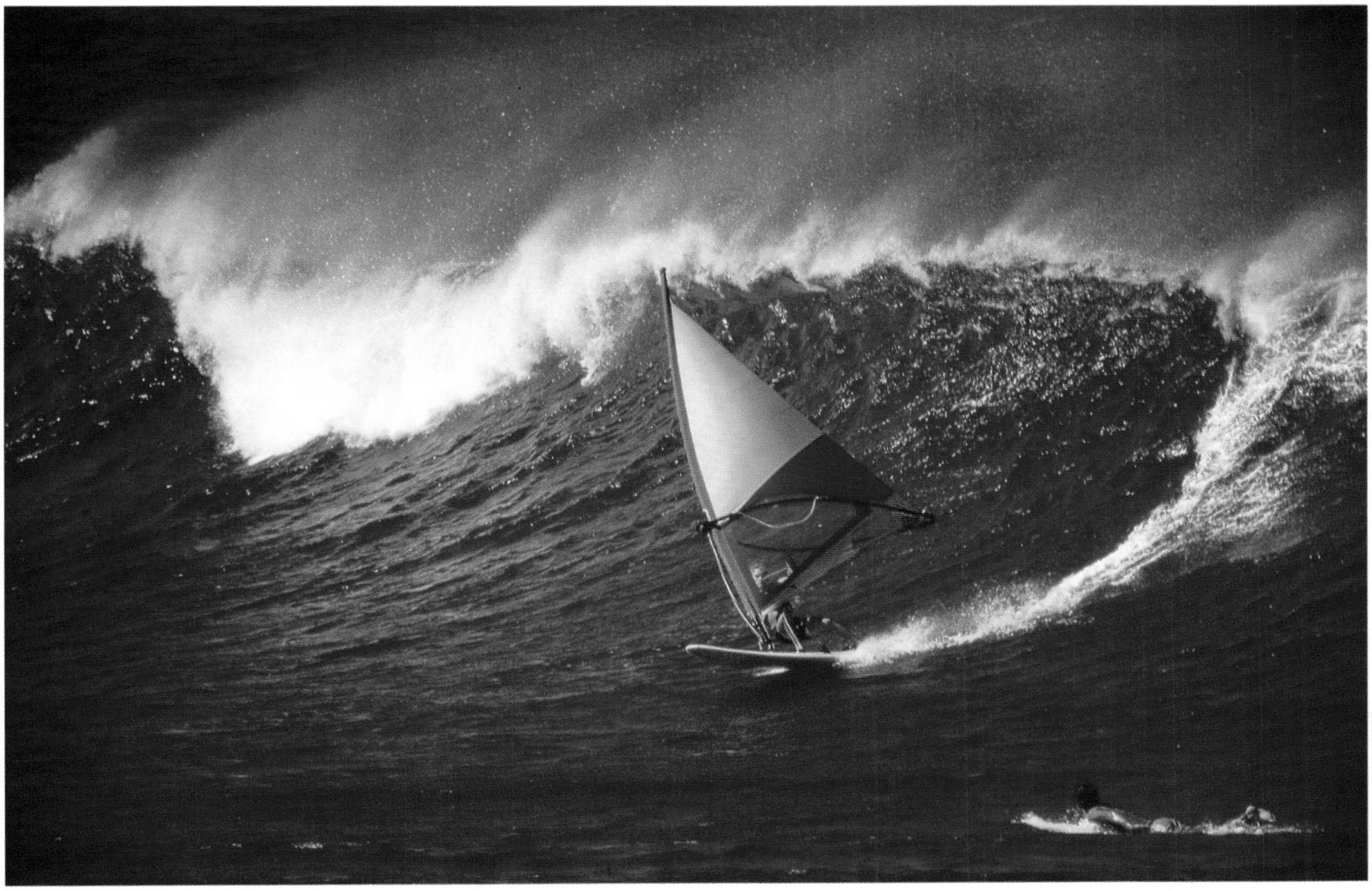

STEVE WILKINGS

PETER CRAWFORD

PETER CRAWFORD

PETER CRAWFORD

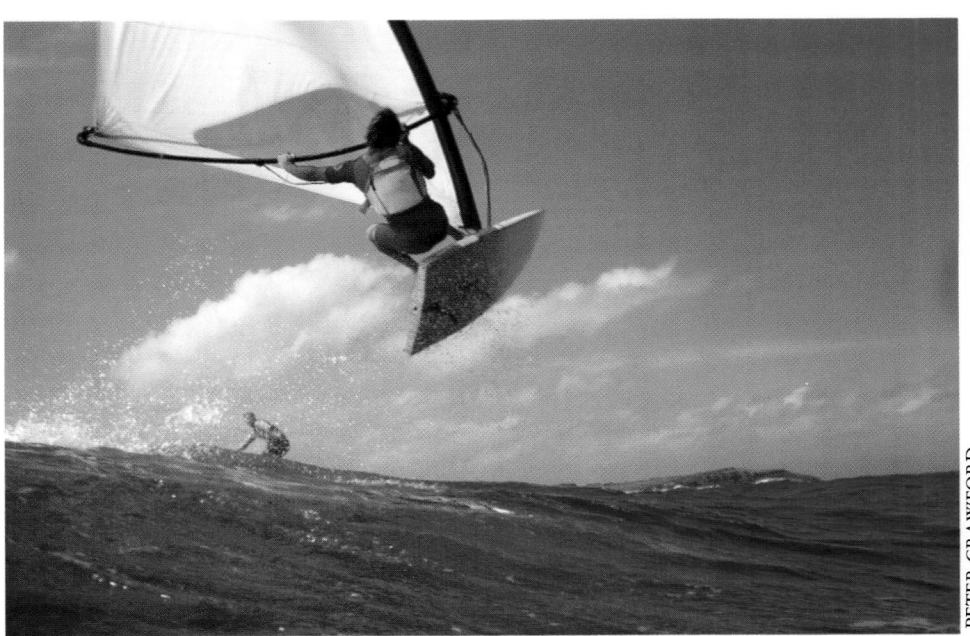

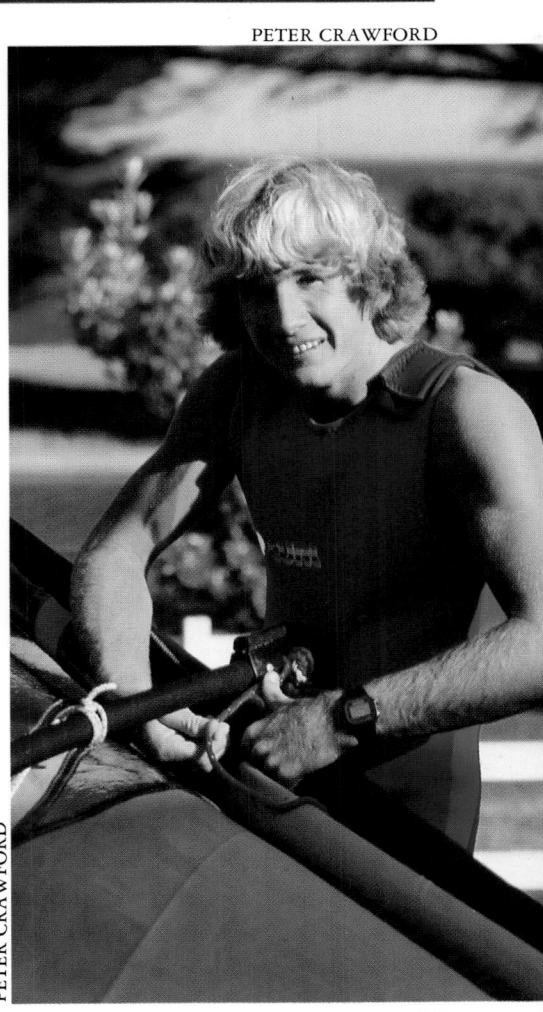

Top: *Mike Waltze: giving credence to the argument that older surfers make excellent sailboarders, especially when it comes to riding waves.*

Above: *Mike Waltze on wide tailed single fin in 1980: the development of the sailboard has closely paralleled the surfboard.*

Right: *Robbie Naish regarded as the world's best all-round sailboarder.*

PETER CRAWFORD

Sequence above: *Robbie Naish coming off the top in good surfing style.*

Below: *Mark Paul: penetrating the surf line requires excellent timing and ability.*

PETER CRAWFORD

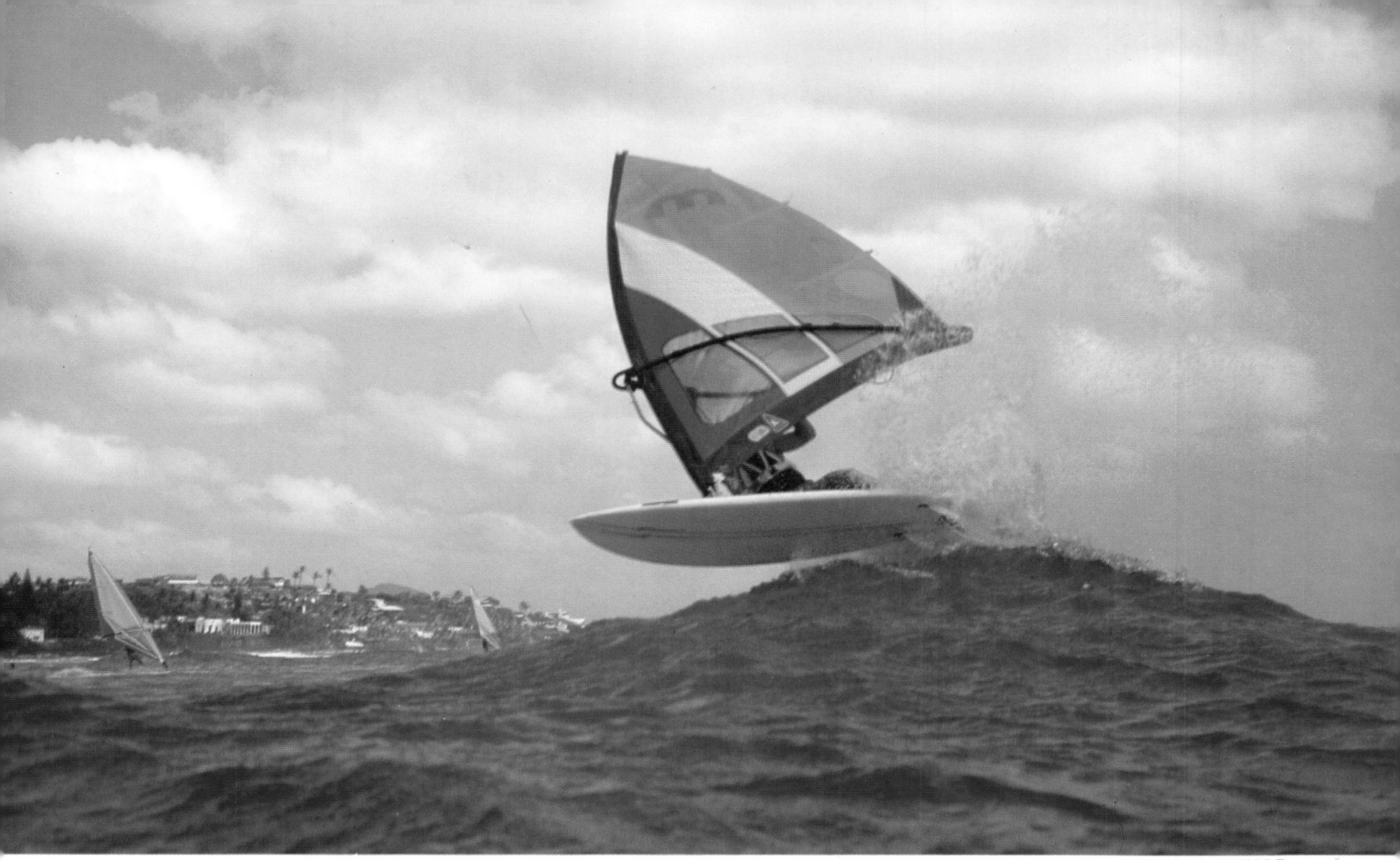

PETER CRAWFORD

Below: *Jason Polakow smacks the lip.*

SYLVAIN CAZENAVE

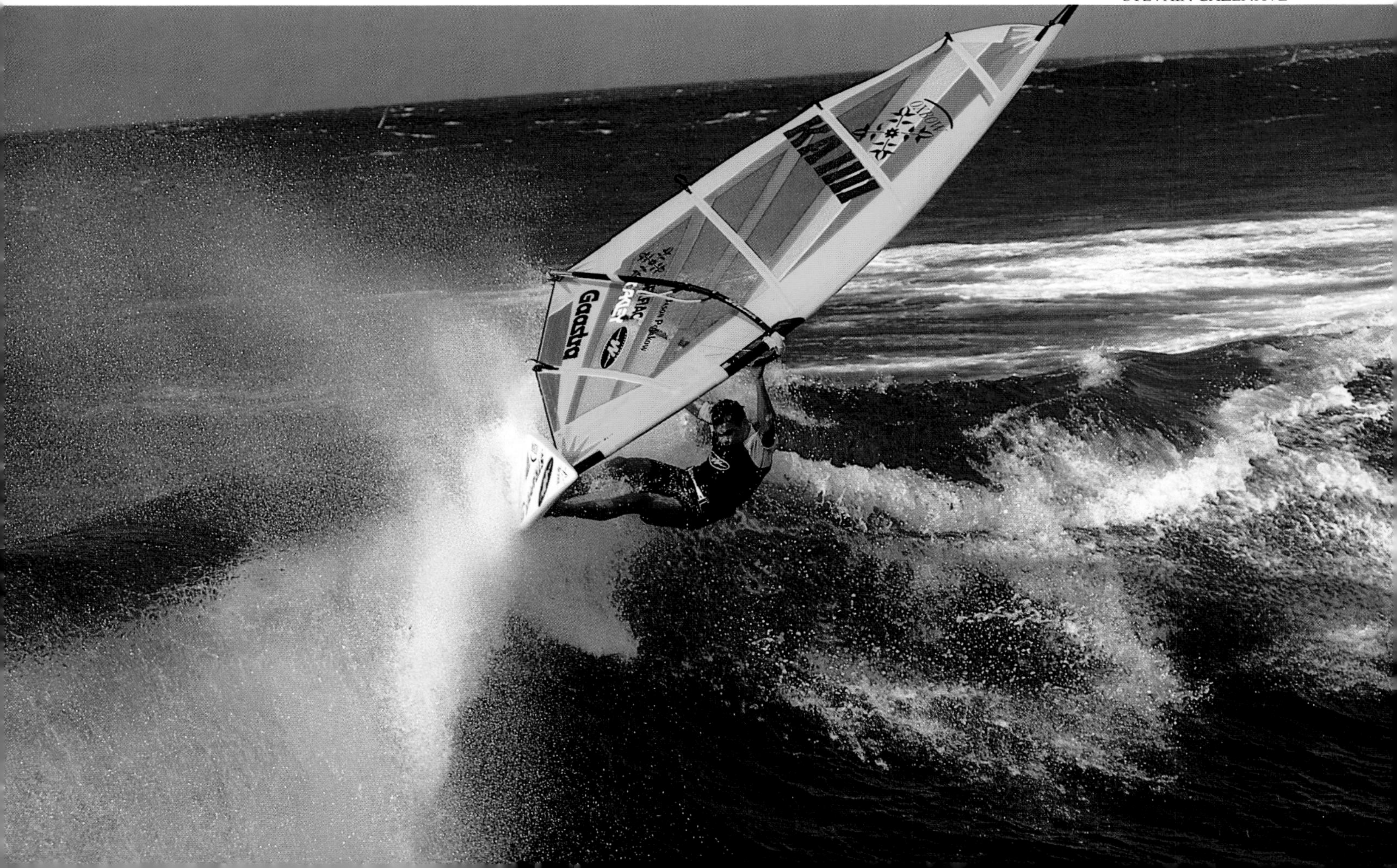

Sequence right: *Re-entry on a close out: about five options are open to Naish whereas the regular board surfer has only one, and that's boring.*

Below: *Mark Paul coming off the bottom with plenty of power.*

PETER CRAWFORD

PETER CRAWFORD

PETER CRAWFORD

'hardcore surfing'. Let's try to define that. 'Hardcore' puts you in the centre. The core. Which means the lifestyle centres on surfing. And hardcore puts you into the rigid regime of keeping up with the latest developments, keeping your equipment hot, and ready; lying in bed at night thinking out tomorrow's plan of attack on that new manoeuvre you're trying to get down; then, in the water, pushing your limitations, going for the radical, having a go. Hardcore also means checking conditions many times a day. Shutting everyone up for those few seconds each night as T.V. weather man Mike Bailey runs down the map, and even buying the latest expensive mag because it's got something you didn't know in it, or a really hot picture of something a bit new. Hardcore means doing all of this, year in year out, year after year, after year.

"OK. That's long-winded maybe, but it pretty much describes hardcore surfing.

"The question is, then, how does windsurfing fit our definition? (Hey! Just to clear up a point first. I don't mean that flat water stuff. That's just the nursery! I mean the real windsurfing. Surfing with a sail in your hands.)

"Well, windsurfing fits the bill. It fits the definition. In fact, it fits better than surfing without a sail does, at the moment anyway. Why? Because apart from all those fun things that hardcore surfing is, hardcore windsurfing is more! It's got new manoeuvres being developed right now! (Like the 'sixties in sailless surfing'). It's got more thrills in an hour than surfing without a sail for a month. It's three times as fast. You surf-hardcore-going out!!! As well as coming in. There's no more paddling! It's totally uncrowded! In fact, we look for people to surf with! Conditions are hot when the wind swings onshore! You can jump! Do sixty foot cutbacks. Surf green waves, white waves, big waves, small waves. Out-

run waves. Beat huge sections of whitewater. It's happening now! Never again will it be new.

"The sail liberates surfing to new frontiers. Open ocean surfing. Where you pick up swells miles out, drop into 'em, carve the base, climb, hit-the-lip, and as it fizzles, hunt another quick bowl. Or riding dribbly two foot surf. With 15 knots plus of sidewind you can still jump six or eight feet high, race sections, do re-entries and racey cutbacks. On the other end of the scale, the fact that you can pick up green swells a stinkin' long way out means the lid is blown off big wave surfing. Keana Point is now possible. Within a few years some guy with minus 50% regard for life will ride a 45-foot wave there, with a sail.

"Now, don't get me wrong. I'm not saying regular surfing is out of it. It hasn't changed. When there's a well-stacked swell, the wind's light and there's nobody out, surfing with just

Right: *Robbie Naish, Diamond Head, Oahu: "It's happening now! Never again will it be new". McTavish.*

PETER CRAWFORD

a board is great. We all know that I've been doing it with great zeal for over 26 years. But let's face it, those conditions are becoming a rarity. And with windsurfing, well, new wonderful equipment has been added to the surfboard. In the 'forties, a fin was added. 'Sixties and 'seventies twins and tris were added. Now a sail.

"We will have to liberate surfboards further. Cheyne Horan could leap sections without a sail tomorrow if we could fit a footstrap device. We're working on it. It's harder than you think. You keep treading on the things, not in them. And we still need a rail that won't suck the deck under when we get totally upside down in the tube. The book of sailless surfing is certainly not closed yet.

"But nevertheless, a surf historian of the future will have to note that a sail was added in the 'eighties. And in these years, windsurfing became not just a part of surfing, but the new

surfing. Ask the guys who have been through it all. Midget. Nat. Wayne. Greenough. And many, many more.

"Finally, let me tell you it was hard in the early 'sixties when we surfers first arose in the bodgie/rocker-dominated coastal towns. Fights. Fear. Misunderstanding. We were new. We just wanted to surf. Now the milk bar bodgie is all but gone (sigh). Surfers rule. Meantime, all we want to do is surf, this time with a sail. So . . . er . . . no milk bar bodgie vibes huh? Check us out when the wind turns strong onshore at Noosa, Currumbin, Lennox, Long Reef, Merimbula or Torquay."

So that's McTavish. Basically I agree with him. And yet, although I am aware of all this coming down, I often ride a surfboard without a sail. Most of the time surfing is still exactly what it was when I was a kid, bloody good fun. Now that I am finally beyond the frustrating kook stage with windsurfing, the problem

is trying to decide which one I want to do most. At the moment I usually take the waves and leave the sail but as I get older and the surf more crowded, surfing with a sail is a realistic alternative.

Surfing never stands still. It shares some characteristics with other sports, such as skiing and hang-gliding. I enjoy them all. Also, as sports develop, they often tend to merge with each other; hence the development of the single snow ski and the windsurfer. It's stupid not to take advantage of these innovations, especially if they bring a new dimension to an existing sport. Whether windsurfing takes off on a direction of its own or merges more and more with traditional surfing, it's an exciting move forward in riding waves.

●

187

Right: *Gary Clisby. Today's surfers are regularly pulling off manoeuvres which would have been impossible not so long ago.*

Below: *John Glomb — out there! The possibilities are limitless.*

CHUCK SCHMID

Right: *This looks dangerous but it's reality for the '90s.*

TOM SERVAIS

Below: *South Africa's Wendy Boffa displaying simple, good clean surfing.*

PETER CRAWFORD

TOWARDS 2000

PETER CRAWFORD

As surfing accelerates towards the year 2000, the question comes up: where do we go from here?

In my opinion surfers today are no different to the surfers of yesteryear. They are all part of a unique tribe of nomads who have wandered this planet in search of rideable waves since the beginning of this century. Both the professional surfer and the amateur qualify as part of this race, which has learnt to overcome the problems of creed and colour.

Surfing is growing up. Every year when the professional contestants reach Australia, you can notice the attitude of the media changing. Surfing has become accepted. The pros themselves have done a great deal to obtain this wide media coverage, exposing their handsome faces and athletic bodies as often as they are asked to. But maybe there's a loss involved as well. When I heard that

the charming South African surfer Shaun Tomson was doing an inner-spring mattress commercial in California I thought to myself: we surfers have become just like all the other pro sportsmen. We're selling out. And in the process we've lost that unique quality which has made us pretty much unacceptable to the general public and the media for the past 30 years. We've become . . . well, almost normal.

I feel we may also have reached the limit of surfboard design potential for a few years and that the next break-through will be technological. There has been no real change in surfboard manufacturing techniques since the advent of foam and fibreglass. Surely it is only a matter of time before more sophisticated moulding and manufacturing techniques catch up with the surfboard and it becomes lighter, cheaper, and much more resistant to damage.

In the meantime most advances may come from that most unpredictable source of all, the surfer himself. Styles and attitudes have changed rapidly in the past few years. Surfers are regularly pulling off manoeuvres which would have been thought impossible some time ago. Each topline surfer brings his own individual approach to what he does and so helps push the state of the art further along. People like Tom Curren, Cheyne Horan and Tommy Carroll . . .

Tom Curren is only 18 years old, a devout Christian, and the first son of Pat Curren, the vagabond shaper who displayed such fine craftsmanship in the early '60s with the sleek-lined 'Curren Guns' that allowed early big-wave riders to tackle huge sets at Sunset and Waimea. Pat introduced his son to wave riding at an early age, and even after the family had split up Pat made sure he was along in 1981 to offer his guidance when Tom rode

PETER CRAWFORD

Cheyne Horan's idea is to achieve neutrality in his boards, what you get out is exactly what you put in.

TERRY WILLCOCKS

the Hawaiian north shore for the first time.

Back in California, Tom, his sister and little brother live close to the ocean in Santa Barbara . . . the mainstay of his young life has been the religious conviction of his mother, which has given him a quiet confidence that he will achieve only what the Lord sees fit. This faith, together with his inherited natural talent has allowed him to become the first serious threat to the Australian domination of the contest scene since Rolf Aurness in 1970. Curren's

struggle from obscurity in minor contests in California to the prestigious position of World Amateur Champion in Australia in July, 1982 was a great achievement. Tommy has had an extraordinary run of success. After his rather amazing victory in Australia he immediately turned pro and stunned everyone by winning his first pro contest (the Stubbies Pro Trials at Trestles).

In Japan, Mark Richards claimed that Tom was the luckiest competitor he had ever surfed against. On two occasions when Tom came up against

Mark and the fast rising Aussie Superstar, Gary Timperley, Mark and Gary both thought they had him whipped but right in the dying seconds of the heat the best wave would fall right in Tommy's lap and he would do it justice with his raw talent and go on to win the event. That win in Japan in October 1982 is unprecedented in pro surfing and gave him much confidence. In February 1983 Curran won the first of the professional contests in Australia, becoming the first non-Australian to win the Straight Talk Tyres Open. Not since 15-year-old Martin Potter came second in both the South Afri-

JEFF HORNBAKER

PETER CRAWFORD

Tom Curren at Sunset Beach (above) and Burleigh Heads. The first Californian to win a major professional contest in Australia!

can pro contests in 1981 has the surfing world been forced to sit up and take such a hard look at a new kid.

The first photograph I ever saw of **Tom Curren** was of his youthful frame spread out in a 3'-4' backside barrel. There he lay suspended on the wall of water, his arms outstretched, his back arched in the same curve as the wave, his ankles looking as if they were straining to hold him over his body's logical balance point. And yet there is no strain, no awkward stiffness associated with holding the body up while executing this amazing

manoeuvre. The layback is just a matter of developing the ability to relax inside a backside tube, of setting it up and flowing with it, no matter how tight the situation gets. It is a perfect example of surfing in the '80s. No-one really knows who did it first and it doesn't seem to matter; rather, the action illustrates the best method devised so far for getting deep in the tube on your backhand, and says a lot about how the youth of today will deal with problems as we move towards the year 2000.

All surfing benefits from break-

throughs in surfboard design: the twin fin everyone just had to have in 1978; the three finned thruster that added so much to the twin in 1981, yet kept a little single fin stability . . . where will it go from here? Four fins? Five fins?

Contest victories have always been indicators of the future direction of surfing, and in 1982 Cheyne Horan was the guy to beat. He won the first two pro contests on the I.P.S. 1982 circuit riding a single fin surfboard. The major difference between Cheyne's boards and the single fins of old are numerous. With his new

191

Tom Carrol won the Surfabout in Sydney and the European Pro in Cornwall, England in 1983, with that incredible projection he has on his forehand.

Top left: *Guess who I just met?*

Top right: *It's slick presentation, when it comes to selling surfboards today.*

Above: *Hans Hedemann at Pipeline. 'Getting in there is only half the battle, it's getting out that counts'. Hans' coach Paul Peterson.*

boards he has solved the problem of stiffness, which was the reason we abandoned single fins in the first place. He has done this by utilising area in the tail, just as multi-fins do. This has given him the looseness of a twin and retained the best attributes of the old single fin (being able to use the stall as a functional move and being able to control your trimming speed across the face). Cheyne's designs start from a very simple, basic principle: achieving neutrality in the board. His idea is to design the board so that it has no built-in tendency to do anything. In other words, whatever performance you get out of it comes as a direct result of the quality of your own performance. However far you push it is as far as it will go.

The only problem with this theory is that if you're feeling slightly sluggish the board reflects your feelings and your surfing becomes slow and uninteresting. I feel we saw this happen to Cheyne in the semis of the '83 Surfabout where a less experienced surfer, Richard Cram, ran rings around Cheyne on his three-fin thruster, displaying much more sparkle and drive because the board which he was riding demanded it. The dynamic acceleration of the multi-fin surfboard is the most important development in surfboards today but the design does have its limitations and every surfer should be aware of them. To put it simply, you have to keep moving. You cannot stand up and cruise as you can on the old single fin. That is why so many older surfers find it a problem adjusting to multi-fin surfboards. When you reach your feet you simply have to make a direction change in order to gain the acceleration produced by the water rushing between the fins. Yet some older surfers who have made the initial adjustment have found that surfing three fins gives them a new zest, making surfing seem almost brand new again.

A lot of how a board works is in the aesthetics. If it looks good then it

PETER CRAWFORD

GUY MOTIL

Above: *Marvin Foster with multi fin acceleration!*

Left: *Young South African Martin Potter.*

probably works, though no-one can really tell until it's been ridden. Cheyne's boards are fat and wide and that has hindered their acceptance. The three-finned boards, being sleeker and more interesting, have been accepted by the majority of the surfing world. The fact that more injuries take place from multi-fins and that more repairs are necessary has not hindered their acceptance.

Tommy Carroll, the goofyfoot, is a good example of the excellence that is possible on a three-finned board. Strong, decisive manoeuvres is the best way to describe Tom's style. To

my mind Tom's surfing is the most interesting in the world today and for one main reason: every manoeuvre he does is with total conviction — and perhaps that is the only thing that could stop him from becoming our new world champion. He's almost too good a surfer. He doesn't bullshit and never has, and that could be his downfall. Over the past few years, especially in the contest arena, we have seen surfers develop an amazing number of manoeuvres which have led to a pinball type of surfing, whether there are rideable waves around or not. Tom's style is more back-to-the-roots and he generally

needs a fundamental ingredient to surf well. Waves.

The final of the '83 Surfabout was held in good rideable waves between Tom Carroll and Richard Cram, another Sydneysider. Tom had deserved a big win for a year or two and no-one on the beach thought that it would end any other way. If Richard won it would have been because Tom had made a terrible blunder or had had a run of bad luck which he could not control. But from the way the surf was building for the final day, that was highly unlikely. The waves were going left, only three to four

195

PETER CRAWFORD

MATSUMOTO

Above: *James 'Bird' Mahelona. Putting the ball decisively in the top pocket.*

Left: *Gary Timperley drawing the bow at the Pipeline.*

Below: *A stylish Marvin Foster keeping his cool!*

JEFF DIVINE

feet but very down the line, with long sections far ahead just made for the acceleration of a thruster.

Richard, like Tom, was surfing three fins and was doing quite adequately on his backhand, but it was difficult for him to achieve that incredible projection which Tom had on his forehand. It was hardly a contest until the second round when Tom made that one mistake; he was too choosey in the waves he decided to go for and ended up not getting good enough waves. Sitting on the beach, watching, I was reminded of how intense the training for professional

competition is. These surfers had gone in the water every day for years to maintain a level of excellence. Now they were being measured by the time they spent in the water minimising the margin for error.

The week after the Japanese leg of the '82 World Contest I remember asking Cheyne Horan why he didn't win. He said simply that he fell off twice. The surfer who wants to win can't afford to make two mistakes. Tom didn't; he made only one and narrowly defeated Richard by taking off on a very high-scoring wave right as the hooter sounded. This gave

Tom the second of the two sets and there was no need for a third. It was a decisive win by the little Aussie battler from Newport, who had bounced back from two serious operations in the past few years. Not that he wasn't ready; he had proved his stamina by beating Cheyne Horan in the '82 Bells contest and going up against M.R. in the final. Tom surfs single fins particularly well and has never used a twin at all. The thruster, however, has done a lot for his style, making his blatant direction changes more acute, and for that reason I doubt if he will ever go back to a single fin.

The old manoeuvre that Tom has revived in his own style is the round-house cutback. George Greenough was the first surfer I ever saw do one, and every talented Aussie surfer from the 'seventies learnt it. Normally on a roundhouse the surfer follows through and comes back over with the white water into the next bottom turn, which sets you up nice and deep for the next section. Tom's variation on this is a quick hard forehand turn, high in the curl, bringing him back right into the curl line.

At this stage Tom can't see any need for changes in his equipment and feels he is still exploring the potential of the thruster; but you can never tell, a new development could be just around the corner. Certainly progress will come from exploring new areas on the wave face and by designing new equipment which alters the surfer's approach to the wave.

I believe that our surfing ancestors in the Polynesian Islands rode waves for the same reason we do; it's fun when the waves are there. No more complexity is necessary. Kids who grow up by the sea will turn to riding in on waves as a logical form of recreation for as long as waves continue to break. If surfing is different now from what it was when I was a kid then the beginners are not aware of it; my son still looks for someone to go surfing with to increase the pleasure.

For myself, I spend most days with one eye tuned to the swell's condition and hunt for the best possible peel-offs in my area. If it's small and just dribbling then a lot of fun can be had on an old Malibu doing big stylised turns and running to the nose, even tandem with wife or daughter; but if I see a well-shaped bank with good waves striking it then I will try to make the time to ride it properly. And I must admit the self-indulgence factor does count. Sometimes I will go for a quick surf or sailboard when I know I should be doing something else. But that's the result of being someone, like hundreds of thousands of others, who is involved in the environment in one way or another: surfing, sailboarding, skiing. Each of

Top: *Chappy Jennings layback. The manoeuvre of the '80s.*

Above: *The essence of surfing — man and wave.*

SURFING MAGAZINE

Above: *Maurice Cole at Hossegor. France offers some of the finest waves in the world at the right time of year.*

KIMIRO KONDO

Left: *Takao Kuga at Isumi river mouth. Young Japanese are fast becoming very proficient at surfing.*

Bottom: *Californian hot rat Chris Barela knows exactly where to put it!*

STEVE SAKAMOTO

those takes a heavy commitment to gain the benefits — developing the ability to appreciate good rideable waves takes a lot of hours in the water and as I get older I trust I can implant this taste for quality in my children, so they too will know what a good wave looks like and have the ability to ride it. So many lessons can be learnt from riding waves; like patience, and how long you have to wait for what you want, and the realisation that the best things in life are free.

I believe most surfers are basically honest people, because of the very nature of the act of surfing. It's so clean, so pure; you can even gain from it a sense of right and wrong. Sometimes surfers screw up, which is a natural tendency with young people. I feel I could have done more, in my surfing career, to impress on young surfers the special qualities of the trip they were getting into. I suppose we all have some regrets. But I am just as convinced now as I was in the early '70s that surfing at a high degree of ability is an art form as much as a sport. When we are at our best, we try to make it so. We try to make *what we do* an art, to make our lives an art form. You couldn't ask for anything more.

DAN DEVINE

Surf Groupies since the beginning of time!

SATO

Nat Young — Ala Moana, Hawaii.
Summer of '82.

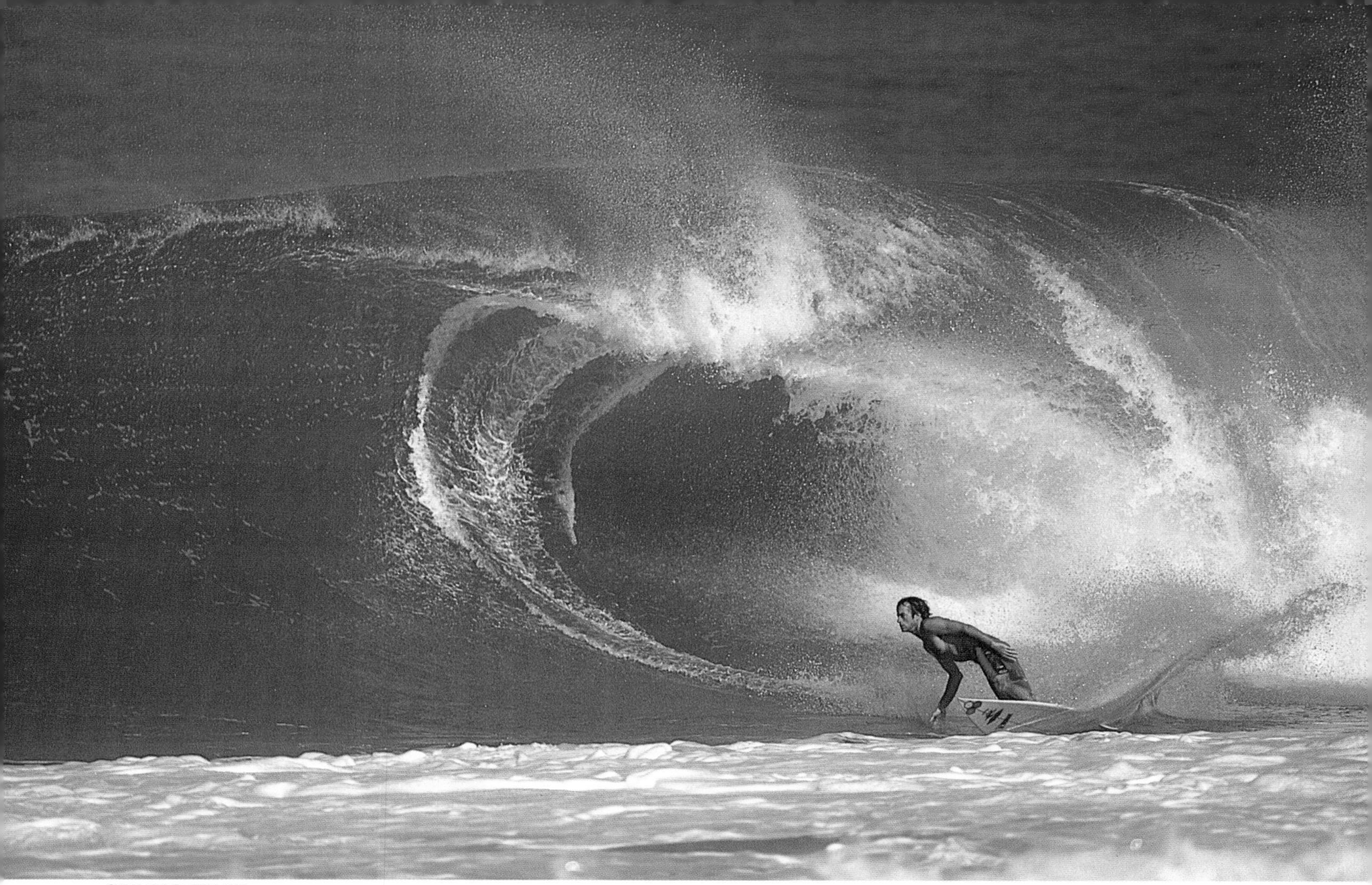

SYLVAIN CAZENAVE

SYLVAIN CAZENAVE

TOM AUGUSTINE

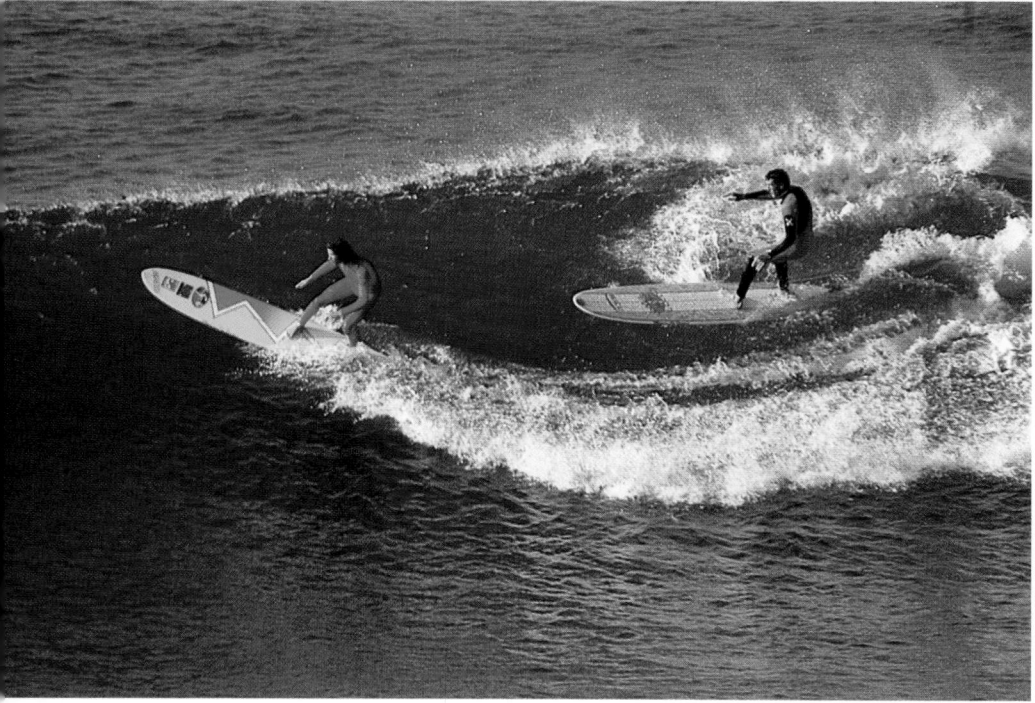

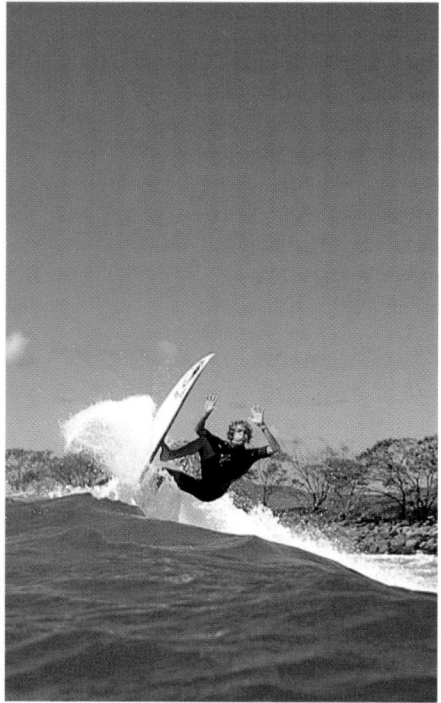

Top: *Tom Curren: style-master of the 1980s.*

Above: *The new and the old: Joel Tudor with Nat Young at Bells Beach.*

Above right: *A Beau Young aerial at Angourie.*

Opposite page: *A victorious Tom Carroll!*

Far right: *Tom Carroll showing supreme confidence at Pipeline.*

THE BEAT GOES ON

Surfing's always been tribal. The sport's consciousness revels in reliving legends, passing on important memories to the next generation, the next country. The cold green islands of Great Britain are unlikely places for legends to meet head on – but communication means surfers worldwide understand the wave riding experience. It connects beaches as far flung as Padang Padang and Pipeline, Tavarua and Narrabeen, Raglan and the Bay of Plenty.

In an ancient smuggler's bar on the old north coast of Cornwall, a bunch of surfer's stood, their arms about each other. On the walls there hung boards from every proud era of the sport – an Hawaiian koawood paddle board, early sixties mals and a professional's thruster from the mid 1980s.

The surfers' ages were as varied. I was on a longboard promotional trip to the UK in 1994, watching the revival of a style of surfing which most – back in 1968 – thought had gone for good. With me were new wave warriors, linking the ballistic 1990s precision, with the grace and poise of the early sixties. Hawaiian

Duane Desoto, California's Joel Tudor and my own 20 year old son Beau, were making this link with the past, which said more about the fun of longboarding and less about pressure to perform in a contest. Almost at the end of this century, surfing is alive and well.

It had been a tough decade in a melting pot of world surfing, which had suffered growing pains. The 1980s were to give us the fully integrated professional surfer, earning enough cash on a world tour to rival the golf or tennis circuits. Gone were the long hairs in beat-up woodies; enter the fine-tuned athletes, the TV networks, the computers, marketable identities. And yet things didn't quite end up that way. The world was getting smaller. There were problems with overcrowding and pollution all piling on the pressures.

Back in 1983, Tom Carroll, 21, was the ideal model for this new form of stardom as the ASP developed. A tough athlete, Carroll went on to take the first of his two world titles in that year (narrowly beating Rabbit). He took Sunset Beach Sunkist

World Cup and 2SM Coke Surfabout at Narrabeen in strong displays of mature versatility. Gary 'Kong' Elkerton arrived on the North Shore on this first trip. His heavyweight talent gave notice of fresh winds of change.

As it happened, big wave riding was creeping back into vogue. That winter, when hurricane Iwa gave Hawaii a battering, the ASP didn't recognise the famous Triple Crown events on the North Shore, because of the small contest purse. Michael Ho went for it anyway (winning the title with a cast on his wrist) but had to pay the fine. He lost his world ranking and didn't get it back. His career suffered. But his standing amongst the North Shore community never faltered.

Other surfers were looking for new ways to carve small waves. Riders like Matt Kechele were punching off the trough, up the face and into the air above the lip, opening up a whole new area of surfing potential.

Back in the contest arena, M.R., Shaun, Rabbit, Dane Kealoha and Cheyne Horan maintained that edge

SYLVAIN CAZENAVE

PETER CRAWFORD

Top: *Professional surfing is very popular in Brazil.*

Above: *A fully prepared Gary Elkerton.*

which meant any changing of the guard would be a hard-fought business. Elkerton was smacking the lip harder than most, Glen Winton surfed the 'Stubbies' with real style and 15 year old Martin Potter made a world debut at the Coke at Burleigh with tube riding way beyond his years. Tour veteran Shaun had to be content with second place. The youngsters were coming.

Martin held the key to surfing's new goal – leaving the wave face on an aerial attack, he offered exciting possibilities with athletic gouges that gave a new generation the direction to surf differently.

The pro tour was growing up fast right around the world. By now, Shaun, one of surfing's great ambassadors, had won more professional contests than any other surfer, apart from four-times world champion Mark Richards. Mark was semi-retired by 1983, but was still rated as the most influential surfer of the last decade. The Wounded Gull, with his knock-kneed driving style and cranked arms, inspired surfers all over the planet to look for speed and turns on shorter boards.

Just as surfing was set to make the twin fin the performance standard, Simon Anderson blew things apart with his revolutionary thruster design.

Ando was a big bloke. He was popular on the Tour and had a lot of respect as a designer/shaper. In his own surfing, Simon skated around too much on twinfins. So he fixed an extra fin near the tail. It was inspired judgement – as his early contest performances proved. Refinements came thick and fast. Someone who jumped right on the new equipment was 18 years old

Tom Curren from Santa Barbara. Tom was on the threshold of a career which would guarantee him a place in surfing's Hall of Fame.

The circuit was running well in the mid-eighties – but there were worries that commercialism would take the heart out of the sport. As an antidote, surfers began to re-discover two old friends – travel and longboarding. It was time to look over your shoulder and over the horizon. Being a sponsored surfer meant certain controls on the freedom which had epitomised the sixties and seventies. It was a hard choice a lot of professionals had to make as the decade ticked by.

Some world rankers had an escape route – Tom Curren carved out a new life with his young family in France, redefining the meaning of 'professional'. In future, Tom chose to surf the contests only *he* wanted. His sponsors would be happy backing this new direction. The magazines still had their photo-shoots. Tom proved there *was* life after the pro-tour.

The women's circuit was emerging too. In the early eighties, American Debbie Beauchamp matched her graceful yet aggressive style to the big and powerful Hawaiian winter tubes. Deep bottom turns at Off the Wall and high slingshot cut-backs at

Sunset, set her up to become a formative influence of the progression of women's surfing.

Debbie had guts – surfing 15 foot Sunset with a broken rib in the 1983 Offshore Masters. She was the spearpoint of a new attack in women's surfing, while Margot Godfrey-Oberg was the elder stateswoman. Now 29, she still had a solid reputation, fine-tuned, since her win in 1968 at the Puerto Rico

Top: *The lineup at Mundaca: Spain has some magnificent waves.*

Above: *Jeff Booth tucking in at Pipe.*

203

SEAN DAVEY

SYLVAIN CAZENAVE

Below: *Lisa Anderson.*
Right: *With daughter Erica.*

Far right: *Jodie Cooper.*
Bottom: *Doing her thing at Sunset.*

HANK

World Championships. Margot had scooped an incredible 7 world titles in a gilt-edged career.

Hawaiian Lynne Boyer was another powerful surfer who was one of the first women to bring skateboard sweeps and turns to the circuit, surfing low down and centred. Lynne's early eighties domination might have found a serious challenger in Isabel McLaughlin. She too, was aggressive and their stylistic rivalry might have set up an interesting edge to female competition.

However those early ASP events generated such little cash that Isabel decided not to go on the Tour. Women surfers had to set about changing their own surfing – and the public perception of feminine competition – to attract large sponsors.

MIKE WAGGONER

Left: *A French girl enjoying summer.*

Right: *Pam Burridge.*
Below: *Pam carving.*

Meanwhile, a tall, 18 year old goofy foot from Manly, Australia, was about to take the stage. Pam Burridge was – for a while – the only woman on the circuit riding a single fin (a Geoff McCoy lazor zap, similar to Cheyne Horan's) in both big and small waves. Pam would stay at the top for the next ten years, combining an ability to surf well in different conditions.

The more dance-orientated surfers still had the talent to be champions. Hawaiian Rell Sunn and Jerico Popler from Long Beach were the main exponents, bringing grace and beauty to the water.

Kim Mearig was another dynamic stylist moving up. A stand-out in the National Scholastic Association in the States (started by ex-World Champ Peter Townend in 1979), the

20 year old Californian was tipped to be the Golden State's top professional, once Margo moved to Kauai.

She began in the 'soul surfer' mould, riding in a speed line style refined around Rincon. Then in 1983, encouraged by Tom Curren, Kim put together a full pack of moves to hold a 180 point ratings lead over Florida's Frieda Zamba. Once again, rivalry was strong, especially as Pam, that year's favourite, was only 350 points behind the top slot.

Frieda was formidable in small surf, and big wave riders like Lynne and Jerico would have to adjust their approach to rip small waves as well as they ripped bigger ones.

Frieda could launch lip punches, 360s and re-entries, in a string of explosive moves from deep water to

the shallows. She won her pro surfing curtain raiser in 1982, against a seasoned crop at the Mazda Women's Surf Sports. From Flagler Beach, she began to change the shape of women's surfing and was the 1985/86 ASP women's champion. What put her there was her fast, positive and inventive style, finding speed and power even in mush.

Waiting in the wings was Jodie Cooper. From Albany near Perth, in Western Australia, Jodie displayed a fast, aggressive style, but lacked a little polish in her early years. But later, Jodie proved her drive and ability in big Hawaiian barrels, never holding back.

Performers like Frieda paved the way for a better deal in the 1990s. The women's Professional Surfing Organisation successfully lobbied sponsors to back all-women pro events. In 1983, Mazda, Hang Ten and Michelob all supported contests. At Christmas that year, $15,000 was up for grabs in the Sunkist World Cup at Sunset – the highest purse yet in women's surfing.

Pauline Menczer was only 17 in 1988, when she took the amateur world title. Suffering from junior rheumatoid arthritis, Pauline struggled to be a professional surfer, following strict diets. Bursting onto the scene in events like the Head Start, she proved to be a major force on the world tour, having the will to win and a radical surfing style. In her early Tour days, wave selection let her down. That's been ironed out and she represented a new wave of committed, talented riders.

Women's surfing is still assessing its appeal and influence. At last, aggressive athleticism seems to be an accepted competitive goal for women, with surfers like world champion Wendy Botha, Toni Sawyer and Lisa Anderson, serve as perfect examples of this new direction. Some say women can't surf as powerfully as men – but that's missing the point. Surfers like Lisa build their surfing from a strength and power still uniquely feminine.

In the 1990s, new surfers like Nea Post, Kylie Webb, Connie Nixon and Michele Donoghoe pushed standards up. Women are still being short-changed. In 1991/92, Women's World Champion Wendy Botha made more than $19,000 in prize money. Her male equivalent, Damien Hardman collected just over $84,000. Both have been professionals for seven years, representing the best in surfing. It's likely that the debate will continue.

For the men, pro-surfing's future looked secure back in 1983. With Ian Cairns as Executive Director, the ASP had been born out of the old IPS, the world governing body of surfing since 1976. The first part of the year focused attention on the Australian 'Grand Slam' – four well run events – though none were ASP sanctioned to allow time for reorganisation. Then, Fred Hemmings refused to allow his Off Shore Pipeline Masters and Sunkist World Cup to be part of the tour, after complaints about rules being counterproductive to the Hawaiian events selection of surfers and seedings.

Rows have rumbled on. The ASP was pulled inside out to meet the needs of tour vets, rookies, sponsors and TV networks. For five years, the schedule was punishing, with little or no break in the year-round contest agenda. The world-wide recession of the late eighties let the steam out of the surf industry. Contest winnings fell by almost 50% over six years.

Now, changes in judging, splitting the Tour into two divisions (bringing in the so-called 'little league' World Qualifying Series) and a shifting away from Hawaii for the traditional year-ender are still splitting the ranks.

More change is in the wind. There's a move to sell the Tour through television, featuring the best surfers, surfing quality waves. The sport needs to spell-out drama and challenge to a mass audience – it's not possible to cultivate that when the best in the world have to fight for money and points in tiny shore-dump surf.

The ASP wants changes. The next five years will tell us if the new direction is the right one.

●

CHANGING THE GUARD

At the start of the 1980s boards were still thickish and boxy, with plenty of foam, full nose and tail widths as the thruster became common currency. There were plenty of single and twin fin designs going through stages of refinement. Split-tail fishes and swallows were popular, with wings ranging from small bumps to large rail steps. Boards of all designs were being pushed to the limits in big and small waves.

It didn't take long before the thruster became the most influential design since the 1968 shortboard explosion. This design 'evergreen' was adapted for all kinds of surfing the world over. Slowly, boards became thinner, narrower and sleeker, with channels both deep and shallow, giving the boards lift and direction.

An extreme deviation from this thruster domination was the work by Cheyne Horan on his lazor zap boards. Cheyne split with Geoff McCoy to develop them using the experimental keel fin. He worked with Ben Lexon, the keel designer of the Australia II yacht which won the America's Cup. Cheyne had done his homework, applying theories about airflow across wings – the sort of work Greenough had done in the sixties with spoon kneeboards and Terry Fitzgerald in the eighties with his 'drifter' boards.

Cheyne was looking for speed and drive in small surf – but the end of the decade saw him return to more conventional thruster designs when he blew out in competition after inconsistent results.

Meanwhile, by the mid-eighties, computer-guided shaping machines with incredible accuracy – pioneered by such visionaries as Frenchman Michel Barland – could knock out a 6 feet thruster in 15 minutes. For the first time, surfers could copy a favourite board. New materials like carbon fibre, epoxy resin and styrofoam were all part of the design brief.

In 1988, Barton Lynch clinched the world titles at Pipeline, on a board inspired by a balsa shape from the 1950s – proving that old designs still had validity. Boards inspired by the new surfing of Tom Curren, Martin Potter and Kelly Slater in small to medium waves, were starting to influence what the sport wanted to try in big waves – but some shapers thought the design envelope may have been pushed too far in the nineties.

The incredibly thin, narrow boards ridden in power displays by Matt Archibold, Derek Ho, Kalani Robb and Shane Dorian, may not be the stock boards which anybody can ride – but the styles of surfing they dictate point to new moves and new directions.

Maybe that's the way it should stay. If the test track for most surfers is waves six feet and under, then part of the fun is to head out into that liquid laboratory and 'rip'. From the 5'9" single fins of the late sixties to the blunt, short twins and scaled-down guns of the seventies, let's get the most out of new ideas and see where they take us.

Even though most of the Tour in the eighties was held in surf four foot and under, it never watered down the desire to ride well in surf over ten foot. Round pins went through a revival, which pushed out swallow, diamond and squash tails. Rockers became flatter with slight nose and tail lifts to deal with heavy drops.

Fin templates shrank as new breakthroughs in sailboarding crossed over with wave riding. Football fins, for instance, with full, sweeping curves were developed by Harold Iggy and Bobby Owens. Shapers like Pat Rawson were experimenting with quads for waves beneath four foot, tris for medium sized swells and long single fins for the big days. Al Merrick, the wizard of Tom Currens' ascendancy, worked almost exclusively with thrusters.

By late 1987, designers were forecasting the stinger come-back. Originally a 1975 design from Ben Aipa, the board was loose and fast. The

Right: Barton Lynch – 1988 World Champion.

SYLVAIN CAZENAVE

sting-thruster combination was heavily tested in Hawaii and California for waves six foot and below. Young Sunny Garcia packed two for his Grand Slam bid in Australia; John Shimooka won a Bud Tour event on one.

At the end of the decade, surfers again got hungrier for big waves. There was increased demand for the skills of long established shapers like Dick Brewer, who turned out some rhino-chasers in the 10'6" range. Boards featured more tail rocker and flatter mid-sections for greater speed. But there was plenty of debate between Brewer and others (like Ken Bradshaw) over the merits of tris over single fins for big waves. Tom Curren arrived on the North Shore in the 86/87 winter, with single fins ranging between 7'4" and 8'4". The narrower tails of the boards gave Tom more curl fade and less off the top, but deeper bottom turns. An older wisdom still held good.

We'll never have total control over our waves and our boards. The search is endless. It is led by the most talented in the sport, sharpened by competition and driven by a quest for bigger moves in critical conditions.

Tom Carroll's grip on the Tour in 1985 was strong. He retained his title after a final battle against Shaun at Bells. Tomson and Carroll had been neck-and-neck as the Tour went into Australia, with Shaun entering the Quiksilver Trials not as a seeded surfer. He would clash with Tom early on and get a chance at the world crown – but he lost in the second round and had failed to do well in the first two 'A' grade events of the season.

Tom was devastating, winning two of the three events on his way to a second grand slam title. Later, a row over apartheid in South Africa caused major political fall-out amongst the pros. Some threatened to boycott the country. Shaun made a passionate speech calling on support for pro-surfing. Some listened, some didn't.

One of the headline grabbers of 1986 was the come-back of MR at the Billabong Pro in 12 foot Sunset. It had been three years since his last win at the Gunston in South Africa. He'd been recovering from torn ankle ligaments for six months but Mark beat Tom Curren, Tony Moniz and Barton Lynch in epic surf.

Tom wasn't down for long. That year he was crowned the youngest world champion of the modern era and the first male American victor since Rolf Aurness in 1970. It was to be the first of three titles. His quiet, considerate personality on land gave no hint of the powerhouse waiting to be unleashed in the water. In competition, Tom combined creative, flowing moves with explosive diversions and few mistakes.

In what's still considered to be an historic clash at the Bells semi-final, Curren took on Mark Occhilupo in epic eight foot surf, both riders scoring near perfect cards from the judges, who said it had been one of the heaviest competition battles of all time.

1987 started with the resignation of Ian Cairns from the ASP after a riot – involving almost 5,000 people and burning cars – at the Huntington O.P. The Association relocated to Sydney and Graham Cassidy took over the helm, in what would prove to be a difficult year. Young Americans like Jeff Booth, Doug Silva and Jamie Brisick started turning up the heat in competitions.

Derek Ho was coming on strong too. His eight second vanishing act behind a big curtain in the semis of the Pipe Masters paved the way to a fine victory and a win in the Triple Crown.

Curren claimed his second world title, and the surfing establishment

Opposite page: *In the 60s, Waimea was crowded with water-men. Now it's crowded with 'wanna-bes'.*

Right & below: *Derek Ho: 1993 World Champion.*

JOLI

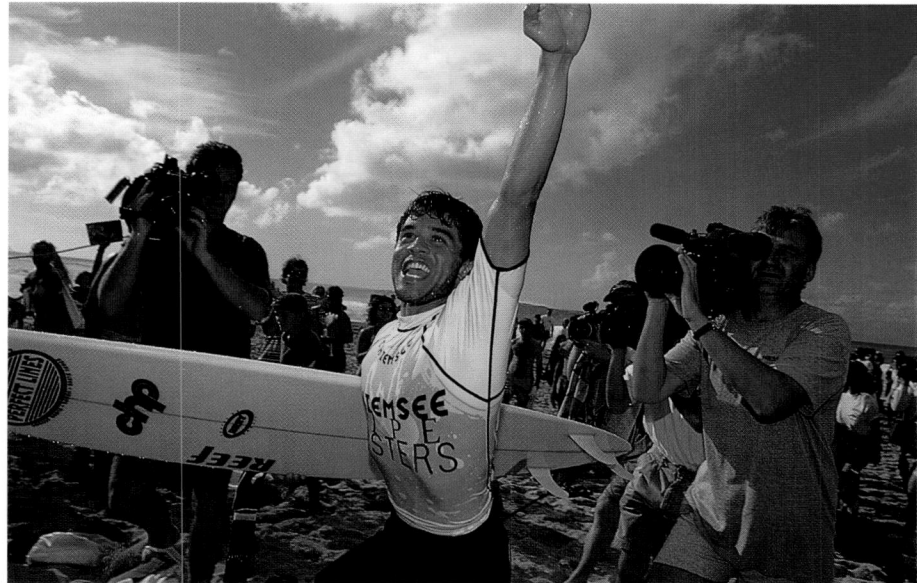

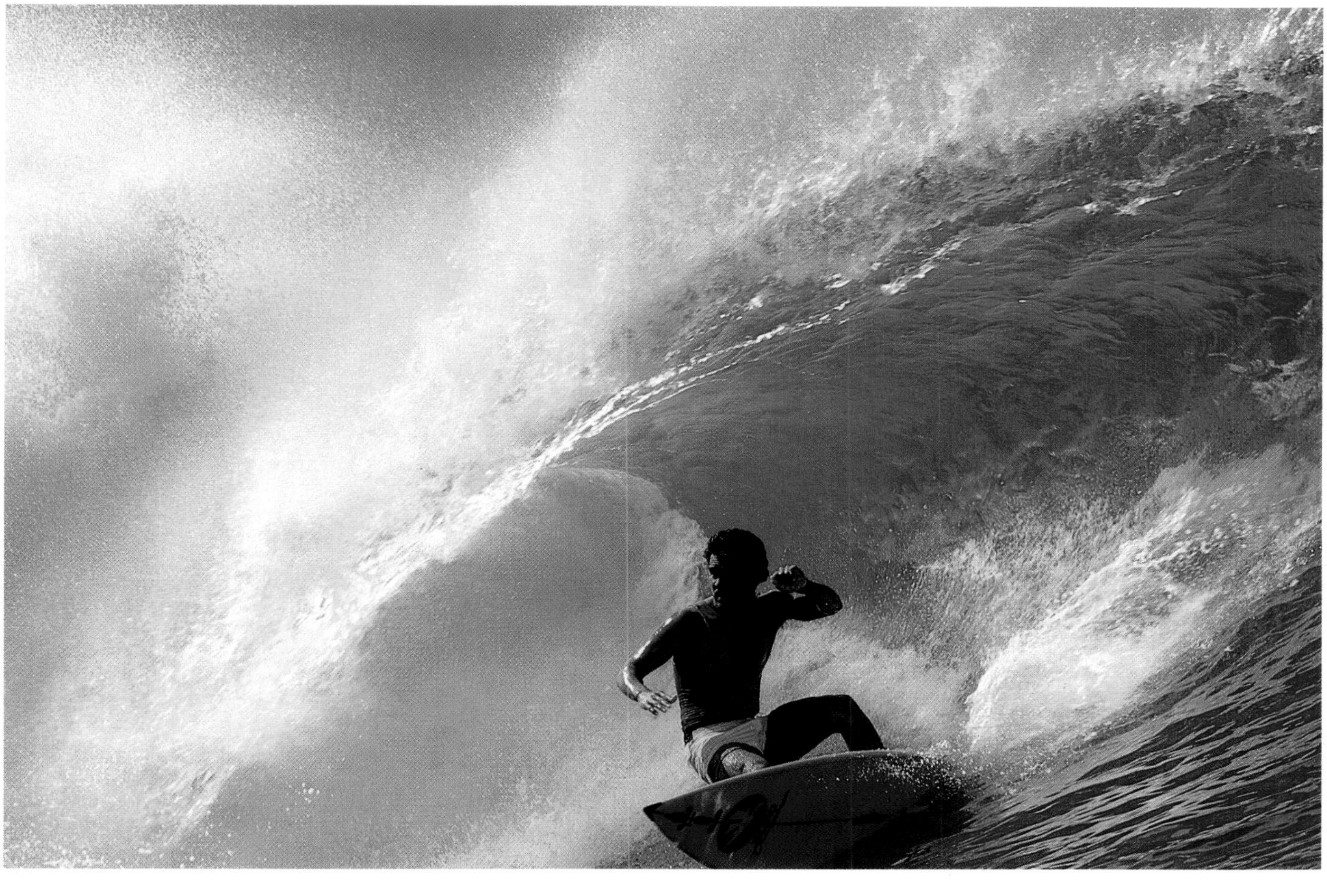

SYLVAIN CAZENAVE

wondered if he was unbeatable in competition. Nicky Wood and Richard 'Dog' Marsh, went through to the finals of the Rip Curl at Bells – the first ever all-trialist final in the history of pro surfing. Nicky at 16, was the youngest surfer ever to win a professional event.

Tom Carroll, meanwhile, who came second on the Tour, was hit by injury problems. He was speared by his board's fins during a practice surf in Japan just before the opening event of the Tour and had to stay out of competition for the next two events. In Hawaii, Tom suffered a broken eardrum after a wipe-out in huge Sunset.

Early cracks were beginning to show as a result of the heavy commitment demanded by the pro tour. Gary Green missed five ASP events and decided to get out after travelling the world for three years. Gary had walked out once before – from the competitors' circle of the Billabong Pro the year before.

He'd watched Rob Bain get worked over in 25 foot sets and decided it wasn't for him. Gary came back to the tour the following season – but the writing was on the wall.

There were plenty of youngsters to take over. Rodd Kerr, Jason Buttenshaw, Merrick Davis and Luke Egan were moving up through the competitive ranks. In Hawaii, it was clear it was going to be an excellent year for Gary Elkerton. Gary dropped the 'Kong' nickname and swept all before him in a display of power surfing at the Hard Rock Cafe World Cup at Sunset and the Billabong Pro.

SYLVAIN CAZENAVE

Damien had done well in Japan and Europe, but had faltered through California and Hawaii. Critics claimed a world champion must rip on the North Shore to be worthy of the crown – but the likeable and determined surfer had many friends on the tour and Damien was a strong champion.

The 1988 season had prospective bookings for 39 events over 11 months. Burn-out fears were growing and there were more complaints that the tour was favouring sponsors and not surfers. The ASP suggested that about 20 double or triple A events would go towards the title with the remaining contests standing as seeding trials. After all, the surfers themselves had voted for such a hectic season. Bigger sponsorship deals were coming forward. Tom Carroll signed a 5 year $1 million contract with Quiksilver.

For the first time since 1983, Hawaii hosted the end of the circuit. Barton Lynch wore the crown. In perfect 12 foot Pipe, Tom Carroll was eliminated after an interference call over Todd Holland. Barton defeated Glen Winton in the semi-finals and said if he had scripted the end of the tour for himself, it couldn't have been better.

B. ALEXANDER

Top: *Damien Hardman was World Champion in '87 and '91, and runner-up in '93.*

Above: *World Champion in 1989, Englishman Martin Potter.*

Never a pretty surfer to watch, Gary nevertheless defined a ruthless ability to demolish some of the heaviest set waves, pushing his surfing up a notch every time Sunset threw something heavy his way. He was almost unchallenged in speed and positioning and his wins took him from 6th in the ratings to equal top – along with Carroll and Narrabeen's Damien Hardman.

By April, Damien had taken the tour lead. In the closest race for the title in the pro-circuit's 12 year history, Hardman had a 285 point lead over Barton Lynch after beating him on his home surf at Manly to win the Coke Classic.

Frieda Zamba won back the women's title – her fourth – from Wendy Botha and semi-retirees, hoping for a domestic circuit for women.

The following year, Martin Potter regained his momentum, to take six firsts in the opening 11 events. At 23 he became the new – and deserving – ASP champion. Martin had been threatening for eight years to do it after finishing 8th in his first season. Over the next 7 years, he finished between 5th and 12th at the end of each year. In the first five events, 'Pottz' took 4 straight firsts and a 5th. Wendy Botha made a similar out-of-the-blocks start and between them they managed to win 13 rated contests.

By now, the European leg of the Tour was the richest and Kelly Slater was on a roll. Kelly could reap the rewards of a clearly defined professional path, carved out by older surfers over the previous decade. At 17 he was intelligent, assured and expressive and had an incredible style.

Tom Curren decided to get off the

Tour merry-go-round to go home to France. New ideas in board manufacture were also turning a few heads. Bob McTavish was building the Pro Circuit Board, featuring an original, copied in a mould. Trials were made on Currens' 6'3" and Barton's 6'1". Sydney based surfer/shaper Greg Webber found the duplicates to be stiffer, yet more buoyant and an interesting match.

In Hawaii, local surfers feared the loss of style, as crowds, commercialism and lack of Tour events increased. There were other things to fear, too. Titus Kinimaka, a big wave hell-man, bottom turned into the bowl at Waimea and tried to pull in. The lip hit him so hard it broke his leg. Karl Palmer from Wollongong helped to keep Titus afloat, while a rescue was mounted – it was Karl's first time out at the famous big wave spot.

Back on the mainland, the Bud Tour was still attracting top money and surfers – Mike Lambresi won the Tour three times as the cash purse went up from $40,000 in 1985, to $465,000 by the end of 1989. Surf helmets were becoming almost standard equipment, especially at beaches like Pipeline. They were offered to all competitors at the Triple Crown, after being invented by Rick Gath from Western Australia. The 1989/1990 season turned out to be the 14th and last on the pro tour for Shaun Tomson, while Cheyne Horan

Above: *Tom Curren with his daughter and shaper Maurice Cole.*

Below: *Christian Fletcher showed the surf world the potential of the aerial in the late 80s.*

made a surprise come-back that year in the AAAAA Billabong Pro, winning the largest cash prize ever in a surfing event – $50,000.

In April 1990, Kelly Slater turned professional and signed with Quiksilver. He tore his way through the French ASP events, in a run which took out Winton, Potter, Wood and Carroll, after blazing through the trials. The surfer who stopped him in France was Tom Curren – heading for another world title. It was a

pretty impressive achievement. Tom survived poor showing at the Hard Rock and Pipe Masters during a Hawaiian winter which wasn't the best. He clinched the title at the Billabong Pro by coming second in his third round heat in the trials. Tom won 7 events of the 11 contests he entered and had come back after staying away from the Tour for a year. Many considered him to be the most influential surfer of the 1980s.

By now, computer shaping was becoming more refined. Bill Bahne, Ray Baum, Bruce Duggan and Tony Channin in San Diego County, had designed a machine to replicate designs by Al Merrick and Gary Linden. Curren rode a computer-shaped 7'6" when he won the world title at the Sunset Beach Billabong event. At a cost of $500,000 investment, the computer used a laser to make more than 1 million calculations from a hand-crafted blank.

The twinzer came onto the scene, another development aimed at breaking the thruster's hold. Developed by Wilf Jobson and Glen Minami, Martin Potter said the board had the speed of the twin fin and forward drive of the tri-fin. Christian Fletcher defined the aerial, with backside ollies, slob airs and double grab frontside airs. By now, Californian surf shops said 40% of their board sales were sticks over 8 feet.

The ASP's new Tour format – the

Kelly Slater: 1992 World Champion, shown here in the perfect carve that his mentor, Tom Curren taught by example (Insert).

WCT and WQS – had begun to promote fresh talent like Ross Williams, Shane Beschen, Dino Andino, Matt Hoy, Kalani Robb, Rob Macardo and Shane Dorian. Meanwhile, Lisa Anderson was making her own statement about women's surfing – in the men's ranks. She entered the Rip Curl Pro Landes trials and surfed through one heat against the men. At the Arena Surf Masters, she blitzed through two men's rounds.

In November, Curren arrived in Hawaii fired up. He surfed the Wyland Galleries Pro on an un-stickered Maurice Cole which caused a real stir amongst sponsors. A month later, Damien Hardman secured the world title – his 2nd in 5 years – when he finished 4th in the Mauri Pipe Masters. Damien's placing finally silenced critics of his performances in surf over 10 foot. Wendy Botha won the women's division, battling against a knee injury which had plagued her all year.

In 1992, Greg Noll decided to make 250 replicas of the famous sixties 'Da Cat' model at $1000 each.

Mickey Dora's originals sold thousands, ranging in length from 9' to 9'8". Barely into the year, Tom Curren split up with OP, his sponsor for more than ten years. Tom went in with Rip Curl in a deal said to be the best ever – $1.9 million.

Rumours about an *Endless Summer 2* were confirmed, when Bruce Brown agreed to direct a sequel to this 1964 classic. Bruce signed up short-boarder Pat O'Connell and long-boarder 'Wingnut'. On the small screen, Kelly Slater landed a part in *Baywatch* which went out to 66 countries. He also came good this year with an ASP title win. The 20 year old wonderkid was the youngest surfer ever to take the crown, when he came 9th in the Alternativa Pro in Brazil.

In the Hawaiian winter season in 1992, the old met the new, head-on. Brock Little surfed 20 foot Waimea on an 11'4" Greg Noll gun. Da Bull used the board in what's said to be the biggest wave ever ridden at Makaha in 1969. Brock found the board – worth $10,000 – a little too

Top pair: *Vetea David showing his form and his quiver.*

Above left: *Japan has quality waves: Kaminoko on the island of Amami Ohshima.*
Above: *Hiroyuki Matsuo in the tube at Kaifu Rivermouth.*

Opposite page top: *Flavio Padaratz: one of Brazil's favourite surfing sons.*

Below: *The talented Australian Mark Occilupo driving hard off the bottom.*

wide and long compared with modern equipment. But function aside, the challenge was an interesting one.

Hawaii's proud traditions found a natural focus in the 1993 ASP champion. Derek Ho won, after taking the Chiemsee Gerry Lopez Pipe Masters in 10 foot surf. The Islands celebrated a worthy champion they could call their own. Little Pauline Menczer took the women's title at last – still fighting the arthritis which had dogged her pro career.

●

SYLVAIN CAZENAVE

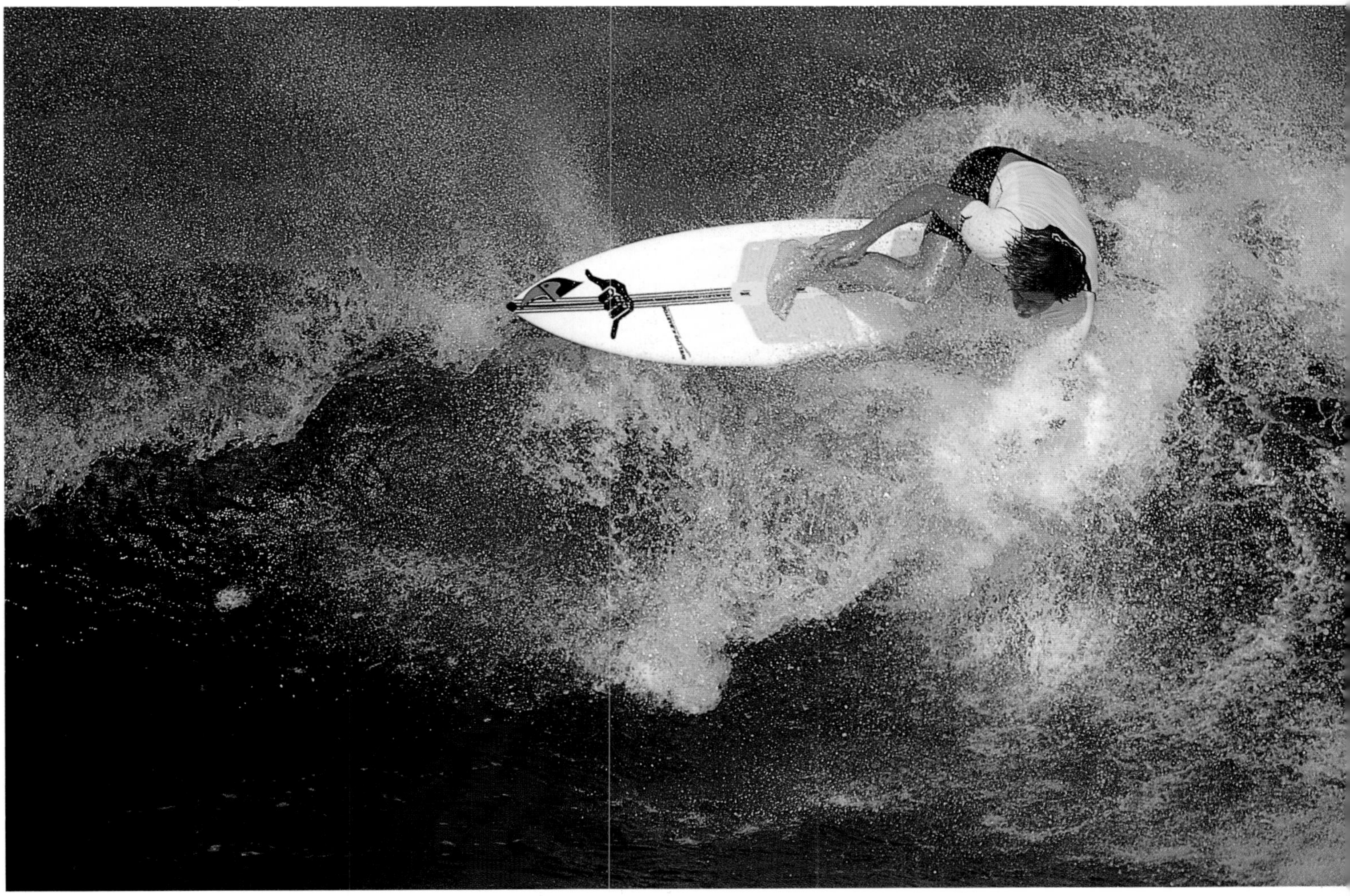

SYLVAIN CAZENAVE

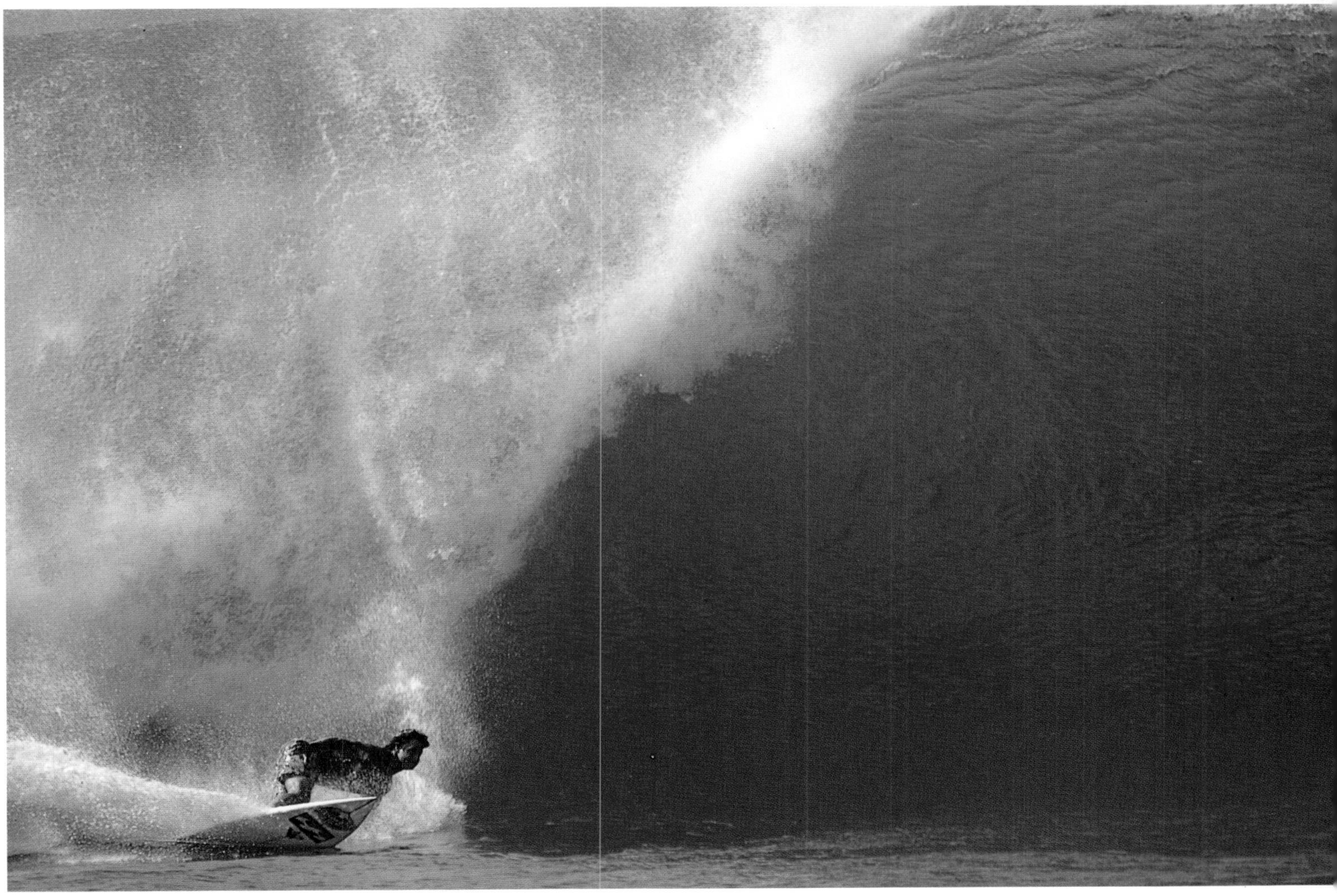

BACK TO
THE FUTURE

SYLVAIN CAZENAVE

Herbie Fletcher summed it up best by saying "the thrill is back". It's hard to think that surfing believed longboarding would disappear for good. The images remained of Wayne Lynch slashing his stubby, wide-backed tracker across the pages of a dozen surf magazines in 1963.

But good things come around again. The revival had its roots in several different places around the world, as the sport took a fresh look at the style of the sixties and what those boards had to offer. That old mal, which had gathered dust up in garage rafters, or weeds at the back of a fence, offered a whole lot of stoke again in a re-awakening that's bringing the generations together – just like surfing used to.

Many old surfers, frustrated by short, light, no-float shapes, gave up in the seventies and went full-on into families and careers. Shortboards offered them little excitement once the surf dropped below four foot.

Surfing mushy waves became a breeze as yellowed old nose riders again took their place in the line-up. Shortboards had taken the elegance, the artistry out of surfing's dance. The sport still had style – but the more sensitive approach to riding a wave was out, as the little boards burned around on their TNT charge.

Lighter foam and glass – a direct product of shortboard design development – became available to tankers who still wanted subtle timing and wave positioning, rather than skyward sweeps at Mach 5. Board builders quickly realised they had an ace up their sleeves – and began refining a new generation of longboards to suit the demands of an old art. There were, though, two distinct schools of thought.

Traditionalists looked for the grace of the old days with the old moves on boards over eight feet – walking the board, stalling, trimming, quasimodos and soul arches all combined into a fluid and functional style. Some felt modern moves on traditional equipment was bad news – longboarding should be viewed as a dance.

But design innovations – including Bonzer-like fins, carbon fibre strips down the centre line, new rail contours and channels, thrusters and wings – meant that longboards were being ridden like shortboards, with off-the-tops, floaters and lip carves. A good half-way-house came out in the form of the minimal, from 7'6" up to 8'6", fusing the glide and force of a longer hull and the fast turn, rail-to-rail potential of the shortboard.

Surfers rediscovered that feeling of lancing down a green wall, cranking a bottom turn, stepping foot over foot to get the thing trimming, arching in the curl, the sheer magic of planing over flat spots with ease, gouging a big slice out of a wall, then pulling into a stall turn and vaulting over the lip in a fire-hose of spray.

The 1983 Malibu Longboard Pro held at Third Point, featured classic longboarding from vets like Dale Dobson, Robbie Dick, David Nuuhiwa, Jay Riddle, JoJo Perrin and Dale Velzy. No leg ropes, no boards under nine feet in length, no money – just trophies and clothes.

Jay Riddle won in the 3 to 5 foot surf, but that wasn't the point. More importantly, surfers from past and present came together to rediscover fun in the sun, at a place where the surfing lifestyle had been defined.

Demand picked up for the work of well-respected shapers like Lance Carson. Reynolds Yater and Joe Quigg who urged new shapers to study old boards and learn from the past. By 1987, there was a longboard division in the Western, Eastern and Hawaiian surfing associations, as well as the ASP. The revivalists were surfers in their teens and twenties, as well as the over forties.

Herbie Fletcher's sons Nathan and Christian, were combining long and shortboarding along with many other youngsters. Leonard Brady in Hawaii put it best – "longboards and shortboards are *both* correct ways to ride waves". It shows good wave judgement to be able to ride the board which most suits the conditions, regardless of length. Meanwhile, with the revival of the longboard pro tour in 1986, I found my feet in the winner's circle again

Opposite page: *Joel Tudor with beautiful form at Guethary in France.*

Top left: *Mike Doyle and Buffalo Keaulana with artistic poses.*

Top right: *Sunny Garcia carving on a longboard.*

Above left & right: *Rusty Keaulana: 1993 World Longboard Champion.*

Below: *The spirit is alive in Hawaii.*

and was world champion during 1988 and through to 1990.

Back in the sixties, Donald Takayama was the first really hot goofy footer, with radical turns and fancy footwork on the nose. Donald has always shaped his own boards – thin, knife-railed high riders. Now he's passing his knowledge on to another generation of surfers, like 18 year old Joel Tudor from San Diego, Duane de Soto from Makaha, Hawaii, who's 17, and 23 year old Takuji Masuda from Japan. Other talented youngsters carrying the traditional torch include Jeff Kramer from San Clemente and Joey Hawkins from Huntington Beach, who was the 1992 ASP longboard champion in France.

Surfing's heritage grows yearly. Longboarding's revival started out with bad press – now it's a valid part of the surfing existence.

Just as longboarding was taking off, equipment at the other end of the scale was making ground – bodyboards. Tom Morey was the father of soft surf-craft. In 1971 in California,

he realised that a soft-skinned stand up board would be perfect for learners. No pointed noses or sharp fins to cause injury. His brainwave created the advanced guard of rippers which spawned the bodyboard generation of the eighties, bringing surfing within everyone's reach.

The idea was simple. Get a rigid foam core and wrap it in high impact, soft plastic. In the late seventies, the board was simple. Early standouts included Dan Kaimi, Jack 'The Ripper' Lindholm and Pat Caldwell. Jack pioneered Pipeline on the little softie, pulling off moves no-one thought possible, like the drop-knee stance. Girls like Phyllis Dameron could rip too, taking on Waimea and Sunset, proving you didn't have to have huge muscles –

Top & above: *Bodyboards are happening! Michael Eppelstun up and flying.*

Opposite page: *The extended breakwall at Port Kembla in Australia improved the wave quality, but the water quality is disgusting. Surfers everywhere have to band together to save our surf.*

just grit and style – to make it on the North Shore.

By the early eighties, Keith Sasaki was dominating, picking up four titles in the Californian small wave events, at the Morey Boogie Pro-Am. But Pipeline continued to be the decade's proving ground, with the Morey Boogie International and Scott Hawaii Classic offering good money – $20,000.

'Sponges' were getting more refined each year. Designers experimented with new plastic construction materials, resulting in boards with more flex and projection. Plan and tail shapes, widths and thicknesses all came under the microscope to create a better board.

Arcel plastic is taking over from polyethylene, because it's stronger and flexes back into shape well after being pulled hard into a bottom turn. Denser foam structure on the outside of bodyboards means less water soak-up.

Bodyboarders like Ben Seversen began charging into a full round-up of bottom turns, drop-knees, off-the-lips, barrel rolls, floaters and tube rides. They track different lines on a wave than thrusters, projecting through longer, drawn out turns. These little boards need the power of The Wedge, Big Rock and Half Point.

The 1990s have seen the emergence of top flight performers. Mike Stewart is an eight times world champion, who's redefining the places surfers go on a wave. Other leaders are Rick Bannister, Adam MacNamara, Harry Antipala, Jay Reale and Guilherme Tamega.

In money terms, the professional bodyboard circuit has some way to go to catch up with the ASP pro tour. But events are starting to shape up in Australia and the 'States. Brazilian Women's world champion, Stephanie Petterson took the 1994 title in six foot Pipe against 40 girls, and is working to promote a full-on tour.

One off-shoot of the sixties hippie movement was the flowering of a greater awareness of green issues. Thirty years on, and surfers have grasped the political nettle to challenge the threat to our seas, to bring the voice of the beach to a wider audience.

Some think Bondi Beach is as much a surfing icon as Malibu, on the West Coast of the 'States. Yet in 1989, 260 million gallons of primary treated effluent a day went into the sea there. The locals started calling it 'Scum Valley'. The smell and taste of the water led some professionals to stay out of the Coke Surf Worx event in mid-November that year.

In 1990, there were worries about pulp mill developments in four Australian States; about tourism pressures in areas like Coffs Harbour; about ozone depletion in Melbourne; more sewage problems at Thirteenth Beach in Victoria, which took the outfalls from Geelong. Two years later in America, heavy rains

MARK NEWSHAM

Sequence above: *Local boat-boy Esai, with only six months' surfing experience, takes off on the set of the day at Cloudbreak on Tavarua (insert). Idyllic islands like this MUST be preserved.*

Right: *Snow-boarding is surfing on the snow…another fragile environment.*

Opposite page top: *Wave pools are a good alternative to the problem of more surfers meaning less waves to go around.*

Below: *Kelly Slater tucked in at 'Wave Flo' in Texas.*

began two large sewage spills, which led health officials to close 100 miles of coast in the San Diego area. All this was bad news for surfing. It was time to organise.

Two of the largest groups – the International Surfrider Foundation and the British Surfers Against Sewage lobby – are expanding. With early support by professional surfers like Tom Curren and Carwyn Williams, the environmentalists are now working towards global policies.

The Surfrider Foundation – set up in 1984 to stop developers ruining prime surf spots – keeps a watch on the 'States, Australia, Europe and South Africa. Success is coming, with their Blue Water Task Force and Respect the Beach campaigns. SAS now has 15,000 members, dedicated to stopping sewage being slopped out of pipes onto European beaches. But they're keeping an eye on new horizons.

"The future means looking beyond your own experience", said SAS organiser, Chris Hines. "Pressures grow daily, not just in the old world, but at emerging surf destinations.

"We must protect idyllic surfing

spots like G-land, Tavarua and countless other remote areas which lie waiting for the traveller. Surfers need a social consciousness if we don't want to ruin these spots with crowds and the problems that human invasion brings. That might call for some sacrifices".

In terms of sewage, SAS says the solution must be at the treatment plant. Rather than pump it into the seas, governments could make the effluent harmless, then recycle the by-products for other uses. Right now, about half the sewage which comes out of Europe's outfalls gets basic screening by passing it through a wide mesh. But there are better ways, like biological digestion, which turns sludge into landfill or fertiliser; sand filtration, micro-screening or disinfection to kill bacteria and viruses.

New research has investigated ultra-violet light disinfection, something which the English Channel Island of Jersey is testing. UV is harnessed to smash up the DNA of harmful viruses. Now, the Bellozane Treatment Works report toxin counts way below the figures quoted by the toughest green lobby.

In America in 1991, surfing had it's greatest victory to date, when The Surfrider Foundation took an offending paper mill to court over pollution in Humboldt Bay. The well publicised win made everyone, even the general media, from 'Time' magazine, to 'Wall Street Journal', realise that surfers were now a political force to be reckoned with. Surfrider President, Robert 'Birdlegs' Caughlin, was ecstatic over the decision, saying – "this is going to send a strong message to polluters around the world, to stop using the ocean as a dump".

Surfers always dream of the perfect wave. The problem's always been that the very force which creates it can also take it away – the seasons, the tides, the winds. Enter the wave pool. The first in Europe in the sixties began with diamond shapes, with swell being pumped out by an air driven generator. Next came

Japan's Surfatorium and the Big Surf venue at Tempe in Arizona. That one broke wall-to-wall with little face to surf on.

Later, engineers refined the shape of pool bottoms and made more powerful machinery to create point waves and surf, which broke at either edge of the pool. Huge ram arms forced out tons of water from the pool's back wall and gushing little foamies would sweep up to the shallow end. New wave pools were

planned all over America and at Allentown in Pennsylvania, the ASP held their first wave pool event during the 85/86 tour. Tom Carroll won it even though there was only enough juice for a couple of off-the-tops and a straight ride to get distance points.

Purists sneered – but here was an interesting new wave frontier. One of the latest projects is the Schlitterbahn Water Park in Texas, where a metal sluice gate throws out a thin, wide fan of water under heavy pressure. The water runs down a gentle slope at the rate of 100,000 gallons a minute. At the end of the slope is a concrete wall, eight feet high. The water flies up the wall and throws back on itself offering a wedging curtain which sets up a right hand barrel.

The project is different from other pools as the wave stays in the same place, just like river rapids. Surfers are trying out thin fibreglass boards, three and four feet long, small keel fins and rudders, to skim around the tube. Wave pool experts say by the year 2000, surfers will be able to enjoy water parks with hard and

easy peaks, half pipes and entry slides. Such a future has a big price tag. To make a wave eight foot high, a developer would need several million dollars.

Small, man-made waves are one thing. The fascination of riding nature's giant waves is another. Shaun Tomson said the real test of a surfer was his ability to charge in Hawaii. Now, experienced watermen are trying a new challenge – the tow-in – which may take surfing into the next century's new power zone.

Tow-ins began in the mid-1970s. Jeff Johnson 'surfed' Avalanche in a 24 foot skiff with outboard motor. In 1987, Herbie Fletcher towed Tom Carroll and Martin Potter into Pipe when the Masters was on hold.

Hawaii's outer reefs – mainly off Maui – throw up to 30 and 40 foot 'blue birds' two miles off shore. Laird Hamilton, Buzzy Kerbox, Bill Hamilton, Darrick Doerner, David Kalama and Pipe Master Gerry Lopez are discovering ways to get into big waves earlier, using fast jet skis, rubber ducks, very narrow

boards and foot-strap technology refined on sailboards.

Power surfing involves being towed into the swell like a water skier. Surfers slip their feet into cushioned straps anchored to boards down to 7'2", though Darrick has preferred more conventional 9'6" and 10'6" Dick Brewer shapes. Widths can be just 14 inches.

The water team have been using Zodiacs, Wave Runners and Jet-skis as tow-in support boats. The smaller boards are pulled into the face and are very fast and manoeuvrable, with air drops, big hops straight across warps in the face, lip bashes, floaters and tube rides all possible.

In the winter of 1993, Backyard was an ideal testing ground. Taking off almost a mile out, big 'S' turns and speed lines on rides lasting more than a minute were common. It's been called the 'unridden realm'. But there are surfers ready and able to make it happen.

●

The future of surfing giant waves in the middle of the ocean – using a Zodiac to tow the surfers into the break. Talented sail-boarder Peter Cabrina making the transition to wave power with Laird Hamilton.

SYLVAIN CAZENAVE

SEQUENCE ERIK AEDER

SYLVAIN CAZENAVE

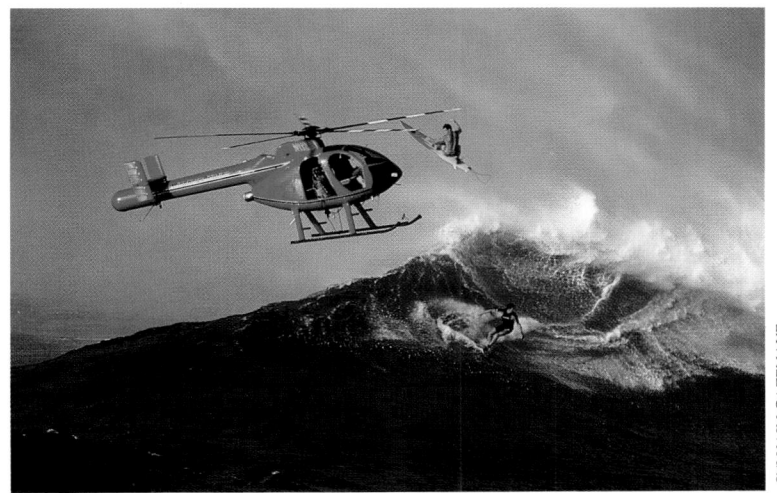

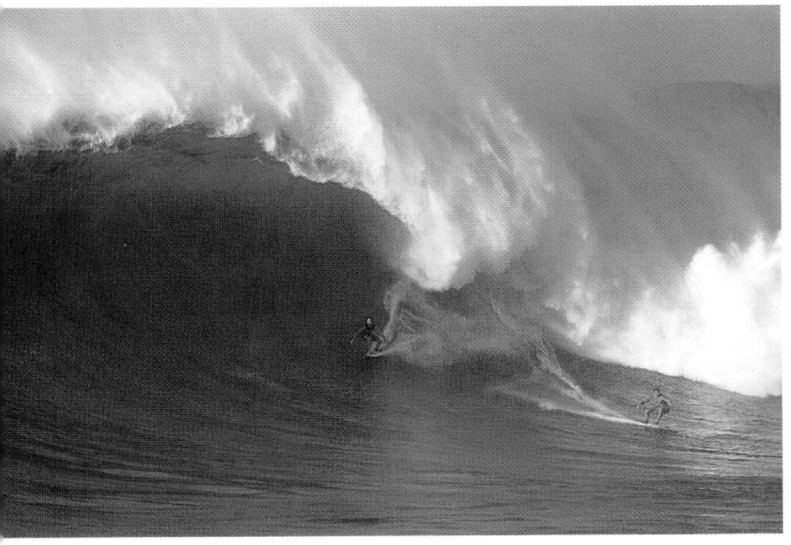

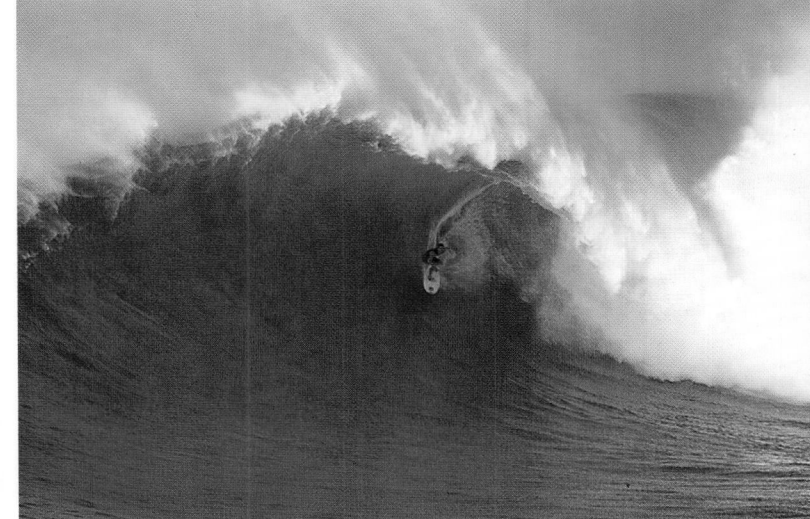

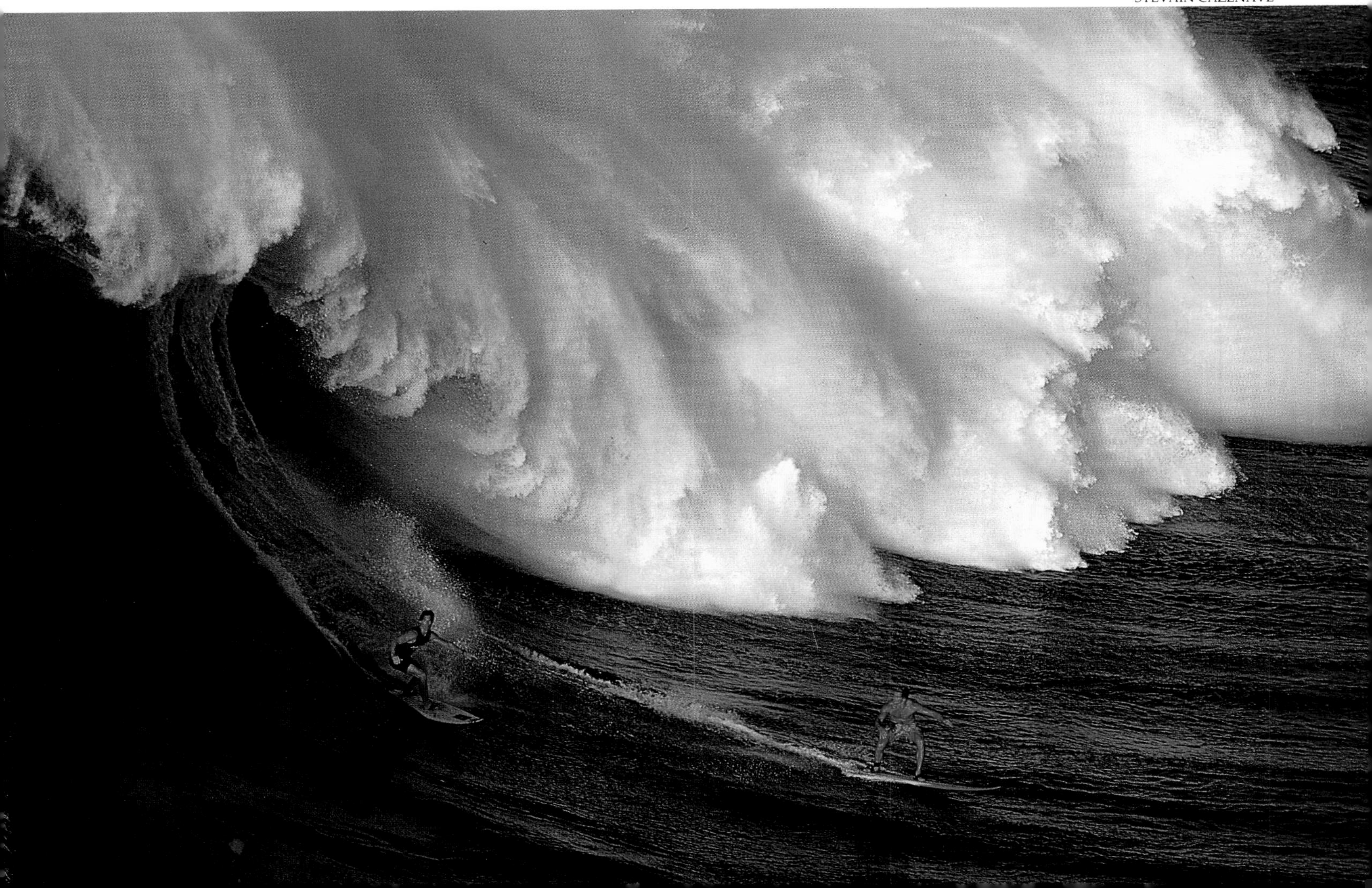

Dedication

This revised edition of *The History of Surfing* is dedicated to the memory of Tom Blake who died of natural causes on May 5th, 1994, aged 92.

Tom, whose picture appears on page 44, is credited with being the first person to put a fin on a surfboard and with many other innovations. Surfers everywhere should feel thankful for his dedication to the sport of surfing.

TOM BLAKE   SURFER MAGAZINE

Every attempt to find the photographers responsible for the pictures in this book has been made, but many were impossible to track down. Therefore I have credited my source. Some very important photographs were in too poor a condition for publication.

Nat Young